NAPLES & CAMPANIA

PASSPORT'S REGIONAL GUIDES OF ITALY

Series Editor: John Julius Norwich

Florence & Tuscany
Laura Raison

Naples & Campania
Martha Pichey

Umbria, the Marches & San Marino
Christopher Catling

NAPLES & CAMPANIA

Martha Pichey

PASSPORT BOOKS
a division of *NTC Publishing Group*
Lincolnwood, Illinois USA

This edition was first published in 1994 by Passport Books,
a division of NTC Publishing Group, 4255 West Touhy Avenue,
Lincolnwood (Chicago), Illinois 60646-1975 U.S.A.
Originally published by A & C Black (Publishers) Limited,
35 Bedford Row, London, England.
Copyright © Martha Pichey 1994
Photographs by Peter Wilson
ISBN 0-8442-9963-4
Library of Congress Catalog Card Number   93-86824

Printed in Singapore by Imago

To my parents, Alberta and Raymond Pichey,
the most enthusiastic travellers I know.

For all their help and encouragement I'd like to thank

Simon Gavron, Ann Pichey, Imelde Sello,
the Toledo Family and Conrad Williams.

CONTENTS

FOREWORD
by John Julius Norwich

Here be dragons, they used to write on the old maps, whenever they got to a
bit of *terra incognita*: not only a warning to the impetuous traveller, but a
comforting reminder of the infinitely preferable state of things back home. To
this day, every native of northern Italy instinctively feels something of the kind
about the south: he will mentally cross himself at the very mention of Campania,
let alone Naples. For him, real civilisation stops at the southern border of
Tuscany: even Rome is hopelessly beyond the pale. Anyone venturing still
further into the wilds will do so at his peril, and is unlikely to be seen again.

The North Italians have, of course, a perfect right to their own opinions, which
– having held them since the early Middle Ages – they are anyway unlikely to
change. But they do not know what they are missing; for the region covered by
this book is among the most rewarding of all Italy. It can boast, in Pompeii and
Herculaneum, the first sites ever to be subjected to serious archaeological investi-
gation; in Vesuvius, what is perhaps the world's most famous volcano; in Paestum, three of the earliest, best-preserved and most moving Doric temples
anywhere; and in the Sorrento Peninsula and its off-shore islands, some of the
most spectacularly beautiful scenery that the world has to offer.

And then there is Naples; and Naples is, of course, the problem. Does it
deserve its reputation? Is it really the running sore on the shin of Italy, the
malignant ulcer that nothing can cure? Or is it in fact a noble, historic city, still
bearing the scars of centuries of misgovernment but preserving at the same time
a strength of character, and a power to fascinate, that many another European
metropolises might envy? I myself have loved it since my first visit over thirty
years ago when, at the instigation of an old Neapolitan friend, my wife and I
found our way to the convent of San Gregorio Armeno and, sitting in the cloister
garth among a riot of baroque statuary, watched the nuns – their black habits
slashed down the middle by a broad band of scarlet – teetering on the tops of
their ladders while they picked oranges and threw them down to their colleagues
below, who held out their skirts to receive them. Later, one of their number
took us into the treasury, where she treated us to our own private miracle: the
liquefaction of the blood, not of San Gennaro but of Santa Patrizia, which took
place – unmistakeably – a foot in front of our eyes.

And there are plenty of other memories too: Capua on its hilltop, commanding the great loop of the Volturno, and the almost palpable presence there of Frederick II, *Stupor Mundi*, the first Renaissance prince, two hundred years before his time; the breathtaking frescoes at Sant' Angelo in Formis nearby; the tremendous Roman arch of Benevento; the sulphurous gurglings of Solfatara; and the excitement of finding, at Sessa Aurunca, a superb 12th-century cathedral of which I had never even heard, with a majolica dome above and a mosaic floor below wrought in that wonderful technique known as *opus alexandrinum* – my first, unforgettable introduction to the Romanesque architecture of the south.

All this and much, much more came flooding back into my memory when I first read the typescript of the book that you now hold in your hand. Its author has travelled every inch of the territory that she describes with such infectious enthusiasm, and she knows its history as well as she knows the land itself – no small achievement with a history as tortuous and tormented as that of Southern Italy has been. But she writes not only with knowledge: she also writes with love – a love that is not limited to Capri, Amalfi and the obvious delights of the coast but which extends, sincerely and genuinely, to Naples itself. When I came upon the title of the chapter 'Naples Explained', I confess to a momentary feeling of misgiving, if not of actual alarm: can anyone explain Naples? Well, they can; and she has.

For the first secret of understanding Naples is not to be afraid of it, as nearly all first-time visitors are. This does not mean to tempt fate, leaving your wallet sticking half out of your hip pocket, or swinging your handbag carelessly from your shoulder; but there are, after all, very few large towns anywhere in which such conduct is to be recommended. What it does mean is that you should forget all those horror stories you have heard and approach the city as you would any other: ready to enjoy it, to seek out its hidden treasures – which are there in plenty, if you know where to look for them – and, quite simply, to give it the benefit of the doubt. Even then, you may not immediately like the place; but Naples – like Marseilles, or Liverpool, or Barcelona, or many other great cities, especially if they happen to be great ports as well – does not set out to seduce. Some people, try as they may, will never see its charm; but there will be others for whom, one day, the veil will suddenly lift, never to fall again.

If Naples is an acquired taste, the rest of Campania is more usually a question of love at first sight. Even there, however, we need somone to direct our steps; not only to the sights that we have come to see, but also – and every bit as important – to the hotels and restaurants and bars where we can suitably reward ourselves after a long, hard day. Hence the very proper stress that is laid on the food and the wine of the region in the pages that follow – aspects of the local culture in which the author of this book is no less an expert than in matters of art and architecture. Put yourself, therefore, confidently in her hands. You will not regret it.

John Julius Norwich

1. INTRODUCTION

Everyone seems to know something about Italy's southern region of Campania. They've seen a picture of the cliff-hugging town of Positano, been transfixed by the casts made of Pompeiians killed by Vesuvius, and perhaps heard the phrase 'See Naples and die'. But how many people, even the Italophiles among them, realize what a vast amount of history, art and architecture lies waiting to be discovered throughout Campania? How many travellers have seen the ancient mosaics in the Archeological Museum in Naples, traversed the underground chambers of Italy's best preserved amphitheatre at Santa Maria Capua Vetere or explored the Greeks' first mainland city of Cumae?

Visitors to the region will be following in illustrious footsteps: Virgil settled in Naples; Giotto, Boccaccio and Petrarch were courted there by King Robert the Wise; Dickens, Ruskin, Shelley and Goethe all criss-crossed this territory. As in other parts of Italy, religion is one of the region's strongest threads. Here in Campania it is responsible for temples to Greek and Roman gods, for Romanesque, Gothic and Norman churches scattered throughout the countryside, and for brightly tiled church domes along the coast which attest to sailors' fascination with Eastern trading posts. Amalfi's cathedral and Padula's monastery are two of the region's most lavish examples of the church's power throughout the centuries. And superstitious beliefs reach the height of frenzy when San Gennaro's blood liquifies each year in Naples, though each town boasts its little miracles and sacred stash of saints' bones.

Campania Felix was what the Romans called this place, because it appeared so blessed with fertile soil and superb scenery – bay after bay on the blue Tyrrenhian Sea, hills covered with olives and oranges, flat green fields full of tobacco and vegetables, wheat harvested by the ton. Hot sun, little rainfall and an average temperature of 60 degrees certainly added to a Roman nobleman's enjoyment.

But the Romans weren't the only ones to appreciate the region. Greeks settled here eight centuries before the birth of Christ; then came Oscans and Samnites, followed by Romans, Lombards, Saracens and Normans. At the end of the 12th century the royal houses of Hohenstaufen, Anjou and Aragon ruled the region, though were finally succeeded by the Bourbons. After 1860, Italy was united under the House of Savoy, which begat its own set of problems for a warm and resilient people now officially part of the arid Mezzogiorno south of Rome.

Italy's dividing line between north and south is, geographically speaking, the Garigliano river. This is Campania's northern border, separating the region from

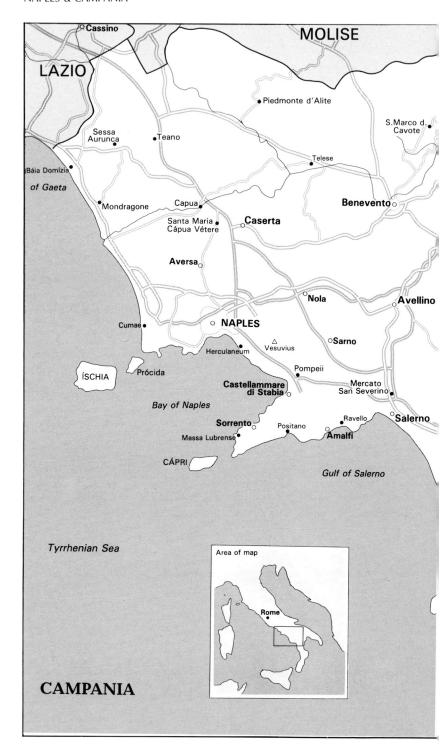

CAPRI

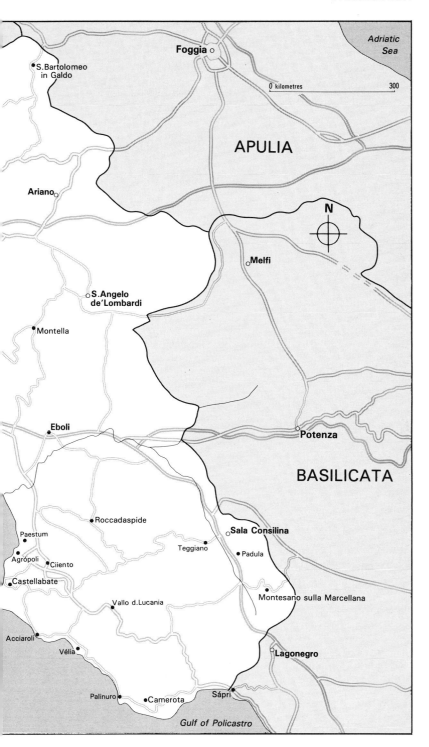

Adriatic
Sea

Foggia ○

● S.Bartolomeo
in Galdo

0 kilometres   300

APULIA

Ariano ○

N

○ Melfi

○ S.Angelo
de'Lombardi

● Montella

● Eboli

○ Potenza

BASILICATA

● Roccadaspide

Paestum
●

● Sala Consilina ○

Teggiano ●

● Padula

Agrópoli
● ● Ciiento

● Castellabate

Vallo d.Lucania ●

Montesano sulla Marcellana ●

Acciaroli ●

Vélia ●

Lagonegro ○

Palinuro ●   ● Camerota

Sápri ●

Gulf of Policastro

Lazio, while its southern limits extend to the Gulf of Policastro, shared with Basilicata. Borders to the east are adjacent to the regions of Molise, Apulia and Basilicata. Campania's inland villages and hill-towns sit low in the valleys or are poised high above them, while the rugged limestone coast is lined with villages tumbling down to the edge of the sea. The islands of Procida, Ischia and Capri encircle the Gulf of Naples, which has struggled with volcanic activity for centuries.

Then there is Naples. A sizeable section of this book is devoted to this raucous city, and with very good reason. Naples is like a huge and dusty antique shop, which initially appears to be unappreciated by its owners. But Neapolitans can quickly, and keenly, catalogue their rich selection of stock for you, and will be happy to show you what is behind a locked door or around the next corner (while also bemoaning the lack of money available to restore their fine buildings). The city is a fascinating study in history, architecture and social custom; the historic centre is a vital and absorbing place to explore.

Naples was a royal capital for almost 600 years, and today's inner cityscape was much influenced by the reign of the Bourbon dynasty from 1734 to 1860. Baroque and Rococo more than flowered: they burst into full exotic bloom. From painters such as Caravaggio and Luca Giordano to architects like Vanvitelli and Fanzago, the city is a rich testimony to the royal courts' patronage of the arts. The museums are outstanding, from the National Picture Gallery at Capodimonte to the National Archeological Museum with its sculptures, wall paintings and mosaics from Pompeii and Herculaneum.

Other parts of Campania are home to similar treasures, and the effort spent tracking them down is a rewarding experience. Caserta Vecchia is a charming walled town north of Naples; the caves and coves along the Cilento coast make beautiful private bathing pools. The landscape is not everywhere an aromatic patchwork of lemon groves and grape vines however, as industrial plants have sprouted like nasty weeds outside the five main provincial cities of Naples, Caserta, Benevento, Avellino and Salerno. To avoid these blights, I have suggested when it's best to drive down the motorway instead of slowly winding through the countryside.

To help get a sense of this region's history and its people, I suggest three 20th-century travelogues: H. V. Morton's *A Traveler in Southern Italy*, Norman Douglas's *Siren Land*, and *Naples '44* by Norman Lewis. I add this guidebook to the list in the hope that I can help you discover the best of what Campania has to offer. But trust the people of Naples and Campania to be your guides as well. If the church door is locked, a restaurant closed, if the street signs seem too confusing, help is always at hand – literally. Italians are famously inventive when it comes to communicating without a common language, and Campanians are no exception.

2. THE FOOD AND WINE OF CAMPANIA

Despite the diversity of the region's geography, and the foreign influences which have played on the Neapolitan's palate, Campanian tastes remain simple and straightforward when it comes to their choice of food and wine. This is partly because they have been blessed with an abundance of flavourful crops in a region of rich soil. But Campania is also part of Italy's Mezzogiorno, the demarkation zone between north and south which implies a peasantry toiling under hot sun for centuries. Historically, this lack of money and its pretensions has meant that Campanians have been forced by necessity to exploit their natural resources to the fullest.

Food

Fruit and Vegetables

Tomatoes grow full of flavour on the volcanic slopes of Vesuvius; fruit and vegetables are planted on the inland plains awash with mineral silt from rivers criss-crossing the region. The food is fresh; most shoppers prefer choosing their own produce at the local seller's stall to the anonymity of convenience stores where they can't chastise a vendor for selling unripe apricots. Their Mediterranean diet is a healthy mix of grains, pulses and vegetables, with seafood eaten far more often than meat. Many families still press their own olives for oil, and their grapes for wine (which is good enough to wash down the midday meal, but rarely of a standard high enough to export).

But the region's fruit and vegetables are shipped throughout the country, with as many as four crops harvested annually on the fertile slopes of Vesuvius. The small San Marzano tomatoes are the stars of any southern sauce. Cherries, figs and apricots are among the best in Italy, along with pungent lemons grown on the islands of Procida and Ischia. Native artichokes, aubergines, broccoli and courgettes are cooked in every conceivable style, bottled and pickled too. They are also breaded and deep fried for what's called the *fritto misto*, an assortment brought hot to the table. Little red peppers are strung to shrivel in the sun, and in early autumn you might come across a caldron of stewing tomatoes outside a family's kitchen – this season being the perfect time for bottling the rich red sauce.

The tomato came to southern Italy by way of South America, by courtesy of the Spanish explorer Hernando Cortes in the 16th century (though some give Christopher Columbus the credit). Other foods came much earlier, and all were made use of by peasants inventively managing with what they had. Grape vines and olive trees had been planted hundreds of years before by the Greeks; later trade with the East brought nuts and spices to the area. Though Campania was under the domination of so many different rulers – Greek, Roman and Byzantine, then French Normans, Hohenstaufens, and Angevins followed by the Spanish Aragonese – those in control of the kitchen kept on a steady course by serving the region's freshest produce, fish and the daily portion of pasta.

Pizza, pasta and gelato

Southern Italy is famous for pizza, pasta and ice cream, and Naples has distinguished itself in all three categories. Where would we be if Neapolitans hadn't had the courage to taste the *pomi d'oro*? Tomatoes were the ideal topping for the flat bread baked in a brick oven, *picea* being a word used since the 11th century to describe this circular bread. Sailors improved upon the recipe by creating *pizza alla Marinara* – not by adding fish but by topping it with garlic, oil and oregano in the 1500s. Then in 1889 the food received the royal stamp of approval with the invention of the Regina Margherita pizza. When Queen Margherita, wife of Italy's King Umberto I, summered at Capodimonte, a pie-maker named Raffaele Esposito was invited to experiment for her. He added mozzarella to the standard tomato pie, along with sprinkling leaves of basil over the top: a celebration of Italian unity in red, white and green.

At its simplest, pizza is just *bianca*, freshly baked dough sprinkled with salt and sold by the etto (one hundred grams, or one-tenth of a kilogram). It's a favourite snack available from bakeries and bars. Also popular in Naples are *taralli*, crusty bread rings flavoured with pepper and a hint of almond. Another bread-based dish is *panzanella alla Napoletana* – a salad layered with bread at the bottom, and piled with tomatoes, onions, anchovies and basil. Then there is the *calzone*, or 'trouser-leg', a crescent-shaped pizza that has been folded in half so that its contents are hidden inside. The choice of toppings for pizza or calzone is endless: mushrooms, olives, anchovies, eggs, clams and artichoke hearts to name a few. The Margherita is still a popular choice, but the more elaborate Quattro Stagioni is often ordered. Divided into four sections to represent the seasons, the pizza is normally topped with black olives, hard-boiled egg, artichoke hearts and either clams or mussels. The Neapolitan pizza is not a thick crusted variety; it is thin and crisp, still baked on wooden pallets in round ovens.

Pasta needs no introduction. But what distinguishes this southern staple from its northern counterpart is that it is most often made with durum wheat and without eggs. Naples and its surrounding towns were once famous for exporting hundreds of varieties of dry pasta, but Campania's wheat is no longer harvested for the factories of Torre del Greco and Torre Annunziata. The traditional image of the *mangiatore di maccurune*, a street urchin slurping up strings of pasta, made its way on to postcards and into theatre scenes, and Neapolitans today are no less passionate about their pasta. It's eaten at least once a day, and more often than not with a simple Neapolitan sauce like this one:

> **A Sarza cu 'a Pummarola** (as the Neapolitans say)
> **Salsa al Pomodoro** (as other Italians would say)
> **Tomato Sauce** (for the rest of us)
> Fry a small, chopped onion in oil, and when it begins to turn golden add one kilogram of fresh, peeled tomatoes which have also had their seeds removed (done by immersing the tomatoes in boiling water for about 30 seconds, then peeling and slicing them when cooled). Also add about six sweet basil leaves. Cook over low heat for about half an hour. When the sauce thickens, add salt and pepper to taste. Pour generously over *al dente* (slightly chewy) portions of vermicelli, and sprinkle with freshly grated parmesan.

Lasagne is a dish traditionally eaten during *Carnevale*, while *maccheroni* pie is another reserved for festive occasions. This is usually made with a pasta such as *rigatoni*, layered with eggs, sausage and mozzarella and smothered in a ragu tomato sauce. Another local favourite in the pasta department is called *Strangolapreti*. As the story goes, a greedy priest ate so many of these little potato dumplings that he suffocated. Commonly called *gnocchi*, the ribbed pasta shapes are made with mashed potato and flour, removed from boiling water as soon as they rise to the surface, and doused with a tasty meat sauce (eat slowly).

Mozzarella

This soft cheese is one of the region's prized specialities, made from the milk of buffalo raised on the plains north of Naples. Don't think you know what it tastes like if you've been subjected only to the plastic-packed version bought outside Italy. Mozzarella is practically impossible to export successfully, since it must soak in a mixture of milk and water in order to remain fresh. But taste mozzarella in Campania and you will be hooked for life. Slightly salty and just a bit spongy, it is at its best when dressed with a rich olive oil. The *insalata Caprese*, slices of fresh tomato and mozzarella with basil, olive oil and salt, originated on Capri but is now found on lunch menus all over Italy. Try it, and try it again.

Another version of mozzarella is called *fior di latte*, made with cow's milk. It doesn't have quite as much flavour as that made with buffalo's milk, but is still very good. *Bocconcini*, or 'little bites', are the smallest forms of this delicious cheese, found in shops called *latterie* and *salumerie* (and good for picnics). One of the best sandwiches in the world is mozzarella combined with a salty prosciutto on a crusty round *rosetto* roll. When mozzarella is fried between two pieces of bread it's called *in carozza* (in carriage), a starter seen on most menus in Campania. Any variation on the theme is bound to be delicious!

Meat and fish

You won't often find Campanian families cooking a roast for Sunday lunch – most meat is reserved for making sauces. Traditionally, meat (especially lamb) was eaten a few times a year during Carnevale in February and other holidays. But today financial constraints have lessened, and you will find veal and pork, as well as lamb and chicken, served at home more regularly. They are always to be found on restaurant menus however, along with regional specialities such as rabbit and wild boar.

The local *salumeria* has always had a varied and tasty stock of sausage and salami. The sausage called *cervellata* is one of the best, made with red wine and packed with fennel seeds. *Morsello* is one of the strongest, with its biting red peppers. The Neapolitan salamis tend to be highly flavoured, full of pepper and somewhat fatty. *Prosciutti* are also fatty, though flavourful – certainly not like the delicate slices from the northern regions that go so well with sweet melon. You'll find that the thick *prosciutto* is used to flavour a variety of pasta sauces.

Fish has been a staple part of the coastal diet for hundreds of years, though surprisingly few seafood recipes have ever made their way inland. Hilltop farmers stayed far away from seafaring pirates, and didn't want to have anything to do with their food either! But in Naples and along the Amalfi coast, housewives and restaurant chefs have always been on the lookout for what's *pescato della mattinata* (caught fresh this morning).

Mussels, clams, squid and octopus make their way into pasta sauces, as well as being stewed in the rich *zuppa di pesce*, which also includes the strongly flavoured scorpion fish. Anchovies, called *acciughe* or *alici*, are cooked in a variety of ways: marinated as a starter, fried with *prosciutto* into fritters called *pizzelle alla napoletana*, and often added to deep-fried courgette flowers called *pasta cresciuta*. They also find their way into stuffed peppers and on to the top of the pizza pie.

Common fish dishes include poached octopus, peppered mussels and *calamari* (squid) with raisins and pine nuts.

Sweets

Most of the region's *dolci* are to be found in Naples, a great place for pastry tasting as you hop from café to café. Coffee is strong, the perfect antidote to light, sugar-covered sweets. At the top of my list come *sfogliatelle*, crispy shell-shaped puff pastries that are stuffed with ricotta cheese and fruit such as candied cherries. Another favourite – though by no means confined to Campania – is a caramel-coloured cone-shaped sponge called the *baba*. This is soaked in rum, a common mid-morning snack for stall sellers and students. Along the Amalfi coast you will find *sproccolati*, deliciously skewered sticks of dried figs stuffed with fennel seeds.

Festivals and holidays have a host of treats centered round them. At Christmas time, one traditional cake made with almond paste is called *Divino Amore*. Another, which makes a popular present among friends and relatives during the holiday, is *struffoli* – fried pastry rings coated in honey and decorated with coloured almonds and candied peel. But Naples is probably most famous for the *pastiera*, or Easter pie, a recipe that dates back to the 14th century. The basic ingredients are ricotta cheese and corn, symbols of well being and family prosperity. The Easter pie has become so popular that you can usually find it throughout the year in this region, as well as in other parts of Italy during the Easter season.

Wines of Campania

'The human body was designed as a funnel for pouring wine' is what Pompeiian wine producers used to say. They saw an awful lot of it being drunk, and when the city was destroyed so was Rome's wine supply. Pompeii was part of the area known to Romans as Campania Felix, so rich was its soil for cultivating grapes and other fruits. The wines, supplied in heavy terracotta amphorae, were called Falernum and Caecubum, deep coloured and full-bodied. Were they better than most produced in the region today, as some wine writers suggest? It's hardly an argument one can prove, though certainly worth debating over a bottle or two on a sun-washed terrace. Certainly Caligula would have been on the side of pessimism: he called the wine of Sorrento 'respectable vinegar'.

It has taken Campanian vintners decades, if not centuries, to overcome prejudice against their wines. Norman Douglas showed very little enthusiasm for them in *Siren Land*. Eighty years ago he described those from around Naples as 'inky fluid . . . the grapes clamber up to heaven out of sight of the peasant, who periodically forgets their existence and plants hemp and maize in their earth. No vine will endure this treatment; personal contact is the first requisite for good results.' As for the wine of Capri, he wrote 'it has now become a noisome sulphur-and-vinegar compound that will etch the bottom out of a copper cauldron.'

Campania's annual wine production is close to 30 million cases, though that's less than four per cent of Italy's total annual output. The region's most outstanding producer is Mastroberardino, in a town called Atripalda near Avellino. This vineyard's wines are among the only ones that meet the standards of Italy's DOC (*denominazione di origine controllata*) label. Less than 15 per cent of all Italian wines are classified as such, but the percentage for Campania is less than one per cent. The red and white Lacryma Christi wines, made from grapes grown on Vesuvius, are also known outside Campania. Other wines of the region with a good reputation come from Ischia, known for its dry whites, and from Ravello, known for its reds.

The Mastroberardino wines are all made from local varieties: the red Aglianico, and white grapes called Greco di Tufo and Fiano di Avellino. The family were wine merchants in Naples during the 16th century; in 1720 they moved inland to Avellino and began producing their own. The vineyard was damaged in the 1980 earthquake, but fortunately their stock of 500,000 bottles survived unharmed in a hillside tunnel. Mastroberardino's red Taurasi is the region's, and one of Italy's, best. Aged for three years, it is a rich and velvety wine always worth ordering if seen on the wine list. When the season has been exceptionally good, the family also bottles a Taurasi Riserva.

Another regional red worth noting comes from Mandragone, on the coast near the northern border. The wine is called Falerno, from the ancient Falernum so popular in Imperial Rome. It's a full-bodied, DOC classified wine. Ravello has also had some success with its reds, produced from Per'e Palummo, Aglianico and Merlot grapes. The best of these is called Episcopio, produced by the Vuilleumier family who own the Hotel Palumbo in Ravello. Competition in the category is with another Ravello hotel family. The Caruso family's Gran Caruso red is not quite of the same standard, but still better than most reds in the region.

For Campania's best white wine, we turn again to the Mastroberardino family near Avellino. Their very dry and weighty Fiano di Avellino ranks with the country's best. Running a close second (and three times cheaper) is the same vineyard's Greco di Tufo, of which they bottle up to half a million per year. The only other Campanian whites that can stand up to Mastroberardino are from Ischia and Ravello. In that gorgeous hill-town, the same two hotel families, the Caruso and the Palumbo, compete again, though both vineyards are less successful with white than red.

Of Ischia's wine, the Don Alfonzo, from the Perrazzo vineyard, is good, along with Biancolella from D'Ambra Vini d'Ischia. Norman Douglas was uncharacteristically enthusiastic when describing the wines of the island. 'Large heart in small grape,' he noted, 'a drink for the gods that oozes in unwilling drops out of the dwarfed mountain grapes.'

3. NAPLES EXPLAINED

One fine morning a northerner was walking along the port, when he saw a fisherman stretched out in the shade by the sea-wall, enjoying his rest.

'What are you doing, lying there?' asked the northerner. 'It is only ten o'clock.'

'I have done my fishing. I have sold my fish. Now I am resting,' replied the Neapolitan.

'If you did a little more work, you would catch more fish,' said the northerner.

'And then?' enquired the Neapolitan.

'Then you would have more money.'

'And then?'

'Then you would be able to buy a net.'

'And then?'

'Why then, my good man, you would get a bigger catch.'

'And then?'

'Well, you would have the money to buy a bigger boat.'

So question followed answer until the exasperated northerner explained the end of all this practical exertion.

'Then you would own a beautiful villa, with servants and everything you could possibly want!'

'Yes, and then?'

The northerner was by this time thoroughly nonplussed.

'Then you could lie down and rest.'

'But that is just what I am now doing,' replied the astonished Neapolitan.

I dare anyone to defy the logic in this Neapolitan's world view. Peter Gunn set down this fable thirty years ago in his *Naples: A Palimpsest*. Today, Neapolitans still give one the impression that despite their city's frenetic pace and grimy exterior, they know how to appreciate life and their city's hidden riches. Neapolitans are survivors: most have not benefited in any material way from the seven dynasties which ruled their city; they managed, barely, through dismal conditions during World War II; yet another earthquake devastated buildings in 1980; present-day poverty and unemployment (as high as 25 per cent) seem to give northern Italians and foreigners grounds to express strong prejudice against the local population.

Clichés here run fairly true to form: Neapolitans really are often like actors who relish their roles in street theatre. Everyone seems to live out of doors; on Friday and Saturday nights, midnight traffic jams are not uncommon. And on a Sunday morning, typically quiet in many parts of the world, Naples is bustling as usual. The park grounds at Capodimonte are chaotic – children bicycling, girls doing handstands, and boys playing football while dodging bicycles are just a few of the acts on view.

The city's architecture – so striking and full of contrast – is an invitation to perform. Encrusted Baroque obelisks are tall defenders of small squares; façades of huge crumbling palazzi give no hint of the soaring staircases within; churches are so numerous that you could find one to visit for almost every day of the year (except that nearly half are usually closed). The Castel dell'Ovo remains a placid extension into the sea which Turner painted so softly in 1819. And the Bay of Naples is the same wide blue arc which beckoned Virgil, Goethe and Dickens, while the wide cone of Vesuvius and the twin peaks of Capri are still part of the ancient backdrop.

Why do today's travellers need to be convinced that Naples is worth the trip? It is an insult to its rich heritage merely to 'pass through' on the way to Campania's more favoured spots, and it is a plain mistake to skirt its wealth all together. I know a Swedish woman who was on her way to Rome by train for a holiday twenty years ago. She slept through her stop at Rome's Termini and two hours later awoke to find herself at the Naples station. Two Neapolitan husbands and four children later, she is still there. Naples can do that to a person.

Neapolitans will welcome you happily if you are prepared to explore its riches with an open mind (and, unfortunately, with a tightly clasped purse). Chapter four is devoted to five walking tours, and you'll find that the city will wrap itself around you like a net of hectic energy, charming you with architectural surprises. Its sights and sounds will engage you completely, and perhaps unnerve you at times. In either case, this city and its vibrant people refuse to be ignored. That is part of what makes a city great, and I for one add Naples to an Italian list that includes Rome, Venice and Florence.

Naples through history

Greco-Roman times

The first references to Naples – Neapolis to the Greeks – are found in the Homeric legends of the sirens, who lured smitten sailors to their unsuspecting deaths. But death comes to beautiful sea creatures too, and legend has it that the siren Parthenope threw herself into the waves over unrequited love for Odysseus. Her body was washed ashore in Naples near the Castel dell'Ovo, and the city is said to have sprung from her burial ground. Surprisingly, no crafty tour guide has invented a geographical resting place for the siren, though Neapolitans often refer to themselves as Parthenopeans.

The oldest inhabitants of Neapolis, or New City, built the port in 6BC just a few kilometres to the east of their first Magna Graecia colony of Cumae. The name Neapolis was chosen to distinguish it from Palaepolis, an older city whose foundations merged with the new. Greek culture was so strong along these shores that the language was spoken in some parts until 1450; linguists studying Neapolitan dialect have found traces of Greek within their language today. The whole of Campania has Greek colonists to thank for the introduction of the olive and the vine.

But Greek culture was challenged by the invasion of Samnites from the northern interior who first captured Cumae in 420BC. Then the Romans expanded southwards. After a series of wars from 343BC to 290BC, they gained control over the Samnites and Campania became part of the Roman Republic. Rome's success during the Punic Wars with Carthage between 264BC and 146BC secured their stronghold of the south. Neapolis had fallen after a three-year seige in 326BC, and was a satellite city to Rome for centuries. Her emperors turned this area into a royal playground. Lavish villas were built at Baia, a town which still exists on the Misenum Peninsula west of Naples. The city itself was considered a relaxed place of high culture. Augustus, Tiberius and Nero travelled down from Rome; Virgil spent his last years here while writing the *Georgics* and the *Aeneid*. He was buried in Naples, and guides are fond of pointing out an historically unproven site for this tomb.

Vesuvius erupted in 79AD and Neapolis to the north east escaped the fates of Pompeii and Herculaneum, thanks to a prevailing south west wind. The city was covered with a thin layer of ash and was rocked by tremors.

The Roman Empire itself was officially extinguished in Naples with its last western emperor, Romulus Augustulus. He died in exile in the Castel dell'Ovo in 476AD, after being humiliatingly deposed by the barbarian Ostrogoths. (They considered him too unimportant to be put to death in public, and banished him with an annual pension of 6000 gold pieces.) During the next century, the Byzantine general Belisarius recaptured Naples; the city was firmly in the hands of Byzantium by 533 and for almost six centuries was ruled by exarchs, Byzantine provincial governors.

City-states and dynasties

As in other parts of Italy, a unified Roman Empire gave way to small city-states throughout Campania during this period. The Franks invaded from the Rhine Valley; Lombards from Hungary (then called Pannonia) made Capua and Benevento their strongholds. Saracen invaders from eastern Europe terrorised the coastal regions. The church was also a gradually strengthening force during these centuries, responsible for controlling Byzantine territory. Finally, it was the Norman crusaders who unified the region in the 11th century. From Palermo, they reigned over a land mass equal to the size of Portugal which became the richest state in Italy.

The royal parade began in 1197, and continued until the unification of Italy in 1860. Seven dynasties ruled from Naples, their histories elaborate and sometimes entangled. In the early 11th century, Norman pilgrims, soldiers and their leaders came to Italy from France; by 1053 Norman warrior Robert Guiscard was awarded the whole of southern Italy and Sicily as a papal fief. Palermo fell to Robert's younger brother Roger in 1072 and his son, Roger II, was named founder in 1127 of what was to become the Kingdom of the Two Sicilies. Naples officially became part of this Kingdom in 1139, and the Normans remained in power until 1194.

They were followed by the Germanic Hohenstaufens, Ghibelline supporters of the Holy Roman Empire who were caught in a struggle with the Guelph-supported Papacy. Frederick II came to power in 1208, an enlightened ruler whom Dante called the father of Italian poetry. He founded the first Italian state university at Naples. But when he died in 1250, the Guelphs began to gain the upper hand. Frederick's son Conrad tried to claim the throne in 1252, but was killed. His illegitimate brother Manfred tried to do the same, and was crowned King of Sicily in 1258. But he was killed in 1266 by troops led by Charles of Anjou, who had been goaded by the papacy to oust the House of Hohenstaufen from Naples.

Manfred's younger brother Conradin then tried to reclaim the throne in 1269. At the age of 15, with 10,000 men and the backing of Ghibellines in Pisa, Verona, Siena and Pavia, Conradin moved south through Italy to Naples. But most of his troops were slaughtered before getting close, and Conradin himself was captured and brought before Charles of Anjou who had him beheaded in the Piazza del Mercato. In 1631, when the Church of the Carmine was being built in that same square, a lead coffin inscribed R.C.C. was found. The letters are thought to refer to Conradin: Regis Corradini Corpus. Inside was found the skeleton of a young man, with its severed skull.

So Charles of Anjou, the brother of King Louis IX, became the first in a line of Angevin kings who ruled Naples for almost 200 years. However, he lost Sicily to the Spanish Aragonese in 1282 after a famous struggle known as the Sicilian Vespers. A conspiracy by Sicilians to undermine the French king's power turned into a massacre after a Frenchman insulted a young Sicilian woman. The Sicilians rose up in revolt at the signal of the evening vespers and killed close to 8000 Frenchmen.

Charles of Anjou's successor was Charles II, who ruled from 1285 to 1309. But it was Robert the Wise, ruling from 1309 to 1343, who helped to cleanse the family name, for the Angevin dynasty was criticised for its ruthless tactics and lack of compassion for Naples' people. Robert was a patron of the arts who encouraged poets, writers and artists to find inspiration in his city. Giotto came here to paint in 1328, though only fragments of his work have been discovered; Petrarch visited twice, and was given the sought-after royal seal of approval from Robert the Wise as a poet fit to receive the laurel crown from the Roman Senate; Boccaccio arrived from Tuscany ostensibly to study banking, but spent his time at court collecting material for some of the wonderful tales of The Decameron which he wrote in the 1350s.

After 1343, the Angevin dynasty was gradually weakened by power struggles within the family that lasted for almost 100 years. This opened the way for the House of Aragon. In 1442, Alfonso the Magnanimous captured Naples, and reunited Sicily with the mainland. The Aragon dynasty was decidedly less enlightened than Naples' previous rulers. Alfonso celebrated his victory by inserting a tall marble arch into the entrance of the Castel Nuovo. 'Pious, merciful, unconquered,' he modestly commissioned stone carvers to inscribe upon the arch. His bastard son and successor was Ferdinand I, who ruled from 1458 to 1496. He had an even worse reputation than his father, for he exploited women, killed feudal barons in revolt, and even mummified his enemies.

Naples was then ruled by a long line of viceroys from Spain, the most influential of whom was Don Pedro de Toledo (1532–54). The city was greatly expanded during this period, the Via Toledo (also called Via Roma) running in a long ribbon from north to south. The narrow streets branching off it first held barracks for Toledo's soldiers; today they are known as the poverty-stricken Spagnolo quarter, full of small and airless homes called *bassi*.

Vasari came to work in Naples in the 1540s; Caravaggio reached Naples in 1606. The first performances in which the famous, earthy, tragi-comic Neapolitan character of Pulcinella appeared occurred around 1620. A brief revolt over increasing taxes started by a fishmonger named Masaniello led to Naples' only popular uprising, in 1647; citizens were freed from Spanish rule for nine whole days . . . before the Spanish viceroy had Masaniello shot. The Count of Onate, viceroy in 1651, is credited with introducing opera to the city of Naples. But staged tragedy became reality in 1656 when a plague hit the city and close to one half of the city's population of 450,000 died.

The Bourbons

After the War of the Spanish Succession, Naples came under the rule of Archduke Charles of Austria through the Treaty of Utrecht. But in 1734, with 27 years of uninspired Austrian viceroys behind it, the city became autonomous under the Spanish Bourbon Charles III. The Bourbon dynasty was to remain in power until 1860, except for 15 years (1799–1815) when Naples was proclaimed the Parthenopean Republic by the French. The early Bourbon kings were considered honourary Neapolitans, speaking dialect and behaving the way the citizenry thought they ought to – holding court as royal patrons and parading in finery through the city streets.

Charles III gave Naples many of its most lavish buildings. He was well versed in the history of architecture, and practised drafting and design. He took a keen interest in the commissions he initiated. Capodimonte and its famous porcelain factory were built; the San Carlo Opera House rose in the city's centre; Dutch architect Vanvitelli (Van Wittel) was commissioned to design the Palace of Caserta; excavations at Herculaneum and Pompeii were begun. Charles III's mother was Elizabeth Farnese, and it is thanks to her inheritance that the Farnese collection now rests in the National Archeological Museum here.

When Charles was called back to rule Spain at the age of 43 in 1759, his third son Ferdinand was crowned King of Naples at the age of seven. (The eldest, Philip, was declared insane and the second son, Charles, later became Charles IV of Spain.)

Ferdinand IV was known as 'King Nosey' by affectionate attendants because of his most prominent feature. He grew up relatively uneducated, and spent more time hunting for boar and wildfowl than in caring for the Neapolitan people. By 1760, the population of Naples had reached 347,000 – one of the largest and poorest cities in Europe. Ferdinand's wife Maria Carolina was Marie Antoinette's sister, far more politically astute than her husband. When Napoleon's army was marching from Rome to Naples in 1799 she was convinced that the guillotine would be her fate as well. But the royal family sailed to safety in Palermo, thanks to the help of British Ambassador Sir William Hamilton and Admiral Horatio Nelson (who was infatuated with Hamilton's young wife Emma). This was probably the most dramatic event in the reign of King Ferdinand IV.

Ferdinand returned to Naples after the Peace of Amiens in 1802, choosing the new title of Ferdinand I, King of the Two Sicilies. But in 1805, the king fled again, when by Napoleon's decree his brother Joseph Bonaparte regained the throne, which was then passed to French marshal Joachim Murat (married to Napoleon's sister Caroline). French rule was brief and chaotic; the Bourbon King Ferdinand returned in 1815 after the Congress of Vienna restored order in Europe.

His grandson Ferdinand II inherited the throne in 1830, known unpopularly as 'King Bomba' for his bombardment of Messina to show the Sicilians what he thought of their demands for a Constitution. But a fair account of King Bomba's reign would show that he constructed the fantastic Amalfi Coast drive, built the first iron suspension bridge in Italy and repeatedly saved the San Carlo opera house from bankruptcy. His successor was Francis II, who ruled Naples until Garibaldi entered the city in September, 1860.

This last Bourbon king fled north to Gaeta; Garibaldi arrived with his troops by train from Salerno the morning after. Neapolitans were on the streets to greet them, waving banners and handkerchiefs, though they didn't seem to have any more or less faith in this new band of rulers than the last. Turin was made the new capital of a united Italy in 1861, and the House of Savoy now ruled with Victor Emmanuel II as the first king. Naples was never again looked upon as a royal capital, though upper class travellers did continue to make a pilgrimage there as part of the obligatory Grand Tour for at least another thirty years.

Grand Tour travellers

Naples was host to a steady stream of travellers well before the 1800s, and its appeal (and in some cases, lack of it) was recorded by many. One Englishman, a member of the Royal Society called John Ray, published his observations of daily life in 1673:

This City is well served with all provisions, especially fruit which is very cheap heer . . . Macarones and Vermicelle (which are nothing but a kind of paste cut into the figure of worms or thongs) boil'd in broth or water, are a great dish heer as well as at Messina, and as much esteemed by the vulgar, as Frumenty by the Countrey people in England.

Elizabeth David has done a better job since in describing the delights of Italian food, but it is interesting that even then a traveller found it worth noting. Observations took on a more cultural aspect in the 1700s, when Sir William Hamilton's presence drew many English travellers to the city. As British Ambassador, he lived in Naples for 35 years, well-known for his serious studies of volcanoes and classical antiquities – an early archaeologist whose family would have inherited valuable treasure if most of it had not sunk in a storm off Sicily on its way back to England. In the 1780s, his young wife-to-be, Emma, was famous for her drawing room performances called 'Attitudes'. Goethe described them during a visit in 1787:

> . . . letting her hair loose, and taking a couple of shawls, she exhibits every possible variety of posture, expression and look, so that at last the spectator almost fancies it is a dream . . . Standing, kneeling, sitting, lying down, grave or sad, playful, exulting, repentant, wanton, menacing, anxious – all mental states follow rapidly one after another.

When Stendhal visited in 1817, finding it hard to find a hotel room, he remarked that, 'there must have been two or three thousand English in the city.' Lady Blessington, who published two volumes in 1839 titled *The Idler in Italy*, observed

> The more I see of the Neapolitans, the more I like them. I have not detected among the individuals of the lower class that have fallen in my way, a single instance of the rapaciousness so generally, and I am inclined to think so unjustly, attributed to them by strangers.'

Travelogues took on a negative tone in the late 1800s. The Bourbons had left, and there were no longer Court balls and hunting parties to overshadow the city's poverty. John Ruskin described Naples as 'the most loathsome nest of human caterpillars I was ever forced to stay in'. At the turn of the century, an American millionaire named Dan Fellows Platt wrote that Naples was 'a motorist's hell'. In that he is right to this day, but Ruskin must have been wearing blinkers.

Naples since Garibaldi

During centuries of royal rule, the average Neapolitan was living in anything but palatial quarters. The citizenry's plight became more obvious after Unification in 1860, and received nationwide attention with the outbreak of cholera in 1884. Soon Naples was involved in a massive urban renewal programme to unweave the tight web of airless slums, and to transport cleaner water to the centre.

But the divide between northern and southern Italy, which had always

17

existed, continued to widen in economic terms. Various government programmes meant better health and a higher rate of literacy, but northern industry was steaming ahead of the agriculturally-based south. Campania and the rest of southern Italy were virtually ignored when Mussolini was in power, except as a place to which fascists exiled the likes of Carlo Levi.

The city was bombed during World War II – first by the advancing allies in August, 1943, when Italy was still aligned with Germany, and then attacked and captured by the Germans after the armistice was signed that September. The American 5th Army ousted them, but not before the Germans had destroyed hotels, the port area, and gas and electricity supplies for the city. Because of a drastic lack of food and other services, Neapolitans earned a well-deserved reputation for imaginative cunning and enterprise during World War II.

American soldiers were charmed by the boisterous warmth of Neapolitan families, and when visiting them would bring welcome gifts of flour, cigarettes and chocolate. What the soldiers didn't realise was that 'selling Americans' was one way to make a little extra cash: a Neapolitan family would introduce their soldier to another local family – for a fee, of course. You've only to read Norman Lewis's wonderful book, *Naples '44*, to understand the true meaning of the verb *arrangiarsi*, to 'get by'. In one passage Lewis describes being

> 'drawn into a corner by a priest, white-lipped and smiling. He opened a bag full of umbrella handles, candlesticks and small ornaments of all kinds carved out of the bones of saints, i.e. from bones filched from one of the catacombs. He, too, had to live.'

Despite the fact that Naples has always been dominated by foreign rulers, some of its citizens still believe that they were better off before a 'unified' national government had a guiding hand in their affairs. Masses of development money from the *Cassa del Mezzogiorno* has not successfully addressed their problems. One typical opinion was expressed by a Neapolitan woman I know: 'Where are all the macaroni factories we used to have? Out of business. Where do we buy our pasta from now? The north. Yes, they give us money, but we spend all of ours on goods produced by them.'

Us versus them, and she even has relatives in northern Italy. Her son has a Bolognese friend who braved Naples to visit him, under the impression that Federico was unusually educated and amiable for a Neapolitan. When his cultured northern friend saw that Federico's sister Maria Teresa had rings on her fingers he was horrified. 'Won't they cut your finger off to steal the ring?' he asked. Stories such as these abound, and they astonish me.

The city's population now numbers more than 1,200,000 and the labyrinthine Spaccanapoli section of Naples is still crowded with many who just manage to scrape by. Old men sell eggs from straw carts, lined with sprigs of sage. Widowed women in black sit on wooden chairs behind their makeshift counters, selling contraband cigarettes in open and accepted transgression of the law. And always there are gangs of young boys, *scugnizzi*, about, making you wonder when on earth school is open in this city. I remember one eight-year-old who took time out from his football game beside the Duomo to have a chat with me. Could he help with my map reading? No? Then he'd go back to score a goal for me. Saying goodbye, he chucked me under the chin with unnerving confidence. Older gangs of Neapolitan boys are not so innocent, however. To pay for drugs, they will steal your bag with speed and efficiency.

The devastating earthquake of 1980 has forced the city to re-examine its programme to overhaul many old buildings. A group of concerned citizens, led by Baroness Mirella Barracco, created the Fondazione Napoli '99, an organisation founded in 1984 to focus world-wide attention on the city's plight. Private donations, and patrons such as Mario Valentino, Mobil Oil and the CIGA hotel chain have enabled the foundation to restore a number of important monuments, including the Castel Nuovo's marble entrance arch and frescoes within the San Gennaro Chapel. Neapolitans have embraced the foundation's philosophy with fervour. 'Open Door' weekends, to view many monuments often closed to the public, have drawn crowds of up to 500,000. Schoolchildren have proudly 'adopted' monuments throughout the city.

The business of constructing new buildings is not conducted with such noble intentions, however. The construction industry is booming, especially in the suburb of Fuorigrotta, but the Camorra, Naples' mainland version of the Mafia, plays an all too visible role in raking off billions of lire. Many of the city's shops and businesses, an estimated 50,000 of them, pay protection money to the Camorra just to be left alone. (Aptly, Camorra is a corruption of the Spanish word *gamurra* meaning extortion money.) Highest stakes are in the drugs game: the sale of cocaine and heroin is masterminded by the Camorra, and sadly the number of drug addicts has risen in proportion to the organisation's ability to sell. And the criminals' tactics are just as sinister as those of the Sicilian Mafia – in 1988 the severed head of Naples' chief prison psychiatrist was found in a tin biscuit box. He had been testing the mental health of jailed Camorra bosses with too much skill.

That is the darkest side of Naples' character, and is not denied by anyone living there. As with the Mafia, the organised clout and control of the Camorra has remained stable in part because national government has been so unstable. Recent arrests of Mafia and Camorra bosses, as well as of corrupt politicians, have left citizens feeling unsettled, yet hopeful. They remain passionately proud of their city, and of themselves. And, *grazie a Dio*, San Gennaro's blood is still reputed to liquify with reassuring regularity.

4. NAPLES
EXPLORED

The five walking tours that follow will take you past almost all of Naples'
most famous sights. I stress *walking* tours, for except in the case of Hilltop
Museum-Hopping, you will be able to see everything easily on foot. The city's
oldest and most evocative quarter is Spaccanapoli, with its tight alleys and
many famous churches. Then heading toward the sea and radiating out from
the Piazza Trieste e Trento are the city's municipal and cultural monuments:
the Palazzo Reale, Castel Nuovo, the Galleria and the San Carlo Opera House.
Another walk takes you down to the seafront, by the Villa Communale and the
port area of Mergellina. On the hills above you will find some of Naples' most
treasured art – in the San Martino Monastery and at Capodimonte. An important
part of Naples' history is also underground, but unfortunately very few of these
subterranean tunnels, grottoes and building foundations are accessible to the
public yet.

Above ground, it isn't difficult to make your way around Naples. Bus and
tram lines are good, and a ticket purchased for 1000 lire (then cancelled by
inserting into the small red machine at the back where you enter the bus) will
take you from one end of the city to the other. Tickets can be purchased from
many newsstands, and from shops with a black and white sign saying 'T' for
Tabacchi. Buy a detailed map of the city from a bookshop or newspaper stand.
The map published by Studio F. M. B. Bologna is a very good one.

Do not take a car into Naples if you can help it. Even if it isn't stolen, you'll
find it difficult to make your way through city streets. Traffic laws were made
to be ignored here, and only at the major intersections (with a traffic warden
present in crisp uniform) will cars consistently stop for a red light. An estimated
800,000 cars are on the move in the Naples area daily, and half of them invade
the historic centre. If you've rented a car, drop it off at the Capodichino airport
7km out of town and take the bus or taxi in. (The coach service runs reliably
every 40 minutes and costs 3000 lire, whereas a taxi costs anywhere from
30000 to 50000 lire.) If you are driving, choose a hotel with a parking garage,
though this can be a costly option – negotiate with the hotel's management
before handing over the keys or you might be in for an unpleasant surprise
when paying the bill.

While walking in Naples, on no account assume that a driver will stop if you set foot on a zebra crossing. Every part of the pavement is dodgem territory for cars and bodies alike. My tactic is to cross with an old man or woman, or a mother and child, but I can't say this is successful in every case. I should add, however, that not once have I seen an accident in Naples. When taking a cab, always check to see whether or not the meter works, and ask about the supplement charged at night and on weekends. Try to establish a fee, if only roughly, for the length of your journey.

From first-hand experience, I also caution you (as will many Neapolitans) not to carry valuables when touring city streets. Leave credit cards, traveller's checks, passports and cash in the hotel safe, and take with you only what's needed for the day's outing. I found it impossible – what with books and camera and notepads – not to carry a bag the last time I was there but Neapolitans will tell you not to roam around with one. If you must, strap the bag across your chest so that it doesn't dangle from the shoulder, and make a record of your credit card numbers. I learned this the hard way, or rather my sister did. She was pushed to the pavement while two teenage boys on a motorino tried to yank my bag away. (They didn't get it.)

The five sections of Naples explored in the following walking tours cover a total area of about six kilometers from east to west, and five kilometers from north to south. Each tour takes about three hours, and you will by no means have exhausted the city's possibilities by walking them. On the other hand, I have tried to fashion them in a flexible way so that you could visit a museum in the morning and then do a portion of one walk in the afternoon. I must stress that if you are only in the city for a few days, do not miss Spaccanapoli and the National Archeological Museum (Walk 1).

In general, museums open from 09.00 until 14.00. Churches open from 08.00 to 12.00 and/or from about 17.00 to 20.00 in the evening, but these hours are notoriously inconsistent; one of the best times to view churches is on Saturday morning. Shops will close in the afternoon from about 13.00 to 16.00, and then open again until about 20.00. The sign *Chiuso per Restauro* (closed for restoration) might hamper you at times, but it's best to look on the bright side when a monument has been 'closed for restoration': Naples is trying to stop the decay of its architectural history, and is hard at work restoring those buildings most badly in need of repair. Where possible, I have been more specific about opening times for major sites, listed alphabetically in the information section at the end of the chapter.

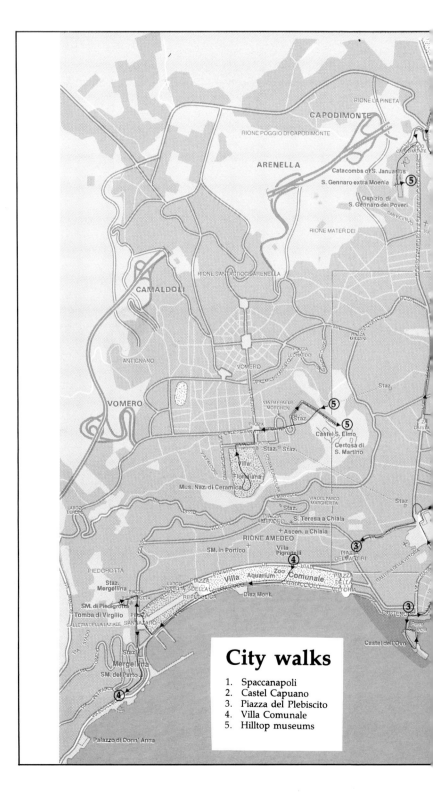

City walks

1. Spaccanapoli
2. Castel Capuano
3. Piazza del Plebiscito
4. Villa Comunale
5. Hilltop museums

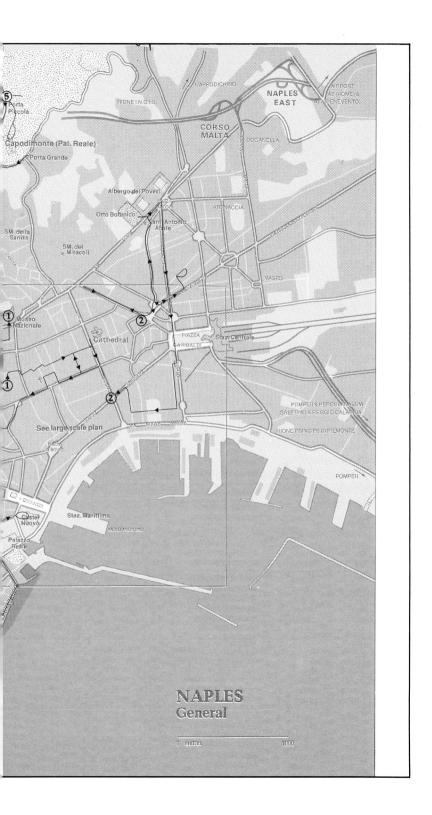

NAPLES
General

0 metres 1000

WALK 1
The inner square: Spaccanapoli

Greco-Roman Naples is almost non-existent if you are looking for ruins to mark the period. What survived best is the original street pattern of the old city, and the section of Naples called Spaccanapoli is right at its heart. This quarter derived its name from the view of Via Roma from the Monastery of San Martino on the hill above. This main street seems to 'split' the city in half, for the verb *spaccare* in Italian means just that; Spaccanapoli is directly east of where the split occurs. The paths of the old city within the quarter can be traced to their Greek nomenclature: the *decumanus major* is Via Tribunali, and *decumanus minor* are Via Forcella and San Biagio dei Librai. This walk is bounded by the superb National Archeological Museum to the north, the Duomo to the east, by the Piazzas Amore and Carità in the southern corners, and by Piazza Dante to the west. The quarter is jam-packed with sights, and though the walk covers the major monuments, there is always more to see. The National Archeological Museum, for example, is worth a full morning's viewing if not a return visit.

The Via Roma cuts through the centre of Naples from south to north into **Piazza Dante**. Many buses begin and end their run here; it's a lively square that serves as a good introduction to the quarter of Spaccanapoli. The high statue of Dante has been watching over the populace since 1872, and the Doric semicircle with statues of twenty-six not very inspiring Virtues was created by Vanvitelli under Charles III. The Port' Alba on the northeast corner of the square is your way in to the quarter. Streets are narrow – a *via* suddenly becomes *vico*, and even this word (meaning alley) takes on its dimunitive in *vicolo*.

People say that you can never really know a Neapolitan until he invites you into his home, and part of Spaccanapoli's irrepressible charm lies in the feeling that you have indeed been invited in. Doors are open wide to the street; people sit in ground floor kitchens having a chat or a game of cards. A girl on a second floor balcony lowers a basket for the red peppers and pasta her mother has bought. Ask for directions and an old man wants to practise the English he picked up from soldiers during World War II. Laundry is draped from one side of the street to the other – like strips of pasta hanging to dry from on high. Plants flourish on balconies, but they'd never survive at street level. All the while cars are edging past *motorinos* which are trying to avoid the passers-by, who are either totally oblivious or suspiciously eyeing anything on wheels.

East to San Lorenzo

Via Port' Alba travels east through the arch and then for a short distance becomes Via San Pietro a Maiella before reaching **Piazza Miraglia**. It might be too early yet for lunch, but make a note of Pizzeria Bellini near the corner of Via Santa Maria di Costantinopoli. It's one of the best in the city, and great fun when lively students from the surrounding university faculties pack it out at lunchtime (though this can make for surly waiters).

The statue of Dante looks down over the Naples piazza that bears his name

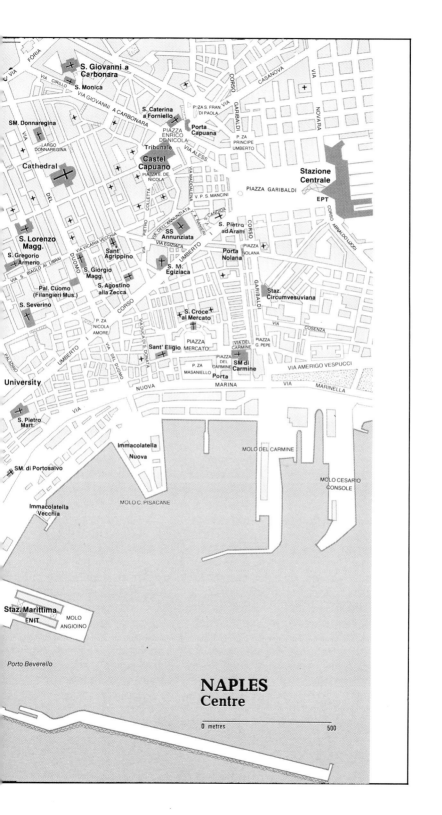

NAPLES
Centre

0 metres   500

On the north west corner of Piazza Miraglia is the elegant **Cappella Pontano**, constructed in 1492 as a funerary vault for Giovanni Pontano's wife Adriana Sassone. The small, simple interior is offset by its beautifully detailed majolica floor. Just beyond the chapel is the church of **Santa Maria Maggiore detta La Pietrasanta**. Building began on Roman foundations under the Bishop Pomponio in the first half of the sixth century, and was among the first four parishes in Naples. But it was rebuilt beginning in 1653, partially redesigned by Cosimo Fanzago. Pietrasanta, or holy stone, refers to the name added in the late 17th century, when a stone within began to attract followers. It was carved with the sign of the cross, and those who kissed it were said to receive plenary indulgences. The fantastic, swirling cotto and majolica patterned floor was restored in 1992. The church's medieval bell-tower is one of Naples' oldest, dating from the 11th century. It is separate from the church and standing to the south east.

A small church with a long name – **Santa Maria delle Anime del Purgatorio ad Arco** is next on the left, at the beginning of Via Dei Tribunali. You are greeted by three bronze skulls on stone columns at street level. Begun in 1604, its façade was reworked by Fanzago in 1652 and again refurbished in 1716. Climb the stairs to a church rich in marble and mother-of-pearl tarsio decoration. The side chapels are as richly decorated with artwork: in the third chapel on the left is Andrea Vaccaro's *Transito di San Giuseppe*, painted in the middle of the 17th century; in the third chapel on the left is an early work by Luca Giordano, *Sant'Alessio Moribondo*, signed and dated 1661.

Farther along on the **Piazza Gaetano** (under which part of the ancient Forum lies) is the church of **San Paolo Maggiore**, built in 1603 by Francesco Grimaldi. The inlaid marble work within is beautiful; frescoes by Massimo Stanzione are on the ceiling, though I think overshadowed by those done by Francesco Solimena in the sacristy. There is a very pretty cloister. This was first the site of the Temple of the Dioscuri, and its two Augustan columns with Corinthian capitals extend out from the church's façade.

San Lorenzo Maggiore

Across the piazza is the entrance to a more interesting church – **San Lorenzo Maggiore**, erected at the end of the 13th century. It is named for the martyred saint who was literally grilled to death over an open flame. The visiting Florentine Boccaccio met his love Maria here in 1334, whom he immortalised as Fiametta in many of his works, including the *Decameron*:

> I found myself in a gracious and beautiful church in Parthenope named after him who, to make himself immortal, endured to be offered on the gridiron. Now while I stood there . . . there appeared to me the marvellous beauty of a young woman . . . my heart began to flutter so strongly that it was as if I could feel it throbbing in the smallest pulses of my body.

I can't guarantee that anything similar will happen to you, but visit San Lorenzo just the same. Erected by the Franciscans, a mix of architectural styles, (thanks to successive earthquakes) is obvious at the entrance, and even more so once inside. The Gothic doorway is set into a Baroque exterior by Sanfelice; within, the Gothic nave with its trio of arches before the high altar has been restored to its simple state, while the apse and its nine radiating chapels were never modernised. In the first chapel to the left of the altar is a *Crucifixion with St Francis and Franciscan Saints* painted by Mattia Preti in 1660; his *Madonna and Child with Franciscan Saints* is on the adjacent wall. The high altar is by Giovanni da Nola, with its statues of Sts Lorenzo, Anthony and Francis; relief panels of the saints are below. Directly to the right is the tomb of Catherine of Austria. With its twisting columns and delicate figures, it is said to be Tino di Camaino's first work done in Naples, commissioned by the Angevin court in 1323.

The 18th-century cloisters of San Lorenzo are entered through doors to the right of the altar, or through a separate door beside the entrance. The four side passages are raised about 2m above the sunken grassy centre, where a forsaken well sits amid toppled columns and broken capitals. This seems an odd and lonely place, but perhaps the thought of Petrarch suffering through an incredible storm here in 1345 aided my impression: 'What a deluge! What trembling of the earth and roaring of the sea! What human shouts!' he wrote. He and the Franciscan monks might have been safest of all in the subterranean passages beneath the church which reveal traces of Greek structures and Roman walls. (Ask the sacristan to lead you down.)

Via San Gregorio Armeno

From Piazza Gaetano, **Via San Gregorio Armeno** runs south, and is worth a detour for its 16th-century church of the same name. Before reaching the church, the entrance to the cloisters is on the right (ring the bell set just within the gate). After Santa Chiara, these are my favourite cloisters in Naples – overflowing with greenery, the yellow-and-green tiled cupola of the church poking up beyond the far wall. Though the Benedictine nuns live in the building above the cloisters, the atmosphere here does not feel confining. In the nineteenth century, girls were sent here to atone for unacceptable behaviour in the eyes of their noble families, and their spirits live on. The nuns here have their own miracle to rival San Gennaro, when the blood of Santa Patrizia liquifies seemingly on request.

The Benedictine nuns have been blessed with visits by restoration experts from Rome; their meticulous work on a cycle of frescoes was finished last year. You will see their handiwork upon entering San Gregorio Armeno – the walls and gilded arched ceiling are covered with the story of the life of the saint. Frescoes between the windows are by Luca Giordano; the Baroque organs here are the most elaborate I've ever seen.

This street is a delight to walk down, filled with the workshops of Neapolitans who sculpt the figurines which fill the Nativity scene of the Christmas creche. In Naples it is known as the *presepio*, a famous part of the holiday tradition. Some churches are renowned for elaborate creche scenes devised 200 years ago. They inspire ordinary citizens to do their best by coming to this street at

Via San Gregorio Armeno, Naples

all times of the year to buy clay and plaster fishmongers, bakers, cheese sellers, wise men, hovering angels and the ubiquitous Christ child in a basket of hay. You can purchase a whole pizzeria in miniature, or a basket of mussels the size of a coin. These delightful representations of daily and divine life make their way to all parts of Italy for sale before Christmas (at many times the Neapolitan price!).

The Duomo

Head back up to Via dei Tribunali, turn right, and walk until you reach Via Duomo. Turn left, and the **Duomo** will be just up on the right. This is not one of the city's most impressive architectural monuments, but the patron saint of Naples, San Gennaro, calls it home. Charles I of Anjou began the French Gothic cathedral in 1294 and Robert the Wise finished the work in 1323. The earthquake of 1456 shattered all but the façade, which had already been rebuilt after an earthquake in 1407.

To the left above the central doorway is the tomb of Charles of Anjou, but the original was destroyed in the earthquake and it's unlikely that any of the man's bones found their way back to his resting place. The ceiling was painted by Fabrizio Santafede in 1621; Luca Giordano and pupils frescoed the 46 saints on the walls above the arches. The third chapel on the south side, with its intricate gilded bronze gates by Cosimo Fanzago, is dedicated to San Gennaro. This is High Baroque at its zenith. The dome was frescoed by Lanfranco; the altarpiece to the right is by Ribera. The head of the saint is stored within a tabernacle behind the altar, along with two phials of his blood.

The cathedral's famous patron saint proves himself worthy by producing a miracle not once, but three times, each year for it is claimed that San Gennaro's blood liquefies within the small phials stored in the chapel. If the ceremony happens quickly, this is a sign of good luck for the city. But if it happens slowly – or, God forbid, not at all – then times will be hard for the Neapolitans. (Ten minutes is quick work; a half hour is agonising.) The head of the saint must always be near the capsules for the miracle to work. Since 1398, the miracle has been documented in this way: on the Saturday before the first Sunday in May the blood liquefies in the church of Santa Chiara (the phials and head taken by procession from the Duomo), then in the Duomo on 19 September and again on 16 December. The churches are packed, but very few people are ever close enough to see whether the hard red substance has turned into liquid. In the late 19th century, a Professor Albini declared the liquid to be a kind of chocolate, but he and his kind were hushed up.

Art experts might argue that the devastating earthquake of 1980 actually produced a different kind of miracle in the Duomo. Strangely enough, the violent tremors uncovered early art works within the side chapels of Santo Spenno and San Massimo on either side of the high altar. Much older frescoes were discovered for the first time and have since been restored, resulting in the layered look of both chapels' walls. One of the most beautiful Renaissance works in Naples lies beneath the main altar. This is the crypt or Capella Carafa, its ornamental work and statue of Cardinal Carafa done by Tommaso Malvito from 1497 to 1506.

Leaving the Duomo, head south on Via Duomo past Via San Biagio dei Librai until you see the **Palazzo Cuomo** on your right, close to the corner of Via D'Alagno. This dark and aggressive façade conceals the **Museo Filangieri**, full of eclectic treasures collected by Prince Gaetano Filangieri. The 17th-century scale model of Naples is one of the most interesting pieces. The model shows that there was slightly more breathing room three hundred years ago, but you'll be able to identify many of the monuments dotted around the city. The museum houses everything from Greek coins and Sevres vases to delicate works in lace.

West along Via San Biagio

Return by Via Duomo to Via San Biagio dei Librai and turn left there. At No.81 you'll come to the **Doll Hospital**. The man who calls himself the doctor here is Luigi Grassi. His grandfather, who designed scenery for the San Carlo Opera House, developed this business as a sideline almost one hundred years ago. But the state of the shop attests to the fact that repairing dolls is no longer a sideline. Signor Grassi is happily entrapped in the limbs of porcelain, wax and wooden creatures. It is a highly 'animated' scene – these dolls, puppets and broken busts all seem to be in the midst of conversation – but you will always be welcome to enter and add to the confusion.

A detour you must take is to the **Cappella Sansevero**, now a private museum. Walking down Via San Biagio, turn right on Via Nilo and then left to 19 Via Francesco de Sanctis. The building (down on the right) was founded in 1590 by Prince Raimondo di Sangro as the family burial chapel, but over the entrance is a sculptural relief of one family member who refuses to be interred. Don Cecco di Sangro is climbing out of his coffin in the hope of heading off to another military campaign.

The chapel's most impressive Baroque work is the *Veiled Christ* by sculptor Giuseppe Sammartino, worked from a single block of marble. Lying in the centre of the chapel, the shroud actually looks like a thin, translucent cover for the body laying beneath; the crown of thorns is at his feet near a pair of pliers with the pulled nails that have released Christ from the cross. The other powerful piece of sculpture here is by Francesco Queirolo from Genoa. Called *Disillusion*, it shows a man said to represent Prince Raimondo's father struggling to free himself from vice, which takes the form of a net incredibly worked in marble. In the chapel's crypt are very strange examples of the Prince's alchemical experiments: the upper bodies of two human skeletons, covered with wires meant to show how and where blood travels through the heart and lungs.

From the chapel's entrance, turn right and return to Via San Biagio by way of **Vico San Domenico Maggiore** to visit the Gothic church of that name. In the piazza to the right, San Domenico was built in the late 13th century and the adjoining monastery, where St Thomas Aquinas once stayed, is run by

The Doll Hospital, Via San Biagio dei Librai, Naples

Dominican friars. Once you have climbed the steps to the basilica, you will find yourself behind the high altar. There are many tombs within, and very good examples of Renaissance sculpture by Malvito, Camaiano and followers, and Jacopo della Pila.

The little church of **Sant' Angelo a Nilo** is nearby, on the square's south east corner. Naples' first Renaissance work is here – the tomb of Cardinal Brancaccio beside the high altar. It was done in Pisa by Donatello, Michelozzo and Pagno di Lapo Portigiano, and shipped here in 1428. Donatello was definately responsible for the delicate relief panel on the side of the tomb facing the altar, called *Assumption of the Madonna*, but art experts no longer think he sculpted the cardinal's head.

Naples never yearned to be the Florence of the south, and its architects were unapologetically more enthusiastic when it came to creating monuments in the Baroque style. Personally, I try to limit my exposure to it, but not when it comes to the city's obelisks. One of the three in Naples is in nearby **Piazza Domenico Maggiore**. Called a *guglia* in Italian, this obelisk was actually started in 1658, two years after Neapolitans voted to put one there after the plague of 1656. But it wasn't finished by Vaccaro until 1737 when a bronze statue of San Domenico was added as the finishing touch at the top.

Piazza Gesù Nuovo and Santa Chiara

The way west now becomes Via Benedetto Croce. On the left, at No.45, you pass the once sumptuous **Palazzo Carafa**, built at the end of the 16th century but modified to accommodate the popular Baroque style at the beginning of the 18th century. Two gryphon-like dogs of stone stand guard at the entrance. You soon reach **Piazza Gesù Nuovo** with its own encrusted *Guglia della Immacolata*, erected in about 1750 through a public collection. On the north side of the square is the church of **Gesù Nuovo**, and its overblown Baroque interior has kept me from entering more than once, despite the appeal made by an old man on the local bus: 'To me it is the most beautiful church in the world. I am only saddened that our city doesn't take better care of it.' Every inch of gold and bronze gleams within, so I'm not sure what he was complaining about. The most interesting thing about the church is the contrast between its stark Renaissance exterior (like that of Palazzo Cuomo) and the completely unexpected explosion of colour inside.

At the southern end of the square is **Santa Chiara** and its famous majolica cloisters (one place you should not miss seeing). The early 14th-century church was badly bombed in World War II but the city wisely decided to return the interior to its original Gothic simplicity. Walk behind the high altar for a look at the tomb of Robert the Wise. Though damaged, Florentine brothers Giovanni and Pacio Bertini sculpted this impressive piece in 1343–45, with the six Virtues upon pillars which support the sarcophagus. On the front and sides are figures representing the king and his family.

Before visiting the cloisters, it is worth spending the small fee to see the presepio nearby. It's a finely crafted representation of the Wise Men visiting

The cloisters of Santa Chiara, Naples

the Christ Child. Exotic animals are crowded next to Neapolitans carrying on with daily life; people hang over balconies or do their shopping, with the requisite ruins in the background. Hanging from the star of Bethlehem is the very thing needed to keep evil spirits away – the *cornuto*, a small horn-shaped amulet hanging from the star's bottom point. What better place for this Neapolitan good luck charm than here?

The **cloisters of Santa Chiara** are a true oasis in the heart of old Naples. The walls, benches and octagonal columns are lined with brightly coloured land and seascapes depicted on majolica tiles. (The name majolica derives from the island of Majorca, where this pottery with its brownish-red base and richly coloured, glossy glazes has been made since the 12th century.) Some of the thickest vines I've ever seen wind their way up toward the overhead arbour, and even the weeds which surround the four-square pathways are lusciously green. The Rococo architect Domenico Vaccaro finished these unusual cloisters in 1742 and they have been used regularly by Neapolitans ever since. To spend a Sunday morning here is to be invited into an eccentric Italian's garden. Children skip rope or help push a younger sibling's pram; some adults read the newspaper while others just meet to exchange local gossip.

Monteoliveto and north to Piazza Dante

The church of **Monteoliveto**, or **Sant' Anna dei Lombardi**, is not far away, and after a trek here you'll be rewarded with a stop at one of Naples' most famous

35

bakeries. On the southeast corner of Piazza Gesù, take the Calatà Trinita Maggiore south, crossing the main road up to Piazza Monteoliveto. But before visiting this church, let me just digress (at the risk of decreasing your appetite) to list the odd assortment of relics kept within **Santa Maria Donnalbina**. The relics of a saint are important to any church's sanctity and identity, but priests here have been more conscientious than most. The following relics are said to lie within: a thorn from the crown worn by Jesus; one of Saint Sebastian's arms; a thighbone from the martyred Saint Arsenio; a breast of Saint Agatha the Virgin; and finally a piece of skin from the body of San Lorenzo said to liquify each year on his birthday. (The church is reached by going south on Via Monteoliveto and taking a left on Via Donn' Albina, but it has been closed *per restauro* for some years now.)

But back to Sant'Anna dei Lombardi, one of the most interesting in Naples for its Renaissance sculpture. The best work here is a terracotta Pietà, with eight figures, in the Chapel of Santo Sepolcro, reached by going right before the high altar and walking to the end of the corridor. The group is by Guido Mazzoni, done in 1492. In the Piccolomini Chapel to the left of the entrance is a lovely sculptured relief, *Adoration of the Shepherds*, by Antonio Rossellino dated 1475. Frescoes by Giorgio Vasari in the vault only convince me that he was better off devoting himself to writing about the lives of the artists than to competing with their talent.

From Piazza Monteoliveto take Via Caravita out to Via Roma and walk north toward Piazza Dante. On your right at No.13 you'll come to a wonderful old pastry shop called Fratelli Cappuccio. Stop in to fortify yourself before making your way to see the Greek statuary and treasures from Pompeii and Herculaneum at the National Archeological Museum. Coffee at Cappuccio is excellent, not to mention the finger-like almond cakes called *cartucci* and the *sfogliatelle* filled with cherries and ricotta cheese.

Via Roma becomes Via Pessina north from Piazza Dante, and you'll see the large building housing the National Archeological Museum up on the far right hand and corner. Walk through the **Galleria Principe di Napoli** on the eastern side of Via Pessina. This three-armed, glass-domed gallery is the oldest in the city, constructed in the 1880s. Like London's Crystal Palace, it was a technological breakthrough with its use of iron struts and glass. But it was never as popular as the Galleria Umberto I built ten years later; most of its original shops now serve as municipal offices.

The Museo Nazionale Archeologico

The northern entrance of the Galleria Principe di Napoli takes you out to **Piazza Museo Nazionale** – not really a square but the beginning of a wide avenue. The 16th-century building, used as a barracks and then as part of the university, was remodelled as a museum in 1790. It houses one of the richest collections of antiquities in the world. When all of its rooms are open it is a huge place to roam around in, with so many important works that it's worth spending quite a bit of time here or coming more than once. I'd suggest that it is worth purchasing the pictorial English guide to the museum in the little shop just inside the entrance. This is mainly to locate objects visually, because some are poorly labelled, if at all, and due to earthquake damage works are occasionally moved as rooms are still being renovated.

The main hall on the ground floor, the *Grande Atrio dei Magistrati*, is full of astoundingly large pieces of sculpture. The marble sarcophagus (No.6705) is from Pozzuoli and carved by Roman sculptors in the third century. Prometheus is at the centre on the bottom row, moulding man from clay, and deities such as Psyche and Zeus surround him. It's an animated scene with an amazing amount of detail in relief. The galleries to the right of the main hall contain a number of fine Greek works: the muscular Farnese Hercules; the Farnese Bull (one of the largest surviving works from ancient Rome, taken from the Baths of Caracalla); a Roman copy of Doryphoros, a boy carrying a spear; the headless statue of Nike; and the Aphrodite Sossandra from Baia, inspired by the original bronze done by Kalamis for the Acropolis in Athens. The Farnese collection has been beautifully restored; an added benefit to visitors is that the process has been well documented and explained, in Italian and English, on side panels beside the works.

On the left hand side of the mezzanine floor are some of Italy's finest treasures – the spectacular mosaics from Pompeii. They are all so well executed and, in most cases well preserved, that I'm hard pressed to single any out. The largest mosaic, of Darius and Alexander at the Battle of Issus, is probably the most dramatic, but not my favourite. I think the Nile scenes, the winged boy on a lion, and the marine creatures are far more compelling. But the most endearing mosaic is by far the least elaborate, that of the small skeleton in black and white. This symbol appeared in many Pomeiian kitchens as a reminder to eat, drink and be merry while in good health because, as the skeleton signifies, life all too soon wastes away. The artist's simple work reminded me a child's efforts to draw the human form. I love the way the artist got away with omitting the hands by having the skeleton carry jugs instead.

The *Gran Salone del Atlante* on the first floor has been under restoration (for its highly decorated ceiling) but should now be open and is the best way through to the wall paintings from Pompeii and Herculaneum. Most were taken from the walls of houses there and many represent scenes from the Greek myths. In room LXXI is Hercules and his son Telephus, who is being suckled by a deer – full of symbolism and strong detail; in the next room is the Sacrifice of Iphigenia being carried away by Ulysses and another young hero while Iphigenia's father, Agememnon, turns his back on the scene; in the same room is Perseus and Andromeda, as he frees her after killing the sea monster. Wall paintings from Stabia, a town south of Pompeii which was also destroyed by Vesuvius, are in room LXXIV. They are much more delicate depictions of lighter subjects, especially the personification of Spring – a young girl, with her back to us, daintily gathering flowers.

WALK 2
Edging beyond ancient boundaries: Castel Capuano and east

This eastern section of Naples is just as dense with people and alleys as Spaccanapoli. Expansion here was more gradual, however; this area does not have the overwhelmingly consistent character that Spaccanapoli does. But the working-class neighborhood here is steeped in history, and in some ways is even more representative of the Neapolitan population as a whole (though you'll see more foreigners in this part of the city, which is full of cheap hotels). Portions of this walk are not pretty; traffic is heavy and persistent. But the churches are well worth viewing, the newly restored English cemetery is a worthy place of pilgrimage, and the market stalls lining Vico Sopramura are a typical part of daily life in Naples.

Castel Capuano to San Giovanni a Carbonara

The walk begins at the immense, white **Castel Capuano**, which doesn't look much like a castle. It was built during the second half of the 12th century, was adapted for use as a royal residence by Frederick II, was restored by Charles I of Anjou in 1266, and was the scene of the assassination of Caracciolo (Joan II's lover) in 1432. Since 1540, it has been the seat of the Court of Justice, but the castle's nickname of La Vicaria represents an unjust act practised just beyond the walls. La Colonna della Vicaria was a marble pillar where debtors were forced to strip and stand naked to declare bankruptcy and to hear the insulting accusations of their creditors. The pillar is gone now, taken to the San Martino Monastery (a museum in Naples' Vomero district) in 1856, but the name lives on. Walking across the bustling Piazza Enrico de Nicola you'll see the slightly less oppressive **Porta Capuana**. This triumphal arch between two squat Aragonese towers was designed by Giuliano da Maiano and erected in 1484. Market stalls and cars encircling the arch are dwarfed by the bulk of the two towers, christened 'Honour' and 'Virtue'. On the north side of this square is the elegant Renaissance church of **Santa Caterina a Formiello**. It was finished in 1593, its design attributed to Florentine Romolo Balsimelli and considered one of the most Tuscan churches in Naples.

Walk north on the Via Carbonara until it becomes Via Cirillo. On the left is the church of **San Giovanni a Carbonara**. The long curving steps up to the Gothic chapel of Santa Monica were designed by San Felice in 1708, but the church's original structure dates to 1343 and was then enlarged by King Ladislas in the early 15th century. Behind the high altar is the king's tomb, erected by his sister Joan II who succeeded him to the throne. Four colossal statues of Virtue hold up the 18m megalomaniac structure. There is some fine sculptural work by Marco and Andrea da Firenze in this piece, but King Ladislas' sister surely went over the top with this commission. Just behind this piece is the Cappella Caracciolo del Sole with a very pretty majolica floor, but the Cappella Caracciolo di Vico to the left of the chancel is really the most interesting part

The vast 15th-century archway of Porta Capuana, Naples

of the church. This unusual circular structure, laden with sculpture, might have been based on a design by Malvito in 1517; but the architect is unknown.

South West to Piazza Garibaldi

Retrace your steps to reach the **English cemetry**. Walk past the Castel Capuano and through Porta Capuana. Then head northeast on Via Martiri d'Otranto until you reach Via S. Maria di Fede on the left. You will come to Piazza S. Maria di Fede, and the cemetery sits on the northern side of the church of the same name. (The bigger Protestant cemetery is just to the east.) Abandoned for decades, this quiet outpost began life as a resting place for illustrious foreigners in 1826 through the efforts of the British Consul Sir Henry Lushington. Its nine statues and funerary munuments have been restored, thanks to the Comune di Napoli and the Fondazione Napoli '99 (see p. 19). The mathematician and physicist Mary Somerville, founder of the Oxford college, is buried here, along with celebrated archeologist Sir William Gell and botanist Friedrich Denhart.

From here, head south on Corso Garibaldi until you reach **Piazza Garibaldi**. Or, if the **Botanic Garden** is open (on Wednesdays and Thursdays from 09.00 until 14.00) head north on Via San Antonio Abate and then left on Vico San Antonio Abate; the garden is directly in front of you. Founded in 1807 by Joseph Bonaparte, it is a rare haven of green, with a gorgeous Neo-Classical greenhouse designed by Giuliano De Fazio. The University of Naples' Science Department has labs and a library here; 8000 species of Mediterranean flora continue to thrive. Beyond the Botanical Garden on the Via Foria is Piazza Carlo III, an uninspiring square dominated by the Albergo dei Poveri which opened in 1829 to house and educate orphans and invalids. It has been wrongly attributed to

A detail of the carving on the Porta Capuana

Vanvitelli, but was in fact initiated in 1751 by Carlo III's second official architect, Ferdinando Fuga. If you've come this far on the walk, hop on a bus that will take you down Corso Garibaldi to the piazza of the same name.

Piazza Garibaldi is the centre of Naples' transportation network. Incessant traffic snakes in a figure of eight around the rectangular square. Buses from here will take you to any part of town; the Metropolitana stops here and in four other places in Naples, while the Circumvesuviana will take you to points east and west beyond the city. The square is lined with Italian and African vendors selling everything from braided bracelets to cheap mechanical toys. The area around almost any city's train station is insalubrious; Naples is no exception.

South towards the marina

On the south west corner of the square, Corso Garibaldi continues down to the new marina. Stop at Piazza Nolana, where the round towers (these two christened 'Faith' and 'Hope') mark the position of city gates constructed in the 15th century. Walk under the arch and then turn immediately left down Vico Sopramuro. The daily **market** here is a busy one: everything from fresh fish and wine to coconuts and dinner plates are on display. Heading south, turn right on Via del Carmine until you are in the busy Piazza Carmine – more of a parking lot than an open public square. The large ruins on the southern end are what remains of the Castello del Carmine, built in 1382 but for the most part demolished in 1906.

The grey and ochre-coloured church of **Santa Maria del Carmine** is at the square's northeast corner, there since the 12th century but enlarged between 1283 and 1300. Conradin is buried where his statue is displayed on the church's left side; the letters RCC mark the spot behind the high altar where he was first interred. When the coffin was discovered by workmen in the 1600s, it is said that the severed head and a sword were lying beside the body. But if the coffin were opened today, no sword would be found. Legend has it that Conradin's mother travelled to Naples and stole the sword (long after she died apparently, as Conradin died three centuries earlier . . .).

The church, with its pretty onion-domed bell-tower and cloisters, is dressed in fireworks for a fantastic spectacle on 16 July in honour of the Madonna 'Bruna' of the Carmine. She is pictured above the entrance, and many Neapolitans have a relationship with this Madonna that rivals tributes to the city's patron Saint Gennaro. On a Wednesday, Santa Maria del Carmine is filled with those praying for miracles because it was on a Wednesday, they say, that the Madonna Bruna healed the sick and wounded who filled her church.

Walk west now toward the Piazza del Mercato, where a small obelisk marks each corner. It is hard to imagine that this large car park was once Naples' most popular square – popular mainly because it was where public executions took place. It is where Conradin, last of the Hohenstaufens, was beheaded in 1268, after trying to recapture the throne at the age of 17. And this is where crowds who had supported Masaniello during a nine-day uprising in 1647 came to jeer as his dead body was dragged around the square.

Continue to walk west along the south side of the square until you reach the church of **Sant'Eligio**. Its original 13th-century structure came to light after the bombing of 1943, and was the first church constructed by the Angevin kings in Naples. That influence is especially seen in the French Gothic entrance, which is just beside the wonderful 14th-century bell-tower with its big round clock – now working again after a silence of fifty years.

South of Piazza Mercato is the new dock area, not especially picturesque unless you thrill to the sight of large ships unloading cargo, and boats ferrying passengers to and from Capri, Ischia, Sorrento and Amalfi. Our walk ends north of here, in the heart of the Rettifilo district. From Via Sant'Eligio, turn right on Via Duca di San Donato and walk north until reaching Corso Umberto I. To the left is Piazza Amore, where trams and buses travel east and west on the wide Corso, and north on Via Duomo.

WALK 3
The political centre: Piazza del Plebiscito and surroundings

If Spaccanapoli is the ancient heart of Naples, then the area around Piazza del Plebiscito is the modern centre of a city that has its share of political emergencies and journalists' deadlines masterminded by upwardly mobile professionals. Bank clerks, café waiters, civil servants and high-ranking public officials all make their way here daily. Via Chiaia, with its elegant shops, is Naples's answer to London's Bond Street, and the stylish cafés in and around the Galleria Umberto Primo cater to a crowd that aspires to be the most cosmopolitan in the city. But the seafront and its salty heritage is not far away, where the Castel dell' Ovo has planted its thick walls in the sea. The quarter of Santa Lucia faces the sea here, a traditional outpost for beached fishermen and fast women, but no longer the colourful scene it once was.

The Castel dell' Ovo

This area of Naples, from Castel Nuovo past Palazzo Reale down to the seafront, is just as full of history as any other. Start your walk by taking the causeway from Via Partenope out to the **Castel dell' Ovo** on the Borgo Marinaro. You are standing in front of the oldest fortress in Naples, the Castle of the Egg. I prefer to call it the Castle of the Enchanted Egg, being charmed by the legend of its foundation. This is where the siren Parthenope was said to have been washed ashore, and in the Middle Ages the legend spread that Virgil built this castle upon a submerged egg that was balanced on the seabed. Official record books tell a more straightforward story: the castle was constructed in 1154,

The imposing fortress of Castel dell' Ovo, Naples

used as a prison, as the site of duels and as a military barracks until recently. Robert the Wise commissioned Giotto to fresco the Chapel of the Saviour in 1309, but no traces of his work have been found by restoration experts.

The castle is now open to the public, though some halls are used for private conferences and lectures. The view of the bay from its upper terraces is superb, and to take a walk through the arched alleyways is to imagine yourself a citizen of an 800-year-old city-state. Appropriately, the Italian Castle Institute has an office here, along with the Alpine Hiking Club. The last time I wandered through I was amazed to see a sign for a poster shop. When I found the room, it was hardly the repository for picturesque landscapes that I thought it would be. The first poster read: 'Contribution of chest X-ray to the functional evaluation of patients with atrial septal defect'. It was the showcase for a European Conference of the International Society of Noninvasive Cardiology. I decided to be noninvasive myself, and went to sit on one of the large paved terraces in the sun.

The borgo surrounding the castle is home to a handful of lucky Neapolitans who have the sea lapping at their islet on three sides. Restaurants line the northern edge, my favourite being a simple little place sandwiched between two fancier ones. The sign above the back door simply says Cucina (kitchen), with a bar counter within and six or seven tables outside by the water. The owner was born 76 years ago in what is now the kitchen, and he'll serve you whatever is brewing on the stove that day – steamed mussels, fried calamari, pasta with those small, rich tomatoes from the slopes of Vesuvius. The fare isn't exceptional, but the setting is and you can't beat it for the price. Looking north from here, you'll see the more expensive restaurants of Ciro and Bersagliere that are packed on Saturday night and Sunday lunchtime. Just beyond, the city's best hotels line the Via Partenope.

From the seafront to the Palazzo Reale

Back on the mainland, turn right and walk to the end of Via Partenope before turning left on Via Console. On the corner here is the three-arched Baroque **Fontana dell' Immacolata**, worth seeing for its statues by Bernini, a fitting entrance to the city's yacht and rowing club, Rarinantes, below. Via Partenope now becomes Via Nazario; fishermen and swimmers clamber over huge volcanic boulders at the water's edge. (To avoid the traffic on this stretch you could cut through the Santa Lucia district in to the left.) Via Sauro bears left into Via Console, and the faded red façade of Palazzo Reale stretches out far to the right. You are now walking up to Piazza del Plebiscito, built during the brief reign of Joachim Murat in the early 1800s. The sweep of this large semi-circular piazza is hard to appreciate with so many cars parked within inches of its Doric columns, but the statues of the Bourbon kings Charles III and his son Frederick IV on horseback manage to rise above the modern turmoil. In the centre of the curving colonnade is the church of San Francesco di Paola, an imitation of the Pantheon in Rome which was designed by Pietro Bianchi in 1817.

Immediately to your right is the façade of the **Palazzo Reale** built from 1600–1602 by Domenico Fontana. Eight Neapolitan kings stand guard in their niches along this wall, but the huge building was not inhabited by royalty until the Bourbons came to Naples in 1764. It had been used by Spanish viceroys before that time. The National Library is on the second floor; the Royal Apartments, now a museum, are on the first floor. The picture galleries at Capodimonte are so much better that I wouldn't recommend spending a lot of time viewing pictures here. However, *Patron Saints of Naples Adoring the Cross* by Luca Giordano, the *Annunciation* by Artemisia Gentileschi, and *Return of the Prodigal Son* by Mattia Preti are all powerful works. The beautiful marble Staircase of Honour on the left side of the inner courtyard is your way up to the museum.

Continue north beyond Palazzo Reale, across Piazza Trieste e Trento, to the **San Carlo Opera House** on Via San Carlo. The opera house is the largest in Italy and second in reputation only to La Scala in Milan. The season runs from September through to June, and you shouldn't leave Naples without attending some event here. (It's open from 09.00 to 12.00 weekdays, except Monday, so you can have a look inside without paying to see a performance, if you prefer.) It was first constructed in 1737 by Medrano, but the theatre was completely rebuilt after a fire gutted the interior in 1816. Verdi, Rossini and Donizetti composed operas for San Carlo; later the famous Caruso sang here for his fellow Neapolitans. Suffice to say that he wasn't well received, and vowed never to sing there again.

Castel Nuovo

Before walking through the famous Galleria Umberto I across from the opera house, continue down Via San Carlo to the **Castel Nuovo**. Neapolitans call it the Maschio Angioino, meaning Angevin fortress or keep. It was built for Charles

I of Anjou in 1279–82, but the structure changed many times in succeeding centuries. The most impressive part of its façade is the triumphal entrance arch – restored and unveiled in the autumn of 1988 with much ceremony. The marble arch was not erected until 1453–67, when Alfonso I of Aragon wanted to remind his subjects how lucky they were that he entered their city. This is one of the finest Renaissance monuments outside Tuscany.

The castle was host to Angevin and Aragon, to the abdication of Pope Celestin V, and to an unexpectedly bloody affair arranged by King Ferdinand I in what is now called the Hall of the Barons. Today it is used as the meeting place for both the City Council and the Regional Council of Campania, but in August, 1486, a different kind of political spirit was at work. King Ferdinand had crushed a revolt of the kingdom's princes, who had banded together and appealed to the Pope to dethrone the tyrants of Aragon. But the king negotiated with such goodwill that the princes were undermined, and to show them that there were no hard feelings Ferdinand suggested that the Count of Sarno hold the reception for his son's wedding at the castle. What a kind invitation! All the rebellious bigwigs were invited, and during a merry feast the drawbridge was lowered and the princes taken to the dungeons.

The Hall of Barons is across the large inner courtyard, up a staircase to the left. In the centre of the courtyard's far side is the gothic Church of Santa Barbara, or Palatine Chapel. It is now part of a civic museum which also includes a first floor picture gallery. The single-naved church was built in the 14th century; frescoes done by Giotto in 1330 once covered the walls. Unfortunately, his *Scenes from the Old and New Testaments* have not survived, save for thin fragments along the window frames. Other frescoes of the late fourteenth century line the walls, done by the Florentine Niccolo di Tommaso, and by lesser painters of the Florentine school. Sculpture done by artists who worked on the castle's entrance arch is also here, notably that of Domenico Gagini, who was an apprentice to Donatello and Brunelleschi.

The Crypt of the Barons is beneath the church, but it is closed to the public. The museum's custodian insists that mummified bodies are still there, but my own demands for proof proved worthless. Traveller Arthur Norway, writing in 1901, described what he found in the crypt:

> Within lies the mummy of a man, fearfully distorted by his agony, his cramped hands clutched desperately . . . the man was strangled, there can be no doubt of it; and there he lies to this hour, fully clothed in the garments which he wore when he came down that little winding stair, hose, buttons, and doublet intact.

The custodian tells a slightly different tale: of four adults and two children who starved to death, chained together but far enough apart so that they would not eat one another. My morbid curiosity was only partially satisfied when the custodian unlocked the rear door to a fantastic, tight spiral staircase. Standing beneath it, dead centre, I felt as if I was being swept up inside a stone cyclone.

Relief scenes on a set of massive bronze doors, recently restored, show Ferdinand of Aragon's victory over the rebelling barons in 1462. Oddly enough,

The triumphal entrance arch, Castel Nuovo, Naples

The soaring arcade of the Galleria Umberto Primo, Naples

a cannonball is embedded in one of the relief panels. One explanation for this mystery was a sudden assault on Castel Nuovo by the Spanish under Consalvo of Cordova, with the French desperately firing at the advancing troops from within. Another hypothesis has the doors sailing to France with other Neapolitan treasures looted by Charles VIII, and caught in the crossfire during the Battle of Rapallo between the French and Genoese. The victorious citizens of Genoa then returned the doors to their rightful owners.

Pizzofalcone

Walk back up the Via San Carlo and directly across from the opera house you will see the entrance to the Galleria Umberto Primo, one of the symbols of the city. The soaring arcade is in the shape of a cross, with four entrances. It opened to the public in 1900, but was badly damaged during World War II when thousands of panes of glass from the roof lay broken on the floor. Now it is full of shops at ground level, with offices on another four. Heading left out to Via Toledo, you are across from the popular café called Caflish, a great place for pastries and a *granita di caffe con panna*, iced coffee with cream.

A break from history and architecture takes you past the shopfronts of such fashionable designers as Armani and Valentino, so from the south-western corner of nearby Piazza Trieste e Trento head down Via Chiaia. This is the place to window-shop, one display vying with the next. Naples' famous chocolate maker, Gay-Odin, is in a wonderful old wooden-fronted shop at No.237 (their factory is open to the public at 12 Via Vetriera). Not much further on, men's shirts are made to order by Giuseppe Buccafusca at No.43; the next shop is Aldanese, selling ribbon, lace, and gorgeous strips of sequins, coral

47

and mother-of-pearl. A wonderful dressmaker, Concettina Buonanno, is at No.30 Piazza dei Martiri.

The funny thing about this district, between Piazza dei Martiri and Piazza del Plebiscito, is that it was once the site of Naples' only volcano, and the crater still exists. The area is known to Neapolitans as Pizzofalcone (falcon's peak), and part of the first Greek colony is said to have risen on its promontory. The spent volcano of Mount Echia has not erupted for centuries, but mineral waters surged through the ground for many decades. The impotent crater is now just a large hole filled with vegetation, suffocated by the surrounding houses near Vico Santa Maria a Cappella Vecchia.

WALK 4
On the waterfront: From Villa Comunale to Mergellina

Naples opens wide on this walk, an area much less dense than those covered in the first three walks. The greenery of the Villa Comunale and the wide avenue of Riviera di Chiaia are centuries removed from a quarter such as Spaccanapoli. The grand sweep of the Bay, the view which inspired the phrase 'see Naples and die', dominates this walk. The city's layout will become more apparent, with the Castel dell'Ovo to the east, and the hills of the Posillipo and Vomero districts above. The walk itself is less than two kilometres from east to west, and takes about three hours.

Villa Pignatelli and Villa Comunale

Your first stop is the **Villa Pignatelli Museum**, half-way down the Riviera di Chiaia. It was built in the 1820s for Ferdinand Acton, who distinguished himself by being in the right place on the family tree, having a famous father in the admiral and a famous son in the author and historian. The villa was later owned by the Rothschild family and then by the Aragonese family of Pignatelli. It was bequeathed to the state in 1952 and became a museum in 1960. Lush gardens of palm and pine surround the white Neo-Classical villa; I think this is one of the prettiest and most peaceful areas of greenery in all of Naples. Many rooms of the museum have been restored to reflect early 19th-century interiors: ornate mirrors and settees, high candelabras, sumptuous silver tableware, and porcelain from Naples and other parts of Italy and Europe. This isn't a museum for picture viewing; the best works are the stately carriages shown in five large rooms near the back of the garden.

Back on the Riviera di Chiaia, cross over to the **Villa Comunale** which runs along the seafront. Spanish viceroys paraded along this leafy stretch, and gathered with other members of the aristocracy. But Ferdinand IV proclaimed

Lush gardens surround the Villa Pignatelli Museum, Naples

it a public park in 1780. It now has a neglected air: its fountains empty and scribbled with graffiti, with traffic whizzing by north and south. The Villa Comunale's best feature is its newly restored aquarium in the centre, said to be the oldest in Europe and founded in 1872 by German Antonio Dohrn. Small tanks, flanked by columns, hold 200 species of marine life which swim in salt water pumped from the bay. A highly regarded marine biology laboratory operates here, and hopes are that its research professors will find a way to counteract the horrendous pollution of the Mediterranean; twelve countries are involved in the effort.

Just to the west of the aquarium is the a statue of Philosopher Giambattista Vico, and this seems a good time for a short philosophy lesson in honour of one of Naples' most famous citizens. The son of a bookseller, he lived from 1668 to 1744 and revived the theory of recurring cycles in history. He was a professor of rhetoric at the university in Naples; his famous *Scienza Nuova* studies and describes the imaginative faculty, along with the nature of poetry and the origins of language. Vico was not well understood during his lifetime, remained in obscurity for decades after his death and is still an unfamiliar name to most people. Yet his ideas helped to shape some of Croce's philosophy, and his writings have continued to influence modern thinking about history and literature.

Santa Maria di Piedigrotta and 'Virgil's Tomb'

From the Villa Comunale, walk toward the seafront and head west on Via Carracciolo for about one kilometre. The walk will end at the Mergellina port area farther along the avenue, but turn right on Via Sannazzarro, and walk through the piazza of the same name up to Piazza Piedigrotta. Up on the left you will see the church of **Santa Maria di Piedigrotta**. Though the church was built in the 14th century, it was completely remodelled in the 1800s and the interior gives no hint of its earlier architectural heritage. Santa Maria di Piedigrotta is famous for its festival in early September. Fireworks, colourful streamers and excited children are all part of the revelry, as well as Neapolitan songs composed especially for the occasion. Naples' second largest train station, Mergellina, is just north.

If you would like to pay tribute to both Virgil and the poet Giacomo Leopardi, author of the lyrical *I Canti*, climb up to the Parco Virgiliano. The little park was created in 1930 to commemorate Virgil's birth two thousand years before, though this spot has been well known to literary travellers since the 16th century. To get there, walk along the church's north side, under the railroad tracks near the tunnel entrance of the Galleria Quattro Giornate. You'll see the entrance to the small park on your left. After walking through the gate and up a steep alleyway you'll come to Leopardi's tomb, moved here from a demolished church in 1939. (Leopardi was from the northern Italian town of Recanati, but died of cholera here in 1837. His devoted friend Antonio Ranieri is said to have saved him from burial in a mass grave, carrying his body through the streets of Naples at midnight to the church of S. Vitale a Fuorigrotta.)

The so-called **tomb of Virgil** (no one seriously believes he is buried here) is above, a niche with its sepulchral urn. A Latin inscription reads: 'Ravaged the tomb, and broken the urn. Nothing remains. Yet the poet's name exalts this place.' Just beyond is the Grotta Romana, a long tunnel now closed which connected Naples to Pozzuoli in Roman times. Neapolitans add to the myth of Virgil as magician by saying that in his wizardry he excavated the grotto himself. The view is excellent, one that must have been very familiar to romantic landscape painters of the Scuola di Posillipo, such as Vanvitelli's father Gaspar van Wittel and Jakob Philip Hackert, who worked not far from here.

Mergellina

Retrace your steps and head for the port area of **Mergellina**. Bow to bow, bumper to bumper, the humble fishing boats here are moored in such a haphazard way that only a Neapolitan could be in charge. Fishermen's shacks line the docks, and they are full of families having their pasta, sorting the day's catch and repairing nets and conical cages. One of Naples' best maintained shrines to the Virgin is near the docks, protected from the elements by a Perspex cover – as if to remind her that sailors need similar protection when braving the sea. Stalls lining the sidewalk sell an array of squirming, silvery fish which I'm sad to say has a reputation for looking better than it tastes. I'd stick to souvenirs of shells and coral.

Panoramic views of the Gulf of Naples can be enjoyed from Posillipo

This part of Naples has a festive atmosphere as the sun sets. Strings of coloured bulbs hung from the restaurant façades blink on like so many stage lights, illuminating various entertaining places for pizza and pasta which are absolutely packed in the summertime. The building behind, which houses the funicular to Posillipo, looks like the entrance to a turn-of-the-century fairground. This is a good spot for people-watching, strolling along the port past stalls that sell salted nuts, coconut slices and cups of lemon ice. The carnival atmosphere is alive and well with sellers of cheap little treasures such as the plastic *cornuto* and shell-covered vases. By bus or funicular, you can climb up to the expensive residential quarter of Posillipo for the famous postcard panorama of the gulf and, at one of the outside bars on Via Petrarca, sip a *cappuccino* with the city spread out below and Vesuvius standing silent guard beyond.

WALK 5
Hilltop museum hopping: Capodimonte and the Vomero

This tour involves walking, but not through narrow streets seeking churches and Renaissance palazzi. Walk 5 is actually two separate tours, within museums mostly, and because they are both on hills above the city you will need to take

51

a cab or public transport to reach them. If you've only got one morning to devote to seeing art then I'd recommend heading for the Museum and National Galleries at Capodimonte, where you can expect to spend about two hours. I especially like the galleries here because you are not overwhelmed – on exhibit are ten to twelve excellent works from each important period of Italian painting with examples by Masaccio, Botticelli, Titian, Carracci and Caravaggio, among others.

The second tour, a bit longer and taking in three sights, is in a residential district called the Vomero. The Carthusian Monastery of San Martino is the main attraction. Portraits, landscapes and maps in its museum elucidate Neapolitan history while giving you a fantastic view of the city. Above the monastery is the huge Castel Sant'Elmo and about one kilometre away is the Villa Floridiana, a ceramics museum surrounded by a park.

Capodimonte

Capodimonte is just that – the top of the hill. This big park and its galleries are in the north central section of the city, and the best way to get there is to take Bus No.24 or 110 from Piazza Garibaldi, or No.160 or 161 from Piazza Dante, then turn left up the hill to the Porta Piccola gates which take you into the park. This is a popular setting for wedding photos, and on weekends hundreds of Neapolitan families come to picnic and relax.

The Bourbon King Charles III commissioned Medrano, the same architect who designed the opera house, to begin the rather severe Neo-Classical **palace** in 1738. He liked this plot of land because it was a good place to hunt, and he wanted a suitable home for the Roman Farnese collection which came to him through his mother, Elizabeth Farnese. It has been said that the paintings suffered while they waited for a home: stacked in hallways and stairways at the Palazzo Reale, visitors complained that bratty delivery boys peed on the Titians and Caravaggios. Carlo also initiated the porcelain works on the grounds of Capodimonte, rivalling his father-in-law Frederick Augustus, Elector of Saxony and King of Poland's factory at Meissen. (The factory no longer produces any porcelain, but some buildings are used as an art college.)

The palace became a museum in 1957. Before viewing the paintings, take time to see the Chinese-style Salottino di Porcellana in room No.94 on the first floor. Everything but the floor and black marble skirting board is made of porcelain, designed by German artist Johann Sigismund Fischer in 1757 for Charles III's wife Maria of Saxony. The white background is festooned with delicate but colourful relief decoration: fruit baskets, birds and butterflies are interspersed with scenes of Chinese men and women. The factory staff was employed full-time for two years on producing the 3000 porcelain pieces needed to decorate the room. Also displayed on the first floor are objects that furnished the Royal Apartments during the 18th century: tapestries, landscape paintings, small ivories, jewellery, gilded chairs and tables, along with more porcelain from the Bourbon collection (though most pieces were taken to Spain by Charles III).

The second floor is where it is worth spending most of your time. (A word of warning however: ongoing renovation has meant that a selection of paintings was moved temporarily to the first floor while the second floor was closed. To avoid confusion, I have not referred to the room number in which a painting hangs.) Notwithstanding, works are displayed in a chronological order and well marked by period, so that one of the first set of rooms you enter is of 14th and 15th-century Sienese and Florentine paintings. The best among them is Masaccio's grief-stricken Mary Magdalen in the *Crucifixion*, a small but very powerful work done in 1426 for the Church of the Carmine in Pisa. Botticelli's *Virgin and Child with Angels* was painted in 1470 when he was just 26. Mantegna is represented by his beautiful soft portrait of *Francesco Gonzaga* who became cardinal at the age of 16, and by his long, dark painting of *Saint Eufemia* holding a white lily. An outstanding work is Bellini's *Transfiguration*.

Parmigianino's restored *Portrait of Antea*, is among the best paintings by the Emilian Mannerists. It's a strange scene — she with the small head, and the ferret baring its teeth. A superb work by El Greco, done in 1577, is called *Youth Blowing on Hot Coals*, with its rich and eerie shades of brown. The *Annunciation* is the first Titian we see at Capodimonte, and one room is devoted to his works — take a close look at his sexy *Danaë* and his unfinished portrait of *Pope Paul III* with his Farnese nephews. There is a change of scene with Flemish Masters, and I didn't expect to be so moved by Pieter Brueghel the Elder's *Blind Leading the Blind* and his allegorical *Misanthrope* which depicts corruption of the church through a boy cutting the money bag (shaped like a heart) from beneath a priest's robe. These paintings seem strangely modern to me, smoky and disturbing scenes painted a year before his death in 1568.

Take time to see Claude Lorrain's large evocative painting of the Roman countryside, *Landscape with the Nymph Egeria*, and my favourite paintings in this museum: Carlo Saraceni's scenes of the life of Icarus — *Flight*, *Fall*, and *Burial*. Art experts don't single this Roman painter out, except to say that he was influenced by Caravaggio. But his touch here is, thankfully, so much lighter than Caravaggio's, full of delicate whimsy and a sensitivity for the tragic folly of Icarus. They are offset by Caravaggio's stormy *Flagellation*, though his *Seven Acts of Mercy* is no longer here, but back in its original position at the church of Monte della Misericordia near the Duomo. Artemesia Gentileschi, one of the few recognised women artists of the period, is represented by her strong portrayal of *Judith* painted in 1630.

The only element I found lacking in the galleries was adequate seating; there is practically nowhere to sit and view the paintings unless you dare to steal a guard's seat for a few minutes. But across from the gates of the park I found an unpretentious place to sit and have a good meal, a pizzeria at No1 Via Bosco di Capodimonte. This was cheap and cheerful at its best, and I had the one of the most delicious pizzas I have ever eaten.

The **Catacombs of San Gennaro** are down Via di Capodimonte (take the stairs and then turn right), behind the Church of San Gennaro Extra Moenia. They are viewed by guided tour (mornings only), a fascinating walk through some of the excavated passages of underground Naples. They were built in two storeys during the second century; the city's patron saint, San Gennaro, is buried within, along with bishops and dukes. The mosaics here are some of the best examples of early Christian art, especially the half-body portraits in the Crypt of the Bishops.

The Vomero

On another hill to the southwest of Capodimonte is the Vomero district, and three funicular railways travel up and down its slope throughout the day. Don't go by bus, because the route skirts the city on the outer highway and takes a long time. Take the Montesanto Funicular west of Piazza Dante, getting off at the second station. (You might be tempted to hum a few bars of the song, 'Funiculi-funicula', written by Neapolitans Peppino Turco and Luigi Danza in 1880. Their song is a wonderful example of the traditional, melodramatic *canzoni napoletane* which are famous the world over.)

If you're interested in ceramics and would also like a walk through dense gardens, make the **Villa Floridiana** your first stop on the Vomero. Walk straight out of the station and down the two sets of steps into Piazza Vanvitelli. Turn left on Via Bernini and right on Via Cimarosa. The entrance to the park will be up on your left.

The Villa Floridiana is a reflection of its neighbourhood – calm and solidly middle class. Young mothers and grandmothers are preoccupied by babies, old men balance canes and cigarettes as they shake hands with friends, and teenage couples steal kisses in more secluded sections of shrubbery. The pathways to the villa are lined by cedars, cypress and pine (and explode with camellias in springtime). From the long terrace at the park's farthest point, you get a fantastic view of the Bay of Naples, and – on a clear day – of Capri.

The **National Ceramics Museum** is housed in the Pompeian-style villa built in 1817 by Ferdinand I for his wife, who took the unlikely name of Duchess of Floridia. The Duke of Martina began to amass his porcelain collection in the second half of the 18th century, with pieces from China, Japan and Europe. The collection of 6000 pieces was donated to the state by the widow of the duke's nephew in 1931.

The next stop on the Vomero is the **monastery of San Martino**. Retrace your steps until you are again in front of the Montesanto funicular station. Facing the station, turn left on Via Morghen, which changes to Via D'Auria. Then take a right on Via Tito Angelini, and up on your left at the end of the street you'll see stairs leading down to San Martino, which lead to a sloped road with the entrance to the monastery at its end. **Castel Sant'Elmo** looms on your left, built in the early 14th century by Robert of Anjou. It was restored in the 1970s and no longer keeps political prisoners within; various cultural organisations for Naples and the province have offices here, and the castle is used frequently for receptions and conferences.

The San Martino Monastery is just below, founded in the 14th century by the Angevin dynasty. The monks became so rich that in the 18th century the

Bourbon King Ferdinand threatened to check their books and cut down on their 'grant'. In the meantime, however, the monks were spending thousands of pounds on paintings, frescoes and sculpted marble, turning the San Martino monastery into an artistic treasure trove.

The lavish Baroque church is just past the entrance on the left. The ribs of the Gothic vaults reveal the character of the original interior, but Baroque was then incorporated and in a much more careful way than in other Neapolitan churches. The best works within are by Ribera, dubbed Il Spagnoletto or Little Spaniard, a court painter who settled in Naples. His twelve larger-than-lifesize *Prophets* are in the spandrels of the arched nave. On the left wall of the choir is the painting some consider his masterpiece, *Communion of the Apostles*, done in 1651. To complete a short study of his best paintings, behind the high altar head to the left through a number of rooms. The last one you come to is the Cappella del Tesoro where Ribera's tender *Deposition* hangs above the high altar.

From the church, pass through the small cloisters and the hallway beyond to enter the museum. The collection in the monastery's museum is eclectic, well displayed and well labelled. If you are interested in the history of the city through art – street scenes, portraits of regal personalities, works of Neapolitan and Campanian masters – then this is the best place in Naples to spend your time. But I have found the museum to be less than illuminating, with too many rooms closed. Room No.25 is one small room that doesn't close, however; it is famous for its exceptional view of the city below. The museum is also known for its Nativity scene called the Cucimiello Crib. It has recently been restored, apparently because the crib had been sent to the Metropolitan Museum of Art in New York City for a special display where harsh lights had wrought havoc on the figurines. 'Mai piu,' explained the custodian sadly. Never again would they let that happen.

From the small cloisters, a long narrow hallway leads to the Grand Cloisters. Sixteen columns line each side, with grey and cream-coloured marble ornamentation above. A well sits in the middle, and only five lonely fruit trees grow in the open square. Its original plan was developed by Giovanni Antonio Dosia at the end of the 16th century, but Cosimo Fanzago had a hand in adding the level above the high arches and completing the decoration. The small cemetery on one side of the cloister with its 16 marble skulls was also his idea.

Fanzago was a prolific artist – an architect, sculptor and decorator – contracted to carry out this work in 1623, which landed him with a lawsuit initiated by the monks. He apparently attacked one of his masons on the job there and was then suspected of murdering him two years later. He always had a hard time working to deadline, and the six-year contract for the Grand Cloisters beginning in 1623 was not completed by 1631. Fanzago had so many commissions throughout Naples that he constantly juggled materials and workers. Employers accused him of taking their materials to another job; he used sculptures meant for the monastery, for example, in a chapel at San Lorenzo instead. And strong as his influence was upon 17th-century Naples, he didn't always receive very good press. But he was an expansive, creative personality who spent generously to entertain his friends. Where were they at the end of his life? He died in poverty, at the age of 87, in 1678.

Practical Information

When to go

The so-called 'tourist season' doesn't exist in Naples, so you don't have to worry about running across busloads of foreigners there. In my opinion, Naples needs and deserves more tourists. But I must caution you to be 'street-wise'. Do not walk around Naples with a wallet or purse which could be stolen. If you can, carry enough cash for the day's outing in a pocket and leave everything else at your hotel. I would also advise against women travelling alone; it is best to travel in company as most Neapolitan men believe themselves to be irresist-ible and will try their best to convince you of this. And lastly, if you are driving do not stop the car for anyone who appears to need your assistance. This is most likely a ploy to disorient you in order to steal your belongings.

To enjoy the best weather while walking the city streets, choose late spring or early autumn. The sun will often be shining and rain will be a only minor irritation. July and August can be stifling, but September and October can still be very warm. December, January, February and March can be cold and wet with occasional strong winds.

Getting there

Most visitors fly into the Capodichino Airport outside the city, but you could instead fly to Rome and drive down through the Campanian countryside. Naples is only 200km from Rome; alternatively, the train ride from Rome's Termini to Naples' Stazione Centrale takes two hours. A hydrofoil service also runs from the Rome airport to Capri and Sorrento (see 'Getting there' information at the end of Chapter Six).

British Airways flies direct from London Gatwick to Naples twice daily, but Alitalia does not fly direct. A British Airways flight doesn't come cheaply, and is more expensive than flying to Rome. The low season Apex fare is about £180 return. But there are very good charter flight deals from companies such as Adelphi Travel, Pegasus and Quo Vadis. Their fares recently ranged from £110 to £140 return, and these agents will often help with hotel reservations, car hire and insurance. A coach runs every 30–40 minutes from Capodochino Airport into Naples, at a cost of 3000 lire. The bus stops at the main train station of Piazza Garibaldi, at the Piazza Municipio in the city centre, and at the main dock of Porto Beverello where boats leave for the islands. It makes sense to use this service, as taxi rates can fluctuate outrageously!

If you decide to rent a car, always book from home – rates within Italy can be twice as expensive. If you want to hire a car when you're already in Italy,

I would still recommend that you telephone a car hire rental company in the UK; believe me, it's worth the price of the phone call.

Tourist Information Offices

The main tourist office in Naples, called the Ente Provinciale per il Turismo, is on 10 Via Partenope, (tel. 081 406 289). They also have a number you can call at the central railroad station: 081 268 779. Another tourist office is located in the lobby of the airport and another is located at the entrance of the causeway to Castel dell' Ovo.

Students looking for less expensive places to stay should contact the Associazione Alberghi per la Gioventú at 9 Via del Chiostro (tel. 081 551 3151). There is also a tourist centre for students at 35 Via De Gasperi 35 (tel. 081 522 0074). The only youth hostel in Naples is behind the Mergellina train station, across from the entrance to Virgil's tomb, on Salita della Grotta 23 (tel. 081 761 2346).

Guided tours are run almost every Sunday between 10.00 and 11.00 from the tourist information office called the Azienda Autonoma di Soggiorno, Cura e Turismo. One office is located at Piazza del Gesù, open 09.00–15.00 every day except Sun (tel. 081 552 3328). The office also has a mobile unit in front of the station in the middle of Piazza Garibaldi, open 08.00–20.00 Mon-Sat; 09.00–13.00 Sun.

Get yourself a copy of the free monthly *Qui Napoli*, written in Italian and English, which is full of useful information – hydrofoil and ferry schedules, sightseeing tours, sports facilities, exhibitions and concerts, church and museum schedules.

Fondazione Napoli '99

If you'd like more information about what this energetic group is doing to help save Naples, or how you can help, write to the foundation at Riviera di Chiaia 202, Naples, 80121 (tel. 081 412 948).

Consulates

Great Britain: 122 Via Crispi (tel. 081 633 511).
United States: Piazza della Repubblica (tel. 081 660 966).

Hotels

Naples is not exactly famous for opulent, old world charm when it comes to hotel interiors. But there is a good deal of choice in both price and location.

I would put GIGA's *Excelsior*, Via Partenope 48 (tel. 081 417 111) at the top of the list for comfort, elegance, services and location. But the superlatives don't come cheaply – room rates start at about £150 for a double. On the corner of the Via Partenope overlooking the Castel dell' Ovo, views from most of its rooms are superb. Special services give you an indication of the clientele: interpreters on request, jet rental, dock space for private boats. Very expensive.

Two other hotels along the waterfront are a bit less posh, and slightly less expensive. Prices at the **Santa Lucia**, Via Partenope 46 (tel. 081 416 566) include breakfast, and this place has a friendly atmosphere.

The **Vesuvio**, Via Partenope 45 (tel. 081 417 044), is right next door, and has gone through some unfortunate modernisation to accommodate more conference business. Its Ristorante Caruso on the 9th floor is this city's answer to Manhattan's 'Windows on the World', with a wonderful view out across the bay. Expensive.

The simply furnished, unpretentious **Hotel Rex**, Via Palepoli (tel. 081 416 388), is around the corner in the Santa Lucia quarter. There is no restaurant, so you have to go out to the local coffee bar for breakfast. Ask for a room with a small balcony, and you'll enjoy a sideways glimpse of the sea. Moderate prices.

The **Britannique**, 133 Corso Vittorio Emanuele (tel. 081 761 4145), has long been a favourite with travellers, halfway up the hill which rises to become the Vomero. It is quiet, with a very pretty garden; moderate to expensive prices.

I can recommend one hotel situated on the central Piazza Garibaldi; make sure you get a room on one of the top floors, some of which have their own terraces with very nice views. The **Hotel Cavour**, Piazza Garibaldi 32 (tel. 081 283 122), has recently been carefully restored, having been a hotel for 100 years; room rates here are moderate. The restaurant attached to the hotel is very good, but expensive.

Restaurants

I have never failed to eat a decent meal anywhere in Campania, and Naples is no exception. Very rarely is dining a three-star experience with a *nouvelle cuisine* platter looking like an underpainted canvas, and that's fine with me. Most often, what you'll get is a one-star meal full of fresh ingredients, from the first-course pasta to a steaming cup of espresso. Trust the waiters' opinions. They've usually had an early meal of the day's specials.

Amici Miei, Via Monte di Dio 78 (tel. 081 405 727), is known for its fresh pasta, especially the lasagna, and ravioli stuffed with ricotta and mozzarella. Moderate.

Bellini, Via Santa Maria Costantinopoli 80 (tel. 081 459 774) is a justly famous pizzeria in Spaccanapoli, though service was poor the last time I ate there. Inexpensive.

La Cantinella, Via Cuma 42 (tel. 081 405 375) is one of only two restaurants in Naples with a Michelin star. It is near the seafront in the Santa Lucia district. Pasta is superb, especially those dishes served with seafood. Closed Sunday and during the month of August; moderate to expensive.

Also in the Santa Lucia district is a good pizzeria called **Da Ettore**, Via Santa Lucia 56, very simple with a warm atmosphere. Inexpensive.

The **Casanova Grill** at the Hotel Excelsior, Via Partenope 48 (tel. 081 417 111), is a very good, though very expensive, restaurant. If you're not staying at this swanky hotel, at least splash out for a meal (or a drink at the bar) if you are looking for some peace and quiet.

The **Cavour**, Piazza Garibaldi 32 (tel. 081 264 730) is an elegant antidote to the chaotic Piazza Garibaldi just outside its doors. *Risotto agli scampi* and pasta with *frutta di mare* are excellent; this is also the place for a tempting array of desserts. Expensive.

At the other end of the port area is a Neapolitan favourite, **Ciro a Mergellina**, Via Mergellina 21 (tel. 081 681 780). Nearby, just beyond Piazza Piedigrotta, is **Il Vicoletto**, Via Piedigrotta. This relaxed, old-style place will be full of Italians who heard about it through word of mouth, and they'll be ordering the fresh pasta made on the premises. Moderate prices.

High up in the Posillipo district is Naples's second Michelin-starred restaurant, **Giuseppone a Mare**, on Via Ferdinando Russo 13 (tel. 081 769 6002). Its speciality is seafood, at very moderate prices, and the position above the gulf can't be beaten.

Price Ranges

Hotel (double room)	*Restaurant (per head)*
Inexpensive: under 60,000	under 25,000
Moderate: 60–120,000	25–50,000
Expensive: 120–200,000	50–90,000
Very expensive: 200,000+	90,000+

Museums and other public sites

Aquarium: Villa Comunale (tel. 081 406 222). 09.00–17.00 Mon–Sat; 10.00–19.00 Sun and hols.

Botanic Gardens: Via Foria (tel. 081 449 759). 09.00–14.00 Wed and Thurs only, or by request through Science Faculty, University of Naples (tel. 081 449 759).

Catacombs of San Gennaro: Via di Capodimonte. Guided tours Fri, Sat and Sun only 09.30, 10.15, 11.00 and 11.45.

Capodimonte Museum and Picture Gallery: Parco di Capodimonte (tel. 081 741 0881). 09.00–14.00 Tues–Sat; 09.00–13.00 Sun and hols. Summer opening hours 09.00–19.00 Tues–Sat; 09.00–14.00 Sun and Mon.

Cappella Sansevero: 19 Via de Sanctis. 10.30–13.30 Mon–Sat, 11.00–13.30 Sun and hols.

Cloisters of Santa Chiara: Via B. Croce (tel. 081 205 561). 09.00–12.30, 16.00–18.30; 09.00–12.30 Sun and hols.

Doll Hospital: 81 Via San Biagio dei Librai (tel. 081 203 067). 09.00–14.00, 16.30–20.00 Mon-Fri.

Filangieri Museum: 288 Via Duomo (tel. 081 203 175). 09.00–14.00 except Mon; 09.00–13.00 Sun and hols.

National Archeological Museum: 35 Piazza Museo (tel. 081 440 166). 09.00–

14.00 Tues–Sat; 09.00–13.00 Sun and hols. Summer opening hours 09.00–19.00 Tues–Sat; 09.00–13.00 Sun and hols.

Palazzo Reale: Piazza Plebiscito (tel. 081 413 888). 09.00–14.00 Tues–Sat; 09.00–13.00 Sun and hols. Summer opening hours 09.00–19.30, 09.00–13.00 Sun and hols.

San Carlo Opera House: Via San Carlo (tel. 081 417 144). Tours 09.00–12.00 Tues–Sat. Ticket office for evening performances open 10.00–13.00, 16.30–18.30 daily except Mon.

San Martino Monastery and Museum: Largo San Martino 5 (tel. 081 377 005). 09.00–14.00 Tues–Sat; 09.00–13.00 Sun and hols. Summer opening hours 09.00–19.00 Tues–Sat; 09.00–13.00 Sun and hols.

Tomb of Virgil: 09.00–13.00 daily. Guided tour by request (tel. 081 413 888, ext. 51).

Villa Floridiana (Duca di Martina Ceramics Museum): Vomero district in park (tel. 081 377 315). 09.00–14.00 Tues–Sat; 09.00–13.00 Sun and hols.

Villa Pignatelli Museum: Riviera di Chiaia (tel. 081 669 675). 09.00–14.00 Tues–Sat; 09.00–13.00 Sun and hols.

5. WEST OF THE BAY OF NAPLES

The Phlegrean Fields

This fascinating part of Campania, less than 16km west of Naples, claims more classical mythology and ancient history per acre than any other place in Italy outside Rome and Sicily. Yet few travellers seem to know much about it. Full of secrets barely concealed, it's as if by putting an ear to the ground you'll hear the whispered prophecies of the Cumaen Sibyl, the Greek recitations of Virgil's *Aeneid*, or Nero's confession to the murder of his mother at Baia. Roman villas have sunk beneath the sea, Cumae's amphitheatre is overgrown with weeds, and the land still rises and falls with underground volcanic activity. This is a mystical land, still so full of hidden promise for the classical archaeologist.

But hidden promise also translates as hard to find in some cases, and other sites, as steeped in myth and history as they are, can no longer be found at all. But with patience and imagination the pieces begin to fit neatly together as you trace your way around the bay. The area's three most important sites, the baths at Baia, the ruins at Cumae and the amphitheatre at Pozzuoli, are all open to the public.

This wide arc of land around the Gulf of Pozzuoli, extending to the tip of Cape Misenum, is called the *Campi Flegrei* – the Burning Fields. You can see why if you visit the crater known as the Solfatara near Pozzuoli. Mud still bubbles up from the ground and many small fumaroles emit sulphuric gases, though this active crater hasn't erupted violently for 36,000 years.

The area's main sights can be seen in a full day, but if you've got less time I would whittle these down to two: the amphitheatre at Pozzuoli and the Italian mainland's first Greek colony of Cumae. Wonderful views await you from Pozzuoli around the bay to Baia, then out to Cape Misenum and up past Lake Fusaro to Cumae. The best plan is to pack a picnic lunch, or buy sandwiches while in Pozzuoli, for a late lunch on the summit at Cumae. Train lines from Naples extend to the Phlegrean Fields (the Ferrovia Cumana e Circumflegrea), but most sights are too far from the stations for the line to be of much use. I would suggest either renting a car (making this a day trip from Naples) or touring with a group arranged by the tourist office in Naples.

The Solfatara and Pozzuoli

The English guidebook for sale on site describes the Solfatara as one of the area's 'innumerable beauties'. Hmmm. Some might prefer to omit this stinking bed of clay in favour of more romantic spots but the Solfatara should be experienced, as it is an extraordinary phenomenon. The Greek geographer Strabo, who lived in Rome after 14AD, described the place in his *Geographica* as the workshop of the god Vulcan, the entrance to the Underworld. A massive eruption 36,000 years ago created this area, 12km wide, and there is record of an eruption in 1198 which poured forth a stream of lava. As you walk across the ash-laden ground, it feels hollow and is hot to the touch. Small rooms have been built to capture the sulphurous steam that is emitted by a number of *fumarole*. A campsite near the Solfatara bills itself as one of the few in Europe to be 'inside a volcano', and many come for the soothing effects of therapeutic steam baths and thermal springs.

If sulphuric fumes have an unpleasant effect on you, travel directly to **Pozzuoli** instead, where the old market area and amphitheatre are worth seeing. The town of 60,000 inhabitants has almost completely engulfed most of the older ruins, and its present troubles are unfortunately the most fascinating aspect of its modern-day character. Pozzuoli has been described as a 'potential apocalypse', very seriously affected by thousands of tremors – a condition called bradyseism. In 1983 about half the population fled as buildings began to crumble. The moving earth, rising over a metre in two years, pushed the piers up so high that ferries from the islands of Procida and Ischia had difficulty docking.

One would have hoped that the past presence of saints (along with being the birthplace of Sophia Loren) could have protected Pozzuoli. St Paul stepped ashore here after the Alexandrian ship 'Castor and Pollux' carried him to Italy from Malta, and San Gennaro survived beastly trials in the amphitheatre. But early warnings by the scientific community seem to be the only cause for hope. Two giant underwater fumaroles were recently discovered offshore, and some scientists think that is a good sign: pressure is being released slowly over a wider area than they had thought. Though the crisis of the early 1980s has passed and Pozzuoli's citizens have returned, other scientists believe it is only a matter of time before mud and lava explode to cover the Phlegrean Fields.

One area that demonstrates the changing sea levels through history is right in the middle of Pozzuoli. Romans came to 'Puteoli' in 194BC, and it became an active trading port. A large marketplace, or *macellum*, still exists near the seafront behind the Via Roma, and its so-called **Temple of Serapis** is the circular area with columns in the centre. But even Serapis, god sacred to merchants, couldn't keep the water from flooding the market square periodically. Three columns standing by the entrance show traces of water marks at different levels along their lengths. In one section they are perforated for a length of about 3m by a species of boring shell which lives underwater.

The amphitheatre, the third largest in Italy after Rome's and Santa Maria Capua Vetere's, is on the hillside behind Pozzuoli off the Via Domiziana (also the way to the Solfatara). You can take the Cumana railroad line from Naples in this case, and walk up the steps behind the Pozzuoli station.

The **amphitheatre of Flavius** was constructed in the second half of the first century, not far from an earlier and smaller amphitheatre. Three tiers of arches define the perimeter (149m x 116m), with a wide entrance at either end and a smaller one on either side. A garden of fragments now surrounds the amphitheatre – headless statues, bodiless heads, portions of a freize, a huge marble foot. What makes this amphitheatre so worth seeing is that it gives visitors a clear idea of how any Roman amphitheatre functioned as a showplace: the floor's middle section opened wide to allow scenery to be drawn up from below, and the extensive underground passages are incredibly well preserved. These can most easily be seen by peering through the sixty openings on the amphitheatre's floor. But the amphitheatre is often fairly empty and you can usually find a way beneath ground level, though due to recent earth movement in the area many passages have been blocked to visitors.

The rectangular openings on the amphitheatre's floor were constructed so that caged animals could be raised through them on a pulley system to the level of the floor. As the cage doors opened, lions and tigers sprang out roaring. In one instance, when Nero was entertaining the Armenian king Tiridates, the emperor became so excited by the fighting that he jumped into the ring and killed several of the animals himself, including two bulls that he speared with one javelin. This is perhaps not surprising when one considers Nero's track record as a pathological killer.

Baia, Bacoli and Cape Misenum

From the main road by the port of Pozzuoli, head west to Baia. Only one main road will take you there, although the Cumana rail line does stop at Baia also. The views here, as you round the bay, are as pretty as those in Naples and once past Bacoli and around the point they are better still. To the east, blocking the Bay of Naples from sight, is the little island of **Nisida**. It is an ancient crater, like so many lakes and lumps in this region. Cicero says that Brutus retired here after Caesar's assassination, in a villa built by the son of the Roman general Lucullus. But no traces remain of this – nor of the delicious wild asparagus described by the naturalist Pliny. This island is nowadays a state-run home for juvenile delinquents.

Before reaching Baia make a detour inland (a right turning off the main road) to **Lake Avernus**, known through Homer's *Odyssey* as home of the Cimmerians and entrance to Hades. It isn't the lake itself but the so-called **Sibyl's Grotto** on the south side which is the attraction here. An overgrown path leads to this long dark tunnel, best seen with a guide who is normally there on weekdays. Legend has it that the cave led the way to a mysterious prophetess similar to Cumae's sibyl, but it is far more likely that the tunnel was built by the Roman general Agrippa around 37BC to escape the advancing troops of Sextus Pompeius.

As a safe harbour for his fleet, Agrippa connected Lake Avernus to the sea by a canal which also ran through the smaller Lucrine Lake nearby. Another tunnel on the northwest side of the lake was dug to Cumae (called the Grotta di Cocceio or della Pace), and ruins on the west side were probably a ship-yard. On the lake's eastern edge are ruins of an octagonal building called the **Temple of Apollo**, thermal baths built by the Romans. And the Sibyl's Grotto, despite romantic legend, was part of Agrippa's overall defence plan – perhaps a place to hide his army and their supplies.

Baia

Drive back out to **Baia**, a picturesque fishing port with so many ruins beneath the sea that fishermen have to be careful where they anchor their boats. Stretched along the hillside are the extensive remains of Roman baths, but there is hardly a foundation wall left to show that Caesar and Pompey, Hadrian and Livy all built luxurious holiday homes along this coastline. Seeing what Vesuvius has preserved at Pompei and Herculaneum, I can understand turn-of-the-century travel writer A. H. Norway's plea, though he isn't exactly sympathetic towards potential human suffering: 'If only the ashes had rained down a trifle harder at Misenum and Baia, what noble Roman buildings might have survived unto this day, conserved by the wisdom of the mountain!' Today the town just seems like a quiet working people's port with modest homes along its shores, hardly a place where midnight orgies raged in damp caves.

The **Roman baths** are reached by a staircase beside the railroad line (to the left as you face the station). Crossing the bridge, you'll see the Temple of Diana down to your right behind the tracks – probably just an extension of the baths at one time. The ingenious Italian who farms this land has created an intimate garden of vegetables among the ruins, with tools and tomato sticks stacked neatly within a subterranean gallery to the side – a typical yet powerful image of an Italy that blends the illustrious past with the ordinary present.

The baths are farther along on your left at the top of the stairs. The **Archeological Park** begins with a long avenue, with ruins far below and just above. This huge Imperial Roman complex was built between the first and fourth centuries, and staircases still connect the different levels. Some rooms were for hot baths, others for cold plunges. Small chambers and pipes supplied and drained water from all over the hill; sulphuric springs were tapped for soothing soaks. Large buildings still stand that were used to collect warm mineral water, the best preserved being the so-called Temple of Mercury. The large circular chamber, with its vaulted roof, is reminiscent of the Pantheon. Because of the water at its base, the building is like an echo chamber – if you whisper on one side your secret will be carried to the other. Directly to the east of this temple are small rooms in a semi-circle, thought to be a theatre. Just below is a large area that served as a swimming pool.

The villas that once lined the shore below the baths are about 4m beneath the sea at Baia, but it wasn't until the early 1970s that archeologists seriously considered excavating. That's when a local fisherman discovered amongst his catch a marble hand holding a cup. Since 1981 about 22 marble statues have been raised from the depths, though progress is slow and government monies hard to procure. Recent discoveries show that more remains of the ancient town are about 1km beyond the shore, but at least 15m below the surface. These finds are exhibited in the 16th-century Aragon castle seen on the hill when travelling out of Baia toward Cape Misenum.

Bacoli

Bacoli is the next stop, a small unpretentious town up beyond Baia. It has two attractions to recommend it. One is the **Cento Camerelle**, or Hundred Little Rooms, a two-storeyed combination of tunnels and arcades near the church of Sant'Anna. The other is the **Piscina Mirabilis**, a big cistern in five sections used to supply water to the Roman fleet at the port of Misenum. The Piscina is a haunting and wonderful experience; a high vaulted ceiling towers above and hundreds of plants hang from the ruins like mossy stalactites.

Bacoli is also supposed to be the scene of the murder of Nero's mother Agrippina. (A ruin known as the Tomb of Agrippina is nearby.) It was a commander of the fleet at Misenum who first helped Nero plan his mother's murder, according to historian Charles Merivale. The commander had designed a boat with movable bolts that could come apart in the water like a broken toy. Persuading his suspicious mother to board the vessel was no easy task for Nero, but she finally assented one moonlit night. Out on the water, however, the boat didn't fall apart as planned. Agrippina jumped overboard and managed to survive. So Nero resorted to more direct tactics. That same night the commander raided her villa and she was murdered in her bed. Perhaps Agrippina deserved her fate, for she is said to have poisoned her husband Claudius so that her son Nero would become emperor.

Nero hardly deserved to enjoy the good life at his villa near Baia. As emperor from 54 to 68AD, he poisoned his stepbrother Brittanicus, killed his wife Octavia and a second wife Poppaea by kicking her when she was pregnant. When his offer to marry Claudius's daughter was refused, he had her put to death. He gained his third wife, Statilia Messallina, after killing her husband. But these incidents were mere trifles when contrasted with his massacre of thousands of Christians and the burning of Rome. To save himself from execution, he committed suicide in 68.

The road which climbs from Bacoli to Cape Misenum affords spectacular views across the Gulf of Pozzuoli, and down into wide blue **Lake Miseno**. This was once linked by a canal to the port area, used as a base for the Roman fleet.

The spectacular view from Cape Misenum

Now the American military has a base here, and long grey metal ships sit like bobbing hippos in the gulf. As you wind slowly inland via Monte di Procida, umbrella pines crown the hills on either side. Scrubby patches of sloping land are cultivated for grapes, olives and tomatoes.

The lives of Campanian citizens here are far removed from those of their cousins in Naples, or even in the busy port of Pozzuoli. Small and somewhat messy rural towns line the twisting road to Lake Fusaro. On a recent autumn visit I was surprised to find myself driving behind a uniformed brass band and a line of decorated wooden carts in one of these little towns. It was a procession to celebrate the *vendemmia*, the season's grape harvest. Vines had been curved to form graceful side arches on the carts, laden with boxes of freshly picked grapes and little girls in frilly dresses. They waved slowly and confidently to the crowd of parents and shopkeepers who lined the streets. The band made its way to a small central square where a platform had been set up for the day's speeches. Neapolitans complain that their festivals and customs don't seem to mean much anymore, but out here on Cape Misenum they still take their harvest traditions very seriously.

Follow the road up past **Lake Fusaro**, stopping briefly at the park bordering the lake if you'd like to see the charming hunting lodge, or *casino*, that Vanvitelli built for Ferdinand IV in 1782. It seems a true folly now, sitting out in the lake with nothing to hunt for miles around. The lake might have been the port for Cumae, 1km north. Until recently, the lake was known for its oyster beds. The fact that it was the crater of an extinct volcano was proven in 1838 when such noxious gases were emitted that all the oysters were destroyed. Vanvitelli's lodge, with a wooden bridge connecting it to the mainland, was restored in 1981 after being neglected for thirty years. It was being used as an outpost to a marine biology station in the big house nearby on the mainland, but both now look empty and neglected, a disappointing example of local restoration efforts wasted through an unclear policy of how to make best use of them.

Cumae

There's nothing more exciting than exploring ruins with no one else around. Although it's completely irrational, whenever this happens I get the feeling that I'm the first to have laid eyes on such a place. I wholeheartedly agree with H. V. Morton in his opinion of Cumae:

> I have not seen a more romantic classical site in Italy. Anyone who is even remotely interested in the classical world who comes to Naples yet fails to visit the Grotto of the Sybil is missing a great experience; should it be a matter of time, I would rather see what is left of Cumae than Pompeii.

The grotto he mentions wasn't uncovered until 1932. In reading older guide-books which are unable to locate the cave I have felt very happy to be a modern traveller, for I can now walk down its long, eerie passage. Cumae was founded about 800BC by Greek colonists, one of their first outposts in a foreign land. The Roman historian Livy has written that these colonists were driven here from Ischia by frequent earthquakes, however; other historians claim it was from the island of Procida due to lack of water. Classical mythology tells the story of the inventor Daedalus escaping from King Minos and landing here on his wings of wax. His son Icarus didn't make it that far, melting his wings by flying too close to the sun and falling to a watery grave. Daedalus rested at Cumae, and then made his way to Sicily where King Minos unsuccessfully pursued him.

Cumae was a powerful port city for centuries. The Etruscans, jealous of her influence, tried unsuccessfully to take the city in 474BC with the help of Umbrian allies. But the Romans did defeat the Cumaeans 140 years later, and it then became a colony of the empire under Augustus. Cumae continued to decline; Saracens sacked the city in the ninth century. Four hundred years later it was such a notorious hideout for pirates and brigands that angry Neapolitans came to burn what was left of the city.

To reach the ruins of Cumae today, you climb a path that leads to a wide tunnel carved in the rock. Just past it, on the left, is the entrance to the **Grotto of the Sibyl**. On either side of the dark entrance are verses from Virgil describing how Aeneas came to consult the Sibyl who he called Deiphobe. In the sixth book of the *Aeneid* Virgil writes:

> On one side of the Eubean rock
> Is cut a huge cavern. To it lead
> A hundred broad ways, a hundred mouths
> From which there tumble out as many voices,
> The Sibyl's answers. As they all arrived

Upon the threshold of the cave the virgin
Cried out: 'The time to question fate is now!
The god is here, the god!' As she spoke
Before the temple doors her countenance
Changed suddenly, her colour changed, her hair
Fell loose about her shoulders and she panted
Violently, her wild heart grew great within her,
She seemed taller, her voice was not a mortal's
Because the god's power had breathed upon her

This scene is not hard to imagine as you walk down the corridor of the Sibyl's Grotto, almost 50m long and over 2m wide. The whole passage is hewn from the rock; its angled walls create the shape of an inverted V with its point lopped off. Six galleries allow light to filter through on the west side, but this is hardly an airy place. When walking through the dank grotto I felt like a citizen of Cumae coming to consult the Sibyl, spooked by whatever fate she had in store for me. She sat in a small room at the end of the tunnel, waiting for her wary customers.

The Cumaean Sibyl was one of the three most venerated oracles in the ancient world, along with those of Delphi and Erythrae. After willing herself into a trancelike state, she was said to make her utterances in perfect Greek hexameters. Her prophecies were written on palm leaves, and collected later into what were called the Sibyline Books. Pliny tells a tale of Tarquinus Priscus coming from Rome to buy the books. The Sibyl offered him the nine books and when he questioned the price she ruined three, offering him the remaining six at the same price. When he continued to quibble three more books were destroyed; the sale was concluded when Tarquin bought three books at the original price. Who knows what wisdom the Roman Senate lost in that transaction! The books Tarquin bought were burned when the Forum was destroyed in 82BC and a committee was elected to go and gather a new collection in Asia Minor. This was safely stored on the Palatine Hill but disappeared after the year 400.

Across from the entrance to the grotto is the puckered rock face of the **Roman Crypt**, a deep underground gallery almost 230m long. The last time I was there it was closed to the public, and the custodian at the entrance had no idea when it might reopen. It is thought that the tunnel continues even deeper through the hills, perhaps connecting Cumae with Lake Avernus to the southeast where the Grotto of Cocceio would be the tunnel's logical exit.

A winding stone staircase above the Grotto of the Sibyl leads to the Acropolis, and the temples of Apollo and Jupiter. A belvedere is on your left, with remnants of statues found in the excavations. From here one has a perfect view out to Ischia and Procida. Now the **Via Sacra** begins, flanked by laurel and oak. The **Temple of Apollo** is just up on the right, with two headless statues at the entrance. Tufts of grass and clover have grown between the big tufa blocks; an interesting section of column rests at one end, constructed in a trefoil pattern. In the sixth or seventh century the temple's foundation was used to construct a Christian basilica.

A series of hewn arches lead to the Sibyl's Grotto

The Via Sacra continues up the hill to the **Temple of Jupiter**. This is the perfect place for lunch – quiet, with a soft breeze coming in off the sea over the summit. Small wildflowers grow between the crumbling brickwork, and the hill is covered with thyme, clover and pine. Arched sections of the Christian basilica built on the temple's remains stand at chest height, and tombs have been discovered beneath the pavement. Amongst the scattered ruins is a circular baptism font in the centre.

Through a small group of trees on the steep hill is a flat area allowing for an expansive view out to sea and south to Cape Misenum. Neatly framed green fields are stretched out far below. Looking closely you will notice just how many low rounded, grassy walls there are in all directions. No larger vegetation has been able to root itself along these humps, for they are all ruins that were once part of the city. If archaeologists resumed excavation here, Cumae would be shown to be much more extensive than just the additional outcropping of ruins (baths and forum) uncovered below to the north-east.

The remains of the city's **amphitheatre** (probably constructed in the first century BC) are beyond the excavated area of the city. Turning right out of the entrance, the hidden oval is near the corner and marked only by a battered yellow metal sign. The site is fairly buried in bushes and high weeds, but with persistence you can find your way through brush and olive groves to the amphitheatre. Many tombs have been discovered nearby, the oldest dating back to the seventh century BC, but they have been badly pillaged for their valuable sarcophagi and other ornaments. The road from the amphitheatre now leads north on the **Via Domiziana** to the elegant **Arco Felice**. This tall triumphal brick archway is squeezed into the hillside to the east, built by the Emperor Domitian in 81–96 to link Cumae with Pozzuoli. Its dark polished Roman paving is still intact beneath, and your way back to modern civilisation is through this lovely arch.

Practical Information

Getting there

Travelling west of Naples to Pozzuoli, Baia and Cumae is best done by car. Avis, Europcar, Hertz and InterRent car rental agencies are all located on Naples's Via Partenope, and also at the airport. If you'd like to go by coach, the following companies in Naples run tours to the Solfatara and Cumae: CIT (Piazza Municipio 70, tel. 081 552 54 26); Cima Tours (Piazza Garibaldi 114, tel. 081 22 06 46); and Tourcar (Piazza Matteotti, tel. 081 552 33 10). By train, the Ferrovia Cumana will stop at Pozzuoli and Baia, leaving from the Montesanto or Corso Vittorio Emanuele stations in Naples. The Metropolitana from Naples's Piazza Garibaldi also stops at the Pozzuoli Solfatara station.

WEST OF THE BAY OF NAPLES

Tourist Information Offices

POZZUOLI   Azienda Autonoma di Soggiorno, Cura e Turismo: 3 Via Campi Flegrei (tel. 081 867 2419).

Hotels and Restaurants

To see the sites here it's really best to stay in Naples, or even base yourself on Procida or Ischia and take the ferry over to Pozzuoli.

BAIA   The place to eat is **Dal Tedesco**, Via Temporini 8 (tel. 081 868 7175), with local pasta dishes served with *frutti di mare*. It's nicest here when you can sit outside on the terrace full of flowers; there are also nine simple and inexpensive bedrooms available if you'd like to stay in the area, though it doesn't open until early June. Inexpensive.

POZZUOLI   Neapolitans will drive out to dine at one of the many restaurants here, since it's well known for fresh fish specialties. The **Castello dei Barbari**, Via Fascione 4 (tel. 081 867 6014) is good, with a nice view to boot and moderate prices.

Price Range
Restaurants (per head)
Inexpensive: under 25,000 lire
Moderate: 25–50,000
Expensive: 50–90,000
Very expensive: more than 90,000

Museums and other public sites

BACOLI   Cento Camerelle: 09.00–16.00; obtain key from custodian at 16 Via Santa'Anna; small fee.
Piscina Mirabile: 09.00–16.00; obtain key from custodian at 16 Via Creco; small fee.
Tomb of Agrippina: Via della Marina.

BAIA   Parco Archeologico, Roman Baths: 09.00–16.00; closed Mon and hols.

CUMAE   09.00–16.00; closed Mon and hols; free parking, snack bar.

POZZUOLI   Amphitheatre: (tel. 081 867 6007) 09.00–16.00; closed Mon and hols.
Solfatara: (tel. 081 867 2341) 09.00–dusk; free parking, snack bar.
Macellum: part of the market place behind Via Roma, seen at any time of day from above, though gates sometimes open 09.00–13.00.

6. NORTHERN CAMPANIA

The fertile fields of the territory north of Naples still deserve the name given to them by the Romans: Campania Felix. Lush soil enriched by river silt, volcanic ash and mountain spring water yield tobacco and olives, fruit and vegetables. The Garigliano River is Campania's northern border with Lazio, and the Matese Mountains separate it from the small region of Molise to the north east. Towns along the Mediterranean coast are packed with holiday visitors in summer, and then completely quiet during winter months.

Inland are many small hill-top towns once protected by now-crumbling castles, whose ancient ancestors saw the likes of Hannibal and Manfred march through on their way to war. Though these foreigners' exploits are part of their history very few towns, even the larger ones such as Caserta and Benevento, are geared to tourism. This certainly adds to their charm, but sometimes also leads to frustration. Streets and historic sites are not always well sign-posted; shops might close just when you're feeling peckish. But if you're interested in architecture and ancient history, and don't need the typical tourist's trappings to keep you satisfied, then this part of Campania is well worth trooping through.

The land area covered in this chapter totals not more than 80km from east to west, and about 50km from north to south. Architectural gems are hiding not far from the main roads. The small Romanesque church of Sant' Angelo in Formis with its complete cycle of frescoes is now totally restored, a jewel polished to perfection. And to paraphrase American writer F. Scott Fitzgerald, a diamond as big as the Ritz sits sparkling in Caserta – the palace and garden complex designed by Vanvitelli for the Bourbon King Charles III. Other less well appreciated sites include the walled town of Caserta Vecchia, Santa Maria Capua Vetere's amphitheatre, the cathedrals of Sessa Aurunca and Teano, and small mountain villages of the Matese.

It's easy enough to make a day trip from Naples out to Caserta, but you'll need a car to reach other smaller towns nearby. With one or two exceptions, the area does not have much to offer when it comes to hotels with character and ambiance. If you'd like to spend a few nights in northern Campania, (and when travelling south from Rome this makes a good place to stop) I recommend staying in the coastal town of Baia Domizia at an unusual hotel called La Baia. Run by three sisters with wonderful taste, it has a distinctive atmosphere with excellent food. I'm sure that warm impressions of northern Campania stem in part from my stay at La Baia. The drive from the hotel to places such as Teano and Sessa Aurunca is less than 45 minutes, to Caserta and Capua just over an hour. And when you're not touring, Hotel La Baia is a great base for eating, drinking and soaking up the sun. During the summer months, a boat takes visitors from Baia Domizia out to the islands of Capri and Ischia.

Sessa Aurunca, Roccamonfina, Teano and Matese Mountains

A short drive east on route 430 from Baia Domizia will bring you to state road No.7, a wonderful stretch of the Via Appia which leads to Sessa Aurunca. The Appian Way, starting in Rome, crosses the whole region of Campania. The Roman official known as Appius Claudius Caecus began the road in 312BC and for about 150 years it simply stopped at Capua. The finished road to Brindisi, passing through Benevento and east on to Potenza, was constructed in 190BC.

The flat road to Sessa Aurunca reminds me of a rural avenue in the south of France where tree tops arch gently to create a leafy tunnel. Low limestone mountains rise in the distance, but beside the road fields are filled with low tobacco plants, and row after row of peach and apple trees. In late autumn nets are cast below limbs to catch olives as they fall, and long tobacco leaves are drying in makeshift sheds.

Sessa Arunca

The hillside town of **SESSA AURUNCA** is 2km north of the main road. Sessa's oldest sight is an arched bridge called the **Ponte degli Aurunci** or Aurunco. It is named for the local population who made this their capital under the Latin name Suessa. The long bridge is just south of the small city, in a solitary place crowded by vegetation, but with portions of Roman paving intact on the road. (Turn left coming into town. Then turn right on Via Adrianea where the Roman paving begins, and the bridge will be at the end of this road.) Built between the first and second centuries, the 21 arches are tall and elegant. It's hard to believe that the bridge has managed to survive this long, considering man's insensitive attempts to domesticate the scene: the archways have been lived in by squatters, and are still used as animal stalls and storage sheds for rusting farm machinery.

The Aurunci fought both the Romans and the Samnites, but were eventually dominated by both. From the influence of Imperial Rome sprang baths and an amphitheatre. Walking along Sessa's medieval streets, you will come across builders' inventive use of old fragments – columns encased in corners and busts protruding from walls, though many have been painted over in recent years. Luckily though, the façade of the **Duomo of San Pietro**, on the Piazza del

Duomo, has remained untouched. It is studded with stone monsters and animals such as wolves, goats and sheep, interspersed with masks from the old theatre. The church's central arch is flanked by lions, who are in the midst of devouring a meal.

The Romanesque cathedral was under construction in 1103, using the remains of the temples of Mercury and Hercules, along with those of the theatre. The portico in front of the church shows St Peter in bas relief above its middle arch. The cathedral's central nave is flanked by 18 columns which separate it from two aisles; the mosaic floor running down the nave is a rich geometric pattern of Arab influence.

The best part of this church's interior is the lovely pulpit. Raised up by six columns riding on the backs of little lions, it is reminiscent of those in both Ravello and Salerno. (Five of the six columns face the centre of the aisle, but the sixth faces the other way. According to locals, the builders were so tired they didn't notice, and didn't have the energy to correct their mistake when it was pointed out to them!) The tight, pieced marble work on the pulpit was done in the 13th century by Taddeo and Pellegrino, masters of their trade. Pellegrino also created the Pascal candelabra nearby, lit for high mass at Easter. A painting by Luca Giordano, *Communion of the Apostles*, is in the Baroque Chapel of the Sacrament.

Roccamonfina and Teano

Back on the road still heading north, you'll be traversing the valley which leads to **Roccamonfina**. The whole group of hills in this area is called Rocca Monfina, the oldest volcanic territory in Campania. It is thought that the hills once rimmed a large crater, which has not been active for thousands of years. On the edge of the highest peak, called Monte Santa Croce, are remains of lava walls that might have been part of a temple in the original settlement of Aurunca. Historians think that the Aurunci abandoned this site in 337BC and moved down to what is now Sessa.

The next stop in this part of Campania is at **Teano** on the slopes of Roccamonfina. Narrow streets wind through the historic centre but the population now numbers 15,000. Its history has seen the Aurunci, Samnites and the Romans file through, along with Lombard domination in the ninth century. Teano is known to modern Italians as the place where, on 26 October, 1860, Garibaldi encountered Victor Emmanuel II – but the position was actually 4km northeast. It is reached by heading north east out of Teano on Route 608 where a granite column was erected in 1960, symbolising the country's unity by a handful of soil from each region buried beneath a plaque.

Teano's Duomo, built in 1116 but renovated on a design by Andrea Vaccaro in 1630, is worth a look for its Crucifix painted on wood above the high altar. The grave, dark cross of the Gothic School is thought to have been painted in 1330 by Maestro di Giovanni Barrile. The church was badly damaged by bombs in World War II, and townspeople say that when its renovation was complete they discovered that the crucifix had been used as a lunch table by the workers!

Just outside Teano, on the way to Capua, is the **Roman amphitheatre**. Excavations there have not been exactly systematic, and the addition of a local family's two-storey home in the middle of the site doesn't add to its appeal.

Matese Mountains

From Teano, heading south means a concentration of rewarding sites in Capua and Santa Maria Capua Vetere. But if you are feeling adventurous, a drive through the slow back roads of Campania takes you north and then west to the beautiful Matese mountains. To find one of the most characteristic villages, Piedimonte Matese, take State Road No.608 north from Teano for about 8km. Then turn right and west on No.372 for 30km until reaching a left turning north on No.158 to Piedimonte.

This territory is dominated by three peaks north of Piedimonte: **Colle Tamburo**, **Monte Gallinola** and the highest, **Monte Miletto** (2050m). They are reflected in the large, clear Lago del Matese below. In the isolated towns just north of here, such as Gallo and Letino, many women still wear the traditional *mappelana*, a headcovering coloured according to marital status: green for the single, red for married women, and black for widows.

But **Piedimonte**, with a population of 12,000, is one of the best places to visit, with interesting churches. And townspeople are used to outsiders – this is becoming a popular day-trip out of Naples for those who want to hike in the mountains, and buy local wine and olive oil. The town was already inhabited during the neolithic age, and almost certainly by the Samnites (who fought their last battle with the Romans on Mount Miletto.)

On Piazza d'Agnese is the Church of San Tommaso d'Aquino, or San Domenico, built in 1414. It sits on the site of the earlier San Pietro, which was built above the ruins of a Roman temple. The church's bell-tower has beautiful green and yellow majolica tiles. On Via d'Agnese is the Baroque church of San Salvatore, designed by Cosimo Fanzago. The majolica paving within is reminiscent of the style found in many Neapolitan churches; the ornately gold-plated organ is an amazing instrument. Just beyond on the left is San Biagio, notable for its cycle of Gothic-inspired frescoes by an unknown artist, Scenes from the Old and New Testament, and the Life of San Biagio, which were completed in the middle of the 15th century. The town's biggest and most Baroque construction is the cathedral of Santa Maria Maggiore, built between 1725 and 1773.

Just north of Piedimonte is the small village of **Castello del Matese**, worth a sinuous sidetrip for its view out to the valleys and down to Piedimonte before heading south toward Teano.

Capua and Santa Maria Capua Vetere

The road south from Teano leads back to state road No. 27, and crosses the motorway which also takes you the 25km down to Capua. The only advantage in taking the slower route 7 instead is that it will lead directly into Capua, and then to Santa Maria Capua Vetere farther south.

Capua

Capua is on a bend of the Volturno River, but the town is not situated to take advantage of the scenery. From the centre of town you'd hardly know the river existed at all, but in fact the Volturno is just behind the Duomo. The draw here is the Museo Campano, with a very good acheological collection housed in the 15th-century palazzo of the dukes of San Cipriano. Walking around, you'll find that Capua is a somewhat sleepy place – typical of so many Campanian towns which have more to tell about their past than future.

Capua was founded in the middle of the ninth century, after the Saracens destroyed the old town further south in 840. Lombard domination is particularly evident; no other city in Campania can boast as many high medieval churches. Restoration experts are struggling to obtain funds in order to reopen the dozen or so that are still intact, some of which have been closed for fifty years. The Duomo itself has mainly been rebuilt, though its elegant bell tower has been standing since 861.

The **Museo Campano** is at the end of Via Duomo; enter a pretty garden through a large stone doorway and climb the steps to the first floor. The museum houses works dating from the Hellenistic to the medieval period. The monumental busts in the first room to the left are strong, severely simple pieces done in the thirteenth century. They once adorned a triumphal arch in Capua, now destroyed, which was built by Frederick II in about 1230. Room No.28 has a small collection of pictures from the 15th, 16th and 17th centuries; the best by far is the *Deposition* by the Venetian painter Bartolommeo Vivarini done in the late 1400s.

The museum's most important works are the strange and solid tufa sculptures on the ground floor. This collection of ancient fertility figures, called Madri (Mothers), represents a rich chapter in Campanian popular art. The statues were uncovered in 1845 near ancient Capua (Santa Maria Capua Vetere) and span the 6th–1st centuries BC. They are *ex voto* offerings to a divinity called Mater Matuta who represented both dawn and birth. When someone offered one of these statues to the divinity, it was in the hope of becoming pregnant, of giving birth to a healthy baby, or offering thanks for the safe birth of a sound child. These sombre women of stone are seated with bundled infants – sometimes as many as five or six – nestled on each arm.

Santa Maria Capua Vetere

Capua's ancient counterpart is a few kilometres south. The drive is down a dreary-looking avenue bordered by signs, shops and petrol stations, which probably once formed part of the Via Appia. Is this really where Hannibal marched into the town that revolted against Rome during the Second Punic Wars and opened its gates to him? I would have had second thoughts about entering the city if the outskirts looked anything like they do today.

The scenery improves once you've passed through the vestiges of Hadrian's Arch at the city's northern edge. (The Appian Way passed through the arch, which was probably dedicated to the Emperor Hadrian who restored the amphitheatre nearby and was a generous patron of the city.) In 215 BC, Hannibal and his Carthaginian troops rested here in style, and exaggerated reports of the perfumed and willing women of Capua have survived the centuries. When I asked the women of Santa Maria Capua Vetere about this reputation, they snorted and said, 'Ridiculous'. When I asked the men, they replied, 'We wish!' Whatever transpired during that period of winter rest is still something of a mystery; some historians have claimed that Hannibal and his troops were then prepared to wage battles throughout Italy while others claim the city's charms softened him for good. Still, it wasn't until the great Roman general Scipio held Spain and its Carthaginian strongholds (defeating Hannibal's brother Hasdrubal) that Hannibal was given marching orders back to Carthage 12 years later.

On the outskirts of Santa Maria Capua Vetere is Italy's second largest **amphitheatre**, a wonderful relic of the town's illustrious past. When H.V. Morton visited here with an Italian professor in the early 1960s, they wandered 'all over the grassy giant as if we were solitary figures in some print by Piranesi, an unusual experience these days when ladies from Bradford and Kansas City are so often to be found seated upon the most remote altars'.

I share the impression; one is often left alone here to explore beneath and around the great shape, 170m long by 140m wide. The amphitheatre sits in its underclothes these days – so much stone has been stripped from the four-tiered façade that it's now more brick than marble. Some of the statues are in the National Archeological Museum in Naples. The best thing about the amphitheatre is the freedom to explore the curving tunnels beneath the floor, trying to imagine the chaos as lions and other beasts were funnelled through as gladiators scrambled into position. Cicero records that it seated 100,000; others claimed it was the model for all other amphitheatres in Italy because Rome's Colosseum was constructed almost 100 years later. A number of fragments are on view in a garden below the ticket entrance, but unfortunately the gladiators' school beyond the amphitheatre (where a slave revolt led by Spartacus is said to have started) is no longer in evidence.

Santa Maria Capua Vetere was originally settled by Oscans, a highly civilised Italic tribe inhabiting the region. But they were overpowered by the Etruscans and Capua became one of the most important cities in southern Italy. It was once the capital of Campania, but that distinction was absolutely out of the question after the citizens' hospitality to Hannibal. To avenge their disloyalty,

Italy's second largest amphitheatre, at Santa Maria Capua Vetere

leading citizens were killed or imprisoned by the Romans; Livy says that some took poison at elaborate banquets to outwit their captors. After the fall of the Roman Empire, the city was under attack by a series of invaders during the next five centuries. First came the Goths, then Vandals and Lombards, and old Capua was finally destroyed by the Saracens in 856.

The small city you drive through today is an amalgamation of many building periods; some structures have survived from the 16th and 17th centuries, especially the brown stuccoed walls bordering the streets. Tall portals with their heavy wooden gates along these dusty walls lead to small courtyards; most of the houses within have, at least in part, been rebuilt to accommodate 20th-century amenities. Streets are narrow and dark; shopkeepers advertising their goods by placing them outside the shop door risk having their fruit and brooms swept away by passing cars.

Life spills out into the squares, and the main one in town is **Piazza Mazzini**. Hundreds of years ago this was the Piazza Seplasia, a market for the famous perfumes distilled from Capuan roses. Just down Via Mazzocchi is the **Duomo**, or the Church of Santa Maria, which survived the Saracen raids. It was first built in 432, enlarged in 787, transformed in 1666, 1700 and 1884. The façade is now Neo-Classical; many of the internal columns are taken from ancient temples in the surrounding countryside. The polychrome marble altars are colourful and well-wrought works of Campanian art, but the dark religious paintings are not the most inspiring of their genre.

More interesting than the Duomo is the **Mithraeum** northwest of Piazza Mazzini off the Via Morelli. This temple to the Persian god Mithras was discovered in 1922. (To enter ask the ticket collector at the amphitheatre to take you there.) This rectangular underground room was the scene of rituals dedicated to Mithras in the second and third centuries centuries AD.

Roman soldiers brought this religion back with them from the Middle East; Mithras was a god ordered by Apollo to kill a bull, symbol of fertility. He wasn't supposed to spill a drop of blood while performing this task. But a scorpion intervened, and the dripping blood from the slain bull represented evil in a then-perfect world. To symbolise this scene, initiates into the cult of Mithras were sprinkled with bull's blood, and promised a better life to come.

A fresco of *Mithras Killing the Bull* is on the back wall of the chamber, a well preserved depiction of the god re-enacting the mythic scene. The stone seating on each side is for members – all male – and the frescoes on the side walls represent the seven stages of initiation into the cult. It wasn't a sinister organisation, though members were sworn to secrecy and always met in underground chambers. The cult was popular enough to arouse the suspicion of Roman politicians, however, who banned members from practising their pagan religion in 395.

Sant' Angelo in Formis and San Leucio: Frescoes, Silk, and a Social Experiment

Two small towns are worth the short detour north from old Capua before heading south to Caserta. One is to Sant' Angelo in Formis, celebrated for its Romanesque church with an incredible cycle of medieval frescoes. The other spot is San Leucio, still producing beautifully embroidered silks in modern, out-of-the-way factories. San Leucio is now a rather isolated place but with such an interesting past that it is worth noting. Besides, you should not miss Sant' Angelo in Formis, and from there you will pass San Leucio on your way south to Caserta.

Sant' Angelo in Formis

When leaving Santa Maria Capua Vetere, head directly north out of town on Via Galatina from the Piazza San Francesco. About 10km on, at the foot of Monte Tifata and just after passing beneath an old archway, is the church of **Sant' Angelo in Formis**. (The caretaker's house is just beyond the arch on the right. He will escort you to the church; a small fee is recommended.)

This beautiful little Lombard Romanesque basilica was known to exist as early as 925, built on the ruins of a large ancient temple dedicated to Diana Tifatina, protectress of the forests. The church you see today was finished under the supervision of the abbot Desiderius from the Abbey of Montecassino in 1073. (That famous and once powerful Abbey is just 20km north in Cassino, in the region of Lazio.) The 1980 earthquake so badly damaged the church that state monies were earmarked for a complete restoration of the structure and frescoes.

The façade of Sant' Angelo in Formis is graced with a delicate portico of five arches, upheld by four Corinthian columns probably taken from the original temple. Inside, the church floor is thought to be from the temple also. The central nave is divided from its side aisles by 14 columns – some granite and others of veiny white cipollino marble. Earthquake damage led architectural experts to realise that the high arched windows were not of the original fenestration; they have been restored as longer lites without as many frames. It was also discovered that the basilica had been fitted with a false ceiling in 1926, and the original ceiling's design has now been duplicated.

Despite its being one of the best examples of medieval ecclesiastical architecture in Campania, Sant' Angelo in Formis is even more important for its cycle of frescoes. Ten experts from the Istituto Centrale del Restauro in Rome came to work on the frescoes for three years. These expressively depicted stories are clearly influenced by Byzantine models. Both those done in the portico and on the walls within were finished in the second half of the 11th century, most likely painted by artists who had also worked at Montecassino. The Life of Jesus is depicted above the arches in the central nave; in the central apse above the altar is Christ Giving His Blessing and opposite, on the back wall above the church's entrance, is a chilling scene of the Last Judgement.

The unattached bell-tower is at least as old as the church, and the big white travertine blocks used in part to construct the tower were taken from the amphitheatre at Santa Maria Capua Vetere. Behind the church are steps leading down into the remains of the temple, soon, we hope, to be open to the public. From the church's forecourt you are treated to a wonderful view: Campania's fertile fields lay below, with Capua straight ahead and Monte Roccamonfina off to your right.

San Leucio

To reach San Leucio, return to the main road travelled on from Santa Maria Capua Vetere, but then turn right on Road No.87 which travels south past Vaccheria. About 2km past the turning for Vaccheria you will come to **San Leucio** and the Piazza della Seta (Silk Square) – more of a roundabout than a proper town square. A left off the piazza leads up the hill on Via Planelli; proceed through the arch and drive up to the parking lot beneath the abandoned palace. On the street to either side are what remains of King Ferdinand's bold social experiment: the 18th-century homes of his silk workers, still inhabited today.

In 1789, the Bourbon King Ferdinand IV had visions of a new town, and with all due modesty planned to call it Ferdinandopoli. Two hundred people would be employed in reviving the manufacture of damasks and brocades, beautifully embroidered silks to be used in the Palace at Caserta and sold to the upper classes. A set of egalitarian laws would be followed, fair to both sexes. Most of this happened, though the town was never called Ferdinandopoli.

It became San Leucio instead, named after a church there dedicated to the saint who was bishop of Brindisi.

Ferdinand's ideas were certainly progressive, though some suspected that San Leucio was merely a playground for the king as benevolent dictator who frolicked there with local peasant girls. King Ferdinand claimed that he was only trying to put into practice the philosophical ideals of Gaetano Filangieri and the social reforms of Bernardo Tanucci. To that end, public health services and education were available to all (school commencing at the age of six); merit was to be the only way of earning individual distinction; people were free to dress however they wished; parents were not allowed to intervene in their children's choice of marital partners; and each factory worker gave a portion of his earnings over to the *Cassa della Carità*, a fund to care for the sick and the aged.

King Ferdinand and members of court came often to San Leucio, a weekend retreat just north of the Palace at Caserta. They stayed in the huge yellow-and-white edifice called the Casino Reale di Belvedere. From the promenade in front there is a wonderful view of Caserta beyond the rooftops of San Leucio. The Belvedere was constructed in 1776. The German painter Jakob Phillip Hackert was invited to reproduce the Campanian countryside on the walls within, and to paint the ceiling of Ferdinand's bathroom where he had requested a bathtub 'big enough to swim in'. A sign tells you that this decaying beauty is now the headquarters of a Scholastic Institute, but I saw no evidence of anyone learning anything. The clock at the top of the façade has stopped; the tall arched windows are broken. The interior must be in a similar state of disrepair.

To King Ferdinand's credit, the manufacturing colony at San Leucio thrived for more than half a century; silks produced here were sought after by wealthy patrons all over Europe. The factories were built behind and to the right of the Belvedere. These buildings are no longer used, as the modern Palazzo dello Stabilmento Serico is in operation just south. The cloth is still highly prized, though it is now made of artificial silk. The Italian government sent state gifts of San Leucio silk to both Queen Elizabeth upon her ascension to the throne and to Jacqueline Onassis when she was First Lady. The only little shop on the Piazza della Seta, called the Bottega della Tessitura d'Arte, sells fantastically intricate bolts of silk in an atmosphere reminiscent of 18th-century workshops.

Caserta and Caserta Vecchia

Caserta is the provincial state capital, dominated by the grand Palazzo Reale designed by Vanvitelli. I highly recommend a visit, for its gardens as well as the sumptuous interiors, despite the fact that there is little else to see in the town of Caserta. As compensation though, the small town of Caserta Vecchia 10km north east is one of the most charming villages in all of Campania. You will have had a very fulfilling day if you visit the Palazzo Reale in the morning, stroll through its gardens, and then drive to Caserta Vecchia in the afternoon.

The gardens at Caserta rival those of Versailles

While Caserta has little to recommend it in the way of restaurants, Caserta Vecchia has a surprising number of good, unpretentious places to eat.

The Palazzo Reale

If you're arriving at Caserta from the direction of San Leucio, state road No.87 continues the five or six kilometres south. But if coming up to Caserta from Naples it's a quick trip north by train or bus, or by car up the A2 motorway. You'll see signs for the **Palazzo Reale**, or **Reggia** as it's also called, when reaching Caserta. You can't miss it, for it's the biggest building for miles around.

The Bourbon King Charles III was again the mastermind behind this impressive architectural centrepiece for the region, and the court architect Luigi Vanvitelli threw himself into planning its construction in 1752. Charles wanted a royal palace and seat of government away from congested Naples, but he never had the opportunity to spend a single night there. He was called back to rule Spain in 1759 before work was completed, and it was then up to King Ferdinand to finish the job in 1774. The palace has been likened to Versailles, and is said to have been influenced by it. I know mine is a minority opinion, but I think Vanvitelli more than satisfied the king's wish to rival Versailles. He positively outdid the French architects – the dramatic staircases and floor plan within, as well as the multitude of diversely planned landscapes behind the palace make it a far more exciting and much less predictable place to explore than Versailles.

The Reggia at Caserta was US General George S. Patton's headquarters after the Allied invasion of Italy, and the scene for Field Marshal Lord Alexander's acceptance of the unconditional surrender of the German forces on April 29, 1945. (2km north east of Caserta is the British Military Cemetery.) I was told

The impressive grand staircase at Caserta, flanked by lions

that the American Army, upon leaving the palace of Caserta, paid to have the marble floors re-polished since so many pairs of heavy boots had detroyed the finish. With 1200 rooms, there is a lot of marble to polish and with 1790 windows, plenty of work for those who wash them.

The main façade of the yellow stucco and travertine building is almost 250m long; the utterly symmetrical, Neo-Classical plan has four identical inner court-yards. The gardens stretch for three kilometres north beyond the back façade of the palace – sculptures, fountains and cascades, along with an English garden and man-made lake with an island are all part of the impressive landscape.

Italian military and other government offices occupy almost half of the Reggia, with one wing open to the public. The second of three front entrances leads to the centre of the building, and at ground level the eye travels straight through to the garden cascades beyond. To the right is the grand staircase, where you are greeted by the stone lions of Clemency and Fortitude, and then led to a wonderfully marbled vestibule – the red star in the middle of the floor is the palace's geometric centre.

The thirty rooms open to the public are entered through the **Hall of the Halbardiers**, where visitors were once discreetly frisked and royal bodyguards would stand in line when the king passed. I found the ornamentation in most of these large rooms overwhelming. The **Appartamento Vecchio** in the left wing is prettier than the Royal Apartment rooms to the right. Allegorical frescoes adorn four rooms named for the seasons, their walls lined with silk from the factories at San Leucio. At the end of this wing are three rooms comprising the library: marquetry borders repeat around the shelf tops and some books are shelved in the lovely conical glass bookcase in the last room. A wonderful, large *presepio* also rests here, with more than 1000 figures and buildings adorning the nativity scene. The **Chapel** and the beautiful 18th-century *Court Theatre*, if open, are worth seeing more than the upper rooms. Ask one of the guards to take you to see them.

At the back of the palace is a bus that travels to the top of the park, for an additional fee of 1000 lire each way. I suggest taking the ride up; you can always walk back. At the top is a snack bar where you can buy a sandwich or slice of pizza, along with illustrated guides and souvenirs. The park is at its best on Wednesday, Saturday and Sunday from about 11.00 to 14.00, when the fountains are on and the long terraced canal is filled with water. Since this is drinkable water, coming from a superbly designed aqueduct in Maddaloni devised by Vanvitelli, the commune decided to limit the supply of this precious commodity to certain days of the week – very sensible, but not so gratifying for the visitor who comes on the wrong day.

Vanvitelli also supervised the park's landscape, which was laid out by Martin Biancour. The most famous set of fountain statues at Caserta is that of **Diana and Actaeon** at the top of the hill beneath a high waterfall. Diana and her nymphs are bathing on one side, while on the other Actaeon has stumbled upon the divine naked figure while hunting. For this innocent accident, Diana punishes him severely; Actaeon sprouts horns and is attacked by his own dogs. To my mind, the dogs are more animated than the other figures in this landscape, but the harmony of composition in such a natural setting more than compensates.

Facing the back of the palace, the **English Garden** will be on your left, and a guide will take you through this section of the park. It was laid out by the Englishman John Andrew Graeffer in 1782, and has many delightful elements. Cedars of Lebanon, palms, pines, and the first camelia imported from Japan to Europe are among the rich variety of botanical species here. The mock ruins are my favourite part of the English Garden. Arched walkways wind around a pond – portions of the vaulted roof and tufa walls are missing while frescoes continue to fade beneath moist brown moss. Another favourite is the **Castelluccia** or miniature castle, a Vanvitelli folly closer to the palace on the west side. It is found past the old fish pond with its central island. The big fishpond, half a kilometre long and forming the first pool before ascending north to the Grand Cascade, was always stocked with fish for the royal kitchens. The way back to the Reggia is along the central avenue with its wide water path of twelve little waterfalls.

The Medieval Borgo of Caserta Vecchia

A winding corniche road to the northeast of Caserta takes you up to the walled town of Caserta Vecchia. Views along the way give you a good idea of what this farming country is like, and what mining has done to the limestone mountains beyond. Stark white patches have exposed whole sides of these mountains, and the regional government no longer allows companies to be so rapacious. But one thing that remains entirely intact in this area is the charming town of

Caserta Vecchia. It's a pleasure to walk its cobbled streets and stand in the unchanged main square with its cathedral and bell tower, with 9th-century castle ruins on a neglected hill above. No more than 300 people live here, and most of the mini Fiats are parked on the town's edge. Unless you're making a delivery to one of the local restaurants, don't try to take a car through these narrow streets.

The town was probably founded in the 8th century by the Lombards, but the oldest existing buildings date from the 11th and 12th centuries when the Normans controlled the region. The **cathedral of San Michele**, finished in 1153, is a fine example of Southern Norman architecture, which in some ways is a blend of styles. The central cupola, added 100 years later, has a Moslem feel to it – a rounded roof, with chequered squares of brown and yellow between delicate intertwined arches on two levels. The bell-tower was built in 1234; Gothic influence means that it's less ornamental but again has the rounded roof of a Middle Eastern dwelling. One of the roadways into the main Cathedral square runs through it.

The cathedral's façade is simple and joyful: two small stone lions jut out on the sides of the main central portal with a little bull above. Over the right-hand entrance are two horselike creatures, and on the left are centaurs. The interior has recently undergone renovation, remaining simple and solemn, and very similiar in plan and proportions to Sant' Angelo in Formis. Eighteen Corinthian columns divide the nave from the aisles; the pulpit and altar are good examples of intricate mosaic marblework.

During the second half of September the town sponsors exhibits and games to celebrate its patron saint of San Michele. I happened upon the *spettacolo* one warm evening when the walled square beside the Duomo was filled with children in splendid silk costumes. Their outfits were half one colour and half another, to represent different teams competing in their version of the *Palio*. The four squads went by the names of the Towers, Walls, Cathedral and St Michael. Before the festivities began, the children sang their way through a half-hour mass. Then they tore back into the square, some hugging the young priest around his middle, imploring him to get the show on the road. The first race began: one runner from each team bore a torch and ran off through the streets, their silken tunics flapping in the breeze. This was followed by more foot-races, and many tries at tug-of-war in the twilight.

I wandered up and down the streets, thinking what a safe and sheltered life they must lead in this perfectly preserved outpost. To grow up in a town that nobody can remember ever having looked any differently – what must that feel like? Perhaps only the names of restaurants here have changed. The five or six here now will beckon you with the smell of roasted peppers and simmering tomato sauce. (Try wild boar too – the local speciality.)

East to Benevento and south to Avellino

Benevento is the capital of Campania's smallest province, important for its place in ancient history. It is surrounded by small, insular towns whose people don't appear to be as open as those in towns and cities along the coast. South of Benevento by about 30km is Avellino, hit so hard by the 1980 earthquake that it's still trying to build itself back into shape. Benevento has more to recommend it than Avellino but, frankly, I wouldn't make a special trip to either place unless you are in search of something of specific interest, or unless your route takes you conveniently past either city.

Avellino and Benevento are quickly reached by motorway from Naples, or by the slower route 7 when coming from Caserta. Route 7, though busy and unattractively lined with small factories just outside of Caserta, traverses interesting countryside before reaching Benevento. Two towns worth stopping in along the way are picturesque **Airola** (with the Church of the Annunciata's façade designed by Vanvitelli) and **Montesarchio** with its Baroque fountain in Piazza Umberto I and a solid 15th-century castle at the top of the windswept hill. You'll drive through a ravine known as the Caudine Forks, where the Samnites trapped the Romans in 321BC, though historians still debate its exact location: between Arienzo and Arpaia, or between Sant' Agata de' Goti and Moiano?

Benevento

Benevento's old town sits on a hill between the Calore and Sabato Rivers, still a throughfare for those travelling between Naples and Apulia. Its Latin name was Malaventum, ascribed to bad air flowing through. Either the air or attitudes changed dramatically, for the Romans renamed this place Beneventum in 268BC. In 571 it became the first independent Lombard duchy, and the remains of walls built during that time are among the oldest in Europe. Benevento was the site of Manfred of Hohenstaufen's defeat by Charles of Anjou in 1266, and the city gained yet more battle scars during World War II when it was badly bombed by the Allies. Benevento is probably best known throughout Italy as the home of Strega, a bitter liqueur made from walnuts. *Strega* means witch in Italian, and the famous yellow mixture takes it name from the superstition that witches gathered around a walnut tree here to celebrate rites on the Sabbath.

Benevento's main sights are grouped closely together, most on or close to the Corso Garibaldi. The 13th-century Romanesque Duomo sits at one end, the church of Santa Sofia and its museum at the other, while Trajan's Arch is down the Via Traiano halfway along the Corso. The **Roman theatre**, built during Hadrian's reign in the second century, is just south east of the Duomo. It is engulfed by homes and apartments, another sad example of how lack of planning can damage an ancient monument. But to the city's credit the amphitheatre is still used for open-air performances.

Trajan's Arch here in Benevento is one of the best preserved in all of Italy, erected across the Appian Way by Trajan in 114. 17m high, it's made of Parian marble and covered with rich bas relief scenes. All the figures are intact, save two on one high outer edge. Those that remain are somewhat hard to identify, but they all depict scenes from the life of the emperor – his coronation, in counsel with Roman senators, and ceremonies of worship, along with mythological scenes. Though the arch is dirty, the only real distraction here is the information booth ridiculously placed in the centre which spoils the arch's lofty proportions.

Benevento's other highlight is the church of **Santa Sofia** and its **Samnite Museum** in the cloister behind. The small church on pretty Piazza Matteotti was built in 762. The internal plan is unusual – semicircular behind the high altar, with six-sided wall sections connecting front to back. The church's central nucleus consists of six columns connected by arches, and a second outer ring of eight pilasters. The overall effect produces a simple and intimate interior, one of the oddest and most pleasing I've ever experienced. Behind the high altar, in the two outer apses, are fragments of an 8th-century cycle of frescoes depicting the Life of St Zacchary.

The cloisters of Santa Sofia are just as delightful as the church. The Samnite Museum is set in airy rooms off this courtyard, and from each is yet another view of the cloisters and its fanciful columns. Each capital, carved in the first half of the 12th century, is full of detail and not a little Arab influence: a camel with driver along one side, a trellis of grapes along the other. On another horsemen gallop and a deer is being attacked. I found every single scene captivating. The museum itself is formed from a provincial archeological collection initiated by Talleyrand in 1806, absentee ruler for nine years who was given the title of Prince of Benevento by Napolean when the French briefly ruled Naples. Statues from Domitian's Temple of Isis are among the most interesting in the collection, but there are also Magna Grecia coins, 6th-century bronze jewellery, ceramics, and paintings by Francesco Solimena, Andrea Vaccaro and Giacomo del Po.

Avellino

The most scenic route from Benevento to Avellino is by winding state road No.88, which takes about an hour. The route wends through a green valley full of small farms. Tobacco is grown here in abundance, and stepped gardens are planted with grape vines and tomatoes. A faster route is by motorway running south east and parallel to state road No.7, and then directly west by motorway A16 to Avellino.

The city of Avellino is capital of its province, with a population of 60,000. It has had the worst luck of any city in the region, being drastically shaken by earthquakes from 1456 until the present day. Perhaps this helps to explain why a high number of Italians from this area have emigrated to other countries, especially the US. After the earthquake in 1980, Italians from many other parts of the country came here to help restore some degree of normality to peoples' lives.

Avellino's medieval nucleus, from the Duomo to the castle ruins just east, is the most interesting section to explore. The cathedral, with its Neo-Classical façade, was originally built in the 12th century but rebuilt in 1868. Beneath the Duomo are remnants of the original Lombard church – **Santa Maria dei Sette Dolori**. Near the Piazza Amendola in the streets around the church are a number of Baroque fountains, along with a clock-tower designed by Fanzago. Avellino's only other attraction is the **Irpino Museum** on two floors of the modern Palazzo della Cultura on Corso Europa. Its archeological collection of prehistoric Irpine, Samnite and Roman objects embraces a period from the neolithic age to the sixth century. There is also a small but valuable selection of Neapolitan paintings, along with a section devoted to the Risorgimento.

Practical Information

Getting there

Travelling north of Naples to Caserta and Benevento is easy to do by train, from either the main station in Naples or Rome. The tour companies listed in the information section at the end of chapter three also run day trips to the palace at Caserta. However, for outlying towns and the coast you must go by car. The A2 motorway is a fast connecting route from Rome to Naples, and many exits along the way are close to the towns mentioned in this chapter.

Tourist Information Offices

AVELLINO   50 Piazza Libertà (tel. 0825 35175).

BENEVENTO   34 Via Giustiniani (tel. 0824 21960).

CASERTA   The main provincial tourist office is located within the central area of the palace complex (tel. 0823 326832). A more accessible office is located on the corner of Piazza Dante at 39 Corso Trieste (tel. 0823 321137).

Hotels and restaurants

AVELLINO   Jolly Hotel, 97a Via Tuoro Cappuccini (tel. 0825 25922) is comfortable but lacking in character. Expensive. Close to the hotel is a very good restaurant called **La Caveja**, 48 Via Tuoro Cappuccini (tel. 0825 38277). Moderate.

BAIA DOMIZIA   In the province of Caserta, my first choice is always **Hotel della Baia**, Via dell'Erica, 81030 Caserta (tel. 0823 721344). In the north west corner of Campania right on the Mediterranean, the small town of Baia Domizia itself is characterised by uninspired post-war buildings, but the hotel is set apart from all that, with a view out to sea. It is a low, cool white stucco building, the floors paved with large glazed terracotta tiles. A tennis court is shared with the hotel next door; the food here is wonderful; taking full or half board is very good value. If it weren't for the fact that the hotel is closed from October to mid-May, the restaurant would undoubtedly be awarded a Michelin star. Moderate prices.

BENEVENTO **The Hotel President**, 1 Via G.B. Perasso, 82100 Benevento (tel. 0824 21000), is in a good position near the church of Santa Sofia. Clean and moderately priced, though without any atmosphere. The basic and inexpensive **Hotel Traiano**, Viale dei Rettori, is just up the street from Trajan's magnificent arch.

Benevento is filled with pizzerias, as well as more formal places such as the expensive **Antica Taverna**, Via Annunziata 41 (tel. 0824 21212), closed Sun; and the moderately-priced **Pascalucci** in the Piano Cappelle district (24548); closed Mon.

CASERTA The large **Reggia Palace Hotel**, Viale Carlo III, PO Box 20, 81100 Caserta (tel. 0823 458500), is clean and comfortable, though impersonal and without character. It is on a main road just south of the palace, 2km from the Caserta Sud exit off the motorway. Food here is good, but the modern décor in the dining room is appalling; there's a pool and a clay tennis court. Expensive. (The hotel is technically in San Nicola La Strada, and other smaller hotels are also on Viale Carlo III, such as the **Pisani** and the **Serenella**.)

One good restaurant in the centre of Caserta is the **Antica Locanda-Massa 1848**, Via Mazzini 55 (tel. 0823 321268), open for lunch, and on Saturday nights. Moderate prices.

CASERTA VECCHIA Unfortunately, there is no accommodation in this charming town, but five or six small and simple restaurants have a long tradition of serving good local fare. They are so close to one another on the town's few walking streets that you can easily survey menus and prices as you stroll along. One I'd recommend is **Al Ritrovo dei Patriarchi** (tel. 0823 371510); closed Wed. Moderate.

TELESE In the region of Benevento, I came across another hotel like della Baia, unusual for its elegance and amenities. It's called **Grand Hotel Telese**, 1 Via Cerreto, 82037, Telese Terme (tel. 0824 940500), located in the small town of Telese about 25km north west of Benevento. It's surrounded by woods, and a large complex of thermal baths are nearby. Reception rooms with floor to ceiling windows are furnished with antiques; bedrooms are plush and inviting, with thick terry-cotton robes supplied. Ask for a room overlooking the front drive and gardens. Full board only; expensive.

Price Ranges

Hotel (double room)	*Restaurant (Per head)*
Inexpensive: under 60,000	under 25,000
Moderate: 60–120,000	25–50,000
Expensive: 120–200,000	50–90,000
Very expensive: 200,000+	90,000+

Museums and other public sites

AVELLINO Irpino Museum, Corso Europa, Palazzo della Cultura. Open 08:30–14.00 Mon–Fri, 08:30–12.00 Sat, closed Sun and hols.

BENEVENTO Samnite Museum, Corso Garibaldi (tel. 0824 21818). Open 09.00–13.00 Mon through Sat; closed Sun and hols.
Trajan's Arch, Via Traiano, viewed at all hours.

CAPUA Museo Campano, Palazzo Antignano, Via Roma (tel. 0823 971402). Open 09.00–14.00 Tues through Sat, 09.00–13.00 Sun, closed Mon and hols.

CASERTA Palazzo Reale and gardens (tel. 0823 321127). State apartments open 09.00–13.30 Tues through Sat, 09.00–13.00 Sun, closed Mon and hols. The park is also open until 16.30 during the months of July, August and September.

SANTA MARIA CAPUA VETERE Amphitheatre, at the top of Piazza Primo Ottobre from Corso Umberto Primo. Open 09.00–16.00, closed Mon and hols.
Mithraeum, Vico Mitreo off Via Morelli. Same hours as amphitheatre, whose custodian will escort you on the ten-minute walk from there.

7. SOUTH WITH HISTORY: *Vesuvius, Herculaneum and Pompeii*

'Blow on a dead man's embers and a live flame will start,' wrote poet Robert Graves. Is there anywhere in the world where this is more true than at the ancient sights of Pompeii and Herculaneum? Vesuvius wrought molten havoc in 79AD, but 1900 years later the tragically encased bodies are still telling us their tales.

Pompeii has been more systematically excavated than Herculaneum, mainly because the fallen volcanic material was not as dense and rock-like as that at Herculaneum. The town's layout is so extensive that you can spend hours in Pompeii wandering from house to shop to temple, getting a good idea of what life must have been like in this market town. But Pompeii is so famous that perhaps people expect too much from it, and some travellers express disappointment with what they find – and don't find. An endless number of unmarked, half-height walls running in all directions appear daunting at first; I do recommend hiring a guide who speaks English to some degree. An important point to remember is that the best works of art found in Pompeii are now in the National Archeological Museum in Naples, except for the cycle of frescoes at the Villa of the Mysteries.

Many more travellers find their way to Pompeii than to Herculaneum and the summit of Vesuvius. If you can devote at least two days' sightseeing to this area of the Campanian coast, it's really best to see all three (along with a trip to the museum in Naples). More than Pompeii, Herculaneum's excavations are a compact and primarily residential quarter which help shed a different shade of light on the period. If you climb to the summit of Vesuvius, wander through Herculaneum, and then spend a day at Pompeii you will have as complete a picture of life suspended in 79AD as anyone possibly can.

After the volcano smothered both towns, they lay hidden for centuries. Rumours of buried treasure at the foot of the mountain were often heard, but nothing was found; in 1503 a cartographer named Ambrogio Leone marked Herculaneum fairly accurately when drawing a map of Campania. But that didn't stimulate enough interest to start digging, perhaps a blessing in disguise considering the amount of damage done by excavating in the 1700s. In the 1590s, an aristocrat who needed water for his villa's fountain at Torre Annunziata dug a channel across the site of Pompeii, and came across inscriptions which named the town. But still nothing was done; he left all stones unturned because he thought the carving referred not to the city but to Pompey the Great, a popular general who conquered the army of Spartacus.

Then in 1709 the building of a monastery well at Resina led to the accidental discovery of Herculaneum. A workman revealed splendidly coloured marbles when he hit seats in the town's theatre, and many objects were then plundered for the nearby villa of an Austrian prince. The theatre was identified correctly only in 1738, and Charles III financed the first excavation, headed by a Spanish engineer. His methods weren't exactly scientific, until a Swiss architect named Weber arrived on the scene. He discovered the famous Villa of the Papyri, still buried under 20m of volcanic matter. Weber diligently tunnelled through many areas, drawing systematic plans of what he found. (These invaluable, though incomplete, floor plans were used for the J. Paul Getty Museum replication in Malibu, California.)

Finally, it was the famous Italian archeologist Amedeo Maiuri who carefully directed the first comprehensive modern excavations of both sights. Past discoveries, especially during the 18th and early 19th centuries, had done their damage – in some cases worse than that inflicted by Vesuvius over the centuries. But Maiuri's work in the 1920s, based on solid research carried out by Giuseppe Fiorelli in the 1860s, has carefully yielded the most fascinating tale of two cities ever told.

Vesuvius

Before visiting Pompeii and Herculaneum, acquaint yourself with their annihilator by climbing to the top of Vesuvius. Still deceptively active, the volcano has erupted eighty times since Pompeii and Herculaneum were buried, though it has been relatively quiet since 1944. While driving up to the summit you'll be able to see where the last lava flow in March, 1944, left its wide dark mark.

The ascent of Vesuvius takes about forty minutes if you're walking up the west face path, reached after passing villages on a winding road that ends at the car park. The trip up Vesuvius can easily be combined with a visit to Herculaneum on the same day, but don't try to fit in Pompeii too; save that experience for a full day's outing.

For the climb up the west face, wear a pair of sturdy, flat-bottomed shoes. The path consists of uneven bits of hard lava and you can lose your footing. Even if it's a warm day, take a sweater or windproof garment because it does get cool on the way up. While climbing, you won't question the position of the cone looming above. But from Naples and the north east, Vesuvius with its two lopsided peaks looks as if it harbours two volcanoes. Before 79AD, the summit was wider and taller, encompassing both peaks as one large mass; but the eruption that wiped out Pompeii and Herculaneum blew away the mountain's top. From the Sorrento side, you can tell which portion of the mountain is a peaked ridge, and which is the cone.

When you get to the summit, at 1277m, you'll be looking down into a cone with a flat barren bottom. In its present state it's hard to believe that this volcano has been capable of spewing forth lava and ash, along with sending low banks of superhot gases and sliding debris toward villages miles away. Vapour continues to escape from cracks along the inner sides and bottom, but fencing prevents anyone from walking down inside for a closer view. Snack bars mark the beginning and end of the trail, selling postcards and garish bits of painted lava.

Vesuvius is an otherworldly place. How could anyone judge its force as the volcano slumbers within and the landscape below looks so tranquil? When Vesuvius is as still as it is today, and was before the great eruption, it's easy to see why Pompeiians were unaware of its destructive power. Tales were told of orange light once escaping from Vesuvius, and in 30BC, the geographer Strabo thought the rocks on the top looked as if they'd been subjected to fire. But this mountain dedicated to Bacchus yielded succulent tomatoes, and its grapes still produce a fine white wine known as Lacrima Christi. This soil full of nutrients was a symbol of plenty rather than ruin.

Even the naturalist Pliny the Elder initially thought the eruption merely curious on that day in August, 79. According to his nephew's account, Pliny sailed closer and closer to Pompeii, both to get a closer look and with the thought of saving people along the shore. Upon arriving at Castellamare di Stabia south of Pompeii, he thought he had time for a little rest and relaxation, and dozed off into a sound sleep. But when he awoke the walls around him were shaking violently; Pliny and his friends were forced to flee with pillows tied to their heads for protection. The air was thick and black with smoke, and Pliny suffocated from the vapours he couldn't help inhaling. Hundreds of people in Pompeii and Herculaneum must have suffered the same fate.

Pliny's nephew's eyewitness account from the shores of Cape Misenum across the bay earned him a scientific honour: the first stage of eruption (fall-out of pumice and ash from a high cloud) has been named the 'Plinian phase'. He recorded that this cloud was

> in appearance and shape like a tree – the umbrella pine would give the best idea of it. Like an immense tree trunk it was projected into the air, and opened out with branches. I believe that it was carried up by a violent gust, then left as the gust faltered.

Sir William Hamilton gives us a light-hearted account of Neapolitan behaviour during a lesser eruption in 1767 in his *Campi Phlegraei*:

> The ashes, or rather small cinders, showered down so fast that the people in the streets were obliged to use umbrellas or flap their hats, these ashes

being very offensive to the eyes. The tops of the houses and balconies were covered above an inch thick with these cinders . . . In the midst of these horrors the mob, growing tumultuous and impatient, obliged the Cardinal to bring out the head of San Gennaro and go with it in procession to the Ponte Maddalena, at the extremity of Naples toward Vesuvius; and it is well attested here that the eruption ceased the moment the Saint came in sight of the mountain.

I have no doubt that Neapolitans would try that ploy again if Vesuvius threatened them. What are the chances of an eruption occuring today? Nobody knows for sure. Many volcanologists are troubled by the disturbances at nearby Pozzuoli – are they a sign that pressure beneath the earth's surface is escaping in a less disastrous way, or is another volcano building up far beneath the flat plain of Vesuvius we see today? The only reassurance is that trained eyes and instruments record every belch and rumble these days, and that there should be plenty of warning before anything drastic happens.

Herculaneum

Herculaneum sits on the western hem of Mount Vesuvius, and on a full day's outing can be combined with an ascent to the summit. The town was named for Hercules by Greek settlers, though the city's origins are not entirely clear to scholars. An Italic people called the Oscans certainly dominated the area 500 years before Christ, building the original walls at Pompeii. But the Oscans were then ousted by another stronger, native tribe called the Samnites who made their way south from the region bordering Campania and Lazio. It wasn't until 89BC that Herculaneum was taken with other Campanian towns by the Roman general Sulla.

As it was part of the Roman Empire, life was relatively peaceful, and Herculaneum was really no more than a satellite to Naples. It was never a commercial centre like Pompeii, and a population of 5000 inhabitants was deduced by counting the seats through tunneling down into the amphitheatre. Large villas were built by the sea, an exclusive suburban enclave similar to Baia which lies west of Naples.

Herculaneum's fate was very different to Pompeii's, due to its position upwind and to the northwest of Vesuvius. After an initial explosion, pumice fell lightly on the town; about 20cm accumulated in 18 hours. But then it was hit by ground surges (clouds of ash and hot gas that hug the ground) and pyroclastic flows (avalanches of pumice, ash and gases). Six successive waves of thick, hot volcanic matter soon flowed into Herculaneum, and the town was buried to an average depth of 22m.

Archeologists had assumed that most of the residents had had time to escape, since less than 12 bodies had ever been found. But in 1980, while workmen were digging a drainage ditch near the marina, they came across a skeleton. Soon they dug up dozens more and in 1982, a capsized boat 10m long. A new theory emerged. Had hundreds of frightened townspeople made their way to the beach, hoping to escape by sea? Groups of up to seven people were found huddled together in vaulted chambers, probably built to store boats. A Roman soldier was found face down with his sword beside him. A 25-year-old woman had been seven months pregnant, her unborn baby's bones as fragile as eggshell. Many had contorted jaws, as if trying to fight the fumes that must have asphyxiated them.

Although much of Herculaneum remains unexcavated, there are important sights to see. (Underground tunnels still lead to the buried amphitheatre and the fantastic Villa of the Papyri, but aren't open to the public and would be difficult to get through even if they were.) The area of the city which has been uncovered comprises five quarters and three main streets, similar to the earliest inner Greek-planned district of Naples. Houses are in a very good state of preservation, including a second storey in some cases. It has been much harder work to uncover ruins here than in Pompeii, but the tough shell of tufa-like material that encased Herculaneum's structures has meant that even some wooden beams and household objects are still in place.

The houses within the excavated area show a variety of different building methods, for a populace which ranged from merchant to patrician. The rich laid claim to the best positions by the seafront, and their homes were filled with decorative frescoes and mosaics. All the public elements of a Roman town are present in Herculaneum: the baths, forum, market, basilica, palestra and theatre. For a lively and informative account of life in the town, I recommend getting hold of a copy of *Herculaneum: Italy's Buried Treasure*, by Joseph Jay Deiss, first published by Harper and Row in 1966 but revised in 1985.

Across from the entrance to the site is a shop selling a detailed visual guide to the ruins, worth purchasing, but I've also outlined highlights here. From the entrance gate, walk south down the avenue and around to your right. The excavated area sits down within high walls, somewhat claustrophobic compared to the open plain of Pompeii.

At the western edge, where you enter, is the **House of the Inn** (Casa dell'Albergo) to the right. This is one of the biggest houses in the southern quarter, and just before Vesuvius erupted had been undergoing renovation to add an apartment and a shop.

Heading up Cardo IV, the first dwelling on the right is the **House of the Mosaic Atrium** (Casa dell Atrio a Mosaico). It once had a beautiful view of the sea, but the shore has since retreated by about 500m. The mosaic in the large atrium is a bold black-and-white geometric design, yet the most amazing thing about it is the floor itself: rippled waves of tile are what you now walk on, caused by the forceful flow of volcanic material beneath the surface. The house is in two sections, with a garden between, and most of the wood in the portico – window sashes, frames and beams – is original. To the left of the entrance was the doorkeeper's area: his mosaic sign to beware of the dog, *Cave Canem*, is similar to the famous Pompeiian version now at the Archeological Museum in Naples.

Just up the same street on the left is the **Wooden Trellis House** (Casa a Graticcio or Opus Craticium, which is the Latin term for this type of construc-

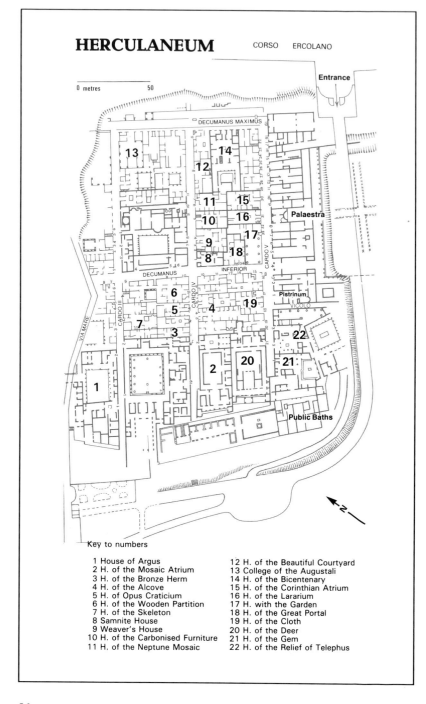

HERCULANEUM

CORSO   ERCOLANO

Entrance

0 metres   50

DECUMANUS MAXIMUS

13

14

12

11   15

10   16   Palaestra

9   17

8   18

DECUMANUS   INFERIOR

CARDO IV   CARDO V

6   19   Pistrinum

5   4   VICOLO

7   3

22

2   20   21

1

Public Baths

VIA MARE   CARDO III

N

Key to numbers

1 House of Argus
2 H. of the Mosaic Atrium
3 H. of the Bronze Herm
4 H. of the Alcove
5 H. of Opus Craticium
6 H. of the Wooden Partition
7 H. of the Skeleton
8 Samnite House
9 Weaver's House
10 H. of the Carbonised Furniture
11 H. of the Neptune Mosaic

12 H. of the Beautiful Courtyard
13 College of the Augustali
14 H. of the Bicentenary
15 H. of the Corinthian Atrium
16 H. of the Lararium
17 H. with the Garden
18 H. of the Great Portal
19 H. of the Cloth
20 H. of the Deer
21 H. of the Gem
22 H. of the Relief of Telephus

tion). Its square wooden frame is simple, consisting of small rooms and a balcony protruding from the second storey. The inexpensive wood and plaster construction was used for poorer dwellings, and the technique was called *opus craticium*. The building has a shop, a back workroom and two apartments; some of the steps to the upper storey are original, and the bedrooms above still contain furniture.

Next door is the patrician **House of the Wooden Partition** (Casa del Tramezzo di Legno), whose façade is one of the best preserved in Herculaneum. Inside, ceilings are high, and traces of fresco decoration are evident from floor to ceiling. The house is named for the wooden screen on bronze tracks used to close off the living room (*tablinum*) from the atrium. Two small bedrooms still have their wooden bed frames.

On Cardo IV's opposite corner is the **Samnite House** (Casa Sannitica), built at least three centuries before Vesuvius erupted and one of Herculaneum's oldest. The atrium is a large airy space dominated by the entranceway, which is flanked by two Corinthian columns. The second-storey gallery is divided by small Ionic columns between a perforated rail. Interior walls were delicately painted in shades of red and sea-green, along with many frescoes.

Across the street are the **Baths** (Terme del Foro), very well preserved and probably constructed between 30 and 10 BC. The men's section is entered at No.7 Cardo IV, the women's at No.8. It's not a luxurious place, but well equipped; some mosaics still survive, along with the characteristic phallic graffiti on some of the walls. In the center of the Baths is the Paleastra, or gym, where both men and women would exercise – perhaps fencing, or playing *pila*, a game in which players would toss a ball (an inflated animal's bladder) to each other. Walking through the Baths, you'll come across separate cold, tepid and hot rooms, as well as waiting rooms and toilets for men and women. Skeletons, perhaps of bath attendants, still remain in the men's waiting room, trapped there when Vesuvius erupted.

Look into two other houses along Cardo IV across from the Baths. The **House of the Carbonised Furniture** (Casa del Mobilio Carbonizzato) still contains its dining couch and a three-legged table.

The **House of the Mosaic of Neptune and Amphitrite** (Casa di Nettuno ad Anfitrite) had its front walls destroyed and lies open to the street, with a shop and its shelves close to the street. The living quarters are toward the back, and the pretty blue-and-green mosaics in the open dining room are only outstripped by the stunning mosaic of a nude golden Neptune and his wife Amphitrite.

Up at the top of the street, turn right on Decumano Massimo. The **House of the Bicentenary** (Casa del Bicentanario) will be on your right, so-called because it was excavated in 1938, 200 hundred years after organised digging started. It was a beautiful house, one of Herculaneum's richest, and lies at the centre of a controversy as a result of a curious discovery within. A wall in one of the upper floor's rooms is marked with the shape of a cross on a patch of white stucco, as if someone had ripped a wooden crucifix from the spot. A small wooden cabinet had been positioned beneath, with a platform in front that might have been used for kneeling in prayer. If that's the case, this would be

The mosaic of Neptune and Amphitrite at Herculaneum

the oldest evidence of the Christian cross in use as a symbol for the group then known by Romans as the cult of the Jew Christus. The Apostle Paul had landed at Pozzuoli 18 years earlier. Was this room's tenant a convert after listening to his radical teachings?

Now turn left into limestone-paved Cardo V, walking past merchant's shops to the **Bakery** (Pistrinum) at No.8. This shop was owned by Sextus Patulcus Felix, as seen by the inscription. Two stone flour mills are intact within, along with bronze baking tins. Over the baking ovens at the back is an upright phallic emblem, a humorous symbol employed to ensure that cakes would rise successfully while baking.

Behind this section of the street is a large gym and exercise area called the **Palaestra**, only partially uncovered among the weeds. But you can see the cross-shaped swimming pool that's been excavated.

Stop into the **House of the Gem** (Casa della Gemma) for a look at the famous graffiti in the loo. Inscribed on the wall is: *Apollinaris medicus Titi imperatoris hic cacavit bene.* In other words: Apollinaris, physician of the Emperor Titus, crapped well here.

The **House of the Deer** (Casa dei Cerveri) is just opposite, named for two little marble statues found inside. It's the last house on the right at the end of the street, and decoration dates it to about 25 years before the eruption. The lavish house is divided into two long sections, and at one time overlooked the bay. Walls were decorated in the black-and-red style of Pompeii; in the enclosed portico are charming paintings of cupids playing hide-and-seek and other games; black-and-white mosaics pattern the hallways, and pots and pans still sit on the charcoal stove. Most of the house's treasures are in the National Archeological Museum in Naples, but the wonderful drunken Hercules, trying to pee, is in one of the little rooms off the garden.

Modern-Day Herculaneum

Excavation continues at the main site, though the extraordinary Villa of the Papyri still remains underground. One of Italy's biggest challenges is to come up with enough money to excavate the site (the J. Paul Getty Museum in Malibu near Los Angeles makes up in part for what we can't see, as it is a modern replica of the structure). Though the villa was partially tunnelled through in the 1750s, archeologists today are still thwarted by the heavy matter encasing it. This amazing suburban villa was named for the papyrus documents retrieved from the library. In total, 1787 volumes were brought to light, and careful unrolling of the scrolls revealed an almost complete collection of the works of Philodemus, the Greek philosopher. Trying to decipher the texts has been a painstaking process for papyrologists at the International Centre for the Study of Herculanean Papyri. But sophisticated microscopes, cameras and computers have all helped to yield interesting results. Ninety pieces of sculpture have come from the villa, among them Hermes at Rest, the Sleeping Faun, and Drunken Silenus, all now at the museum in Naples. It seems a travesty that work to rescue the villa has gone this slowly. When so many valuable works have been uncovered, who knows what remains to be revealed?

Beyond the ruins, Herculaneum has other treasures to offer in the form of elaborate 18th-century villas which have been renovated and opened to the public. These Vesuvian villas are a ten-minute walk south from the excavations, well sign-posted. They were constructed when Bourbon King Charles III was in power and his summer court was transferred to Portici, just north of Herculaneum. Neapolitan noblemen followed suit, and the 'golden mile' was a patch of real estate glittering with 121 late Baroque villas designed by Vanvitelli, Fuga, Vaccaro and Sanfelice. When Charles left Naples for Spain, however, the area lost its appeal and the aristocratic owners began renting these luxurious quarters to local families. Many of the villas were lost through fire and neglect, or subdivided into numerous apartments; the frescoes and elaborate mouldings fell into disrepair.

In 1977, the regional government purchased one of the best examples in the form of Villa Campolieto, designed by Vanvitelli and now beautifully restored. It is a surprising sight after passing crumbling palazzi and auto mechanics' shops. The villa, an elegant Neo-Classical structure in pale yellow and white, is used for conventions and events such as summer theatre. The swirling staircase within is a Vanvitelli trademark, and rooms on the first floor are absolutely covered with floral frescoes. It is the 18th-century answer to the first century's luxurious and elaborately decorated Villa of the Papyri.

Pompeii

The town of Pompeii, originally a native Oscan settlement founded in the 7th century BC, is 16km south of Herculaneum. The city was conquered by Greeks, Etruscans and Samnites, and finally became a Roman colony in 80BC along with Herculaneum. Pompeii was a thriving, noisy market town of about 20,000 inhabitants, filled with shops and bars and small family factories. Traders constantly came and went, while wine and a potent fish sauce were Pompeii's most popular exports.

On the day Vesuvius erupted, Pompeii was the scene of a different but no less deadly series of catastrophes. Many more pumice stones showered down here than at Herculaneum, while dense layers of ash settled at the rate of about 15cm per hour. Roofs began to collapse, and the town was in almost total darkness. The people who died waited too long inside their homes, trapped by fallen timbers or barred from leaving by the pumice still falling. Then they were unable to breathe from the gases and ash surging southward early the next morning. But archeologists think that only one-tenth of the population died that way; many more might have suffocated, like Pliny the Elder, on the roads outside the city while trying to flee. If some of the population did in fact survive, it still isn't clear where they went.

The excavated city today is much larger than Herculaneum, covering an area of about one kilometre east to west, and about half a kilometre north to south. Plan on spending at least four hours here. Apart from the amphitheatre, however, you won't find many places to sit and rest and the site is not well shaded. Wear flat-soled shoes too, since the pavement is uneven. I recommend spending the morning in Pompeii, having a meal outside the gates at lunchtime (or a picnic in the amphitheatre), and then exploring the Villa of Mysteries north of the main excavations in the afternoon.

Though the 1980 earthquake damaged some buildings, many have now been re-opened. And, ironically this most recent earthquake was the catalyst for renewed enthusiasm, and funding, for Pompeii. The Soprintendenza Archeologica di Pompeii was founded in 1981, and an exciting interdisciplinary approach to restoration has evolved: archeologists, biologists, art historians, botanists, climatologists, physicists and computer scientists are all working to maintain and enhance the ancient city of Pompeii.

The most important sites are accessible to the public, and others can be entered with a guide. You'll see the guides milling around looking for business, and you should consider paying their small fee as they'll also take you to see the licentious wall paintings hidden to the general public (listen to their entertaining tales with a historical grain of salt, as many guides can't resist embellishing the facts).

When Goethe visited the site in 1787, he wrote:

> the city still manages to demonstrate, even in its utter desolation, that all its inhabitants had a love of painting and the arts which today's would-be dilettante is incapable of understanding or appreciating.

The excavated city of Pompeii

Add to that Percy Bysshe Shelley's impression of the whole scene in 1818:

> I had no conception of anything so perfect yet remaining. They lived in a perpetual commerce with external nature, and nourished themselves upon the spirit of its forms. Their theatres were all open to the mountains and the sky.

When Pompeii was uncovered in the 1700s, it sparked a resurgence of the four 'Pompeian Styles' of painting found in the town's villas, baths and theatres. The first style is really just a wall covering without any human figures – swirls of colour to represent marble, or simple squares of colour on stucco slabs. The second style, dating from the first century BC, is illusionistic figure painting of religious and mythological scenes. The third is more complex and was popular about one hundred years later – bands or tablets of intricate mythological scenes and landscapes with more figures, the edges often festooned with colourful decorative motifs. The fourth style followed from this, often employed after the earlier earthquake of 63AD. Large panels are of a more impressionistic nature so that decorative elements are less well-defined, best seen in the Villa of Mysteries outside the main area where its cycle of frescoes is still in place.

Enter Pompeii from the west entrance at the Porta Marina near the railroad stations. Close to sixty sites have been excavated, most of them open to the public, and 12 of the most interesting are highlighted here. As in Herculaneum a thorough descriptive guide, with photos, is helpful.

The **Antiquarium**, a museum just inside the western gate, opened in 1948. Recently closed for extensive renovations, it should re-open by the end of 1994. The museum's most famous objects are the plaster casts of bodies caught in

Key to numbers
1 Temple of Venus Pomeiana
2 Basilica
3 Temple of Apollo
4 Temple of Jupiter
5 Macellum
6 Sacrarium of the lares
7 T. of Vespasian
8 Building of Eumachia
9 Comitium
10 H. of the Wild Boar
11 H. of Holconius
12 Palaestra Sannitica

POMPEII

0 metres   300

13	Teatro Grande	27	Thermopolium	47	Casa delle Nozze d'Argento
14	Teatro Piccolo	28	H. of P. Parquins	48	Casa del Centenario
15	Quadriporticus	29	H. of Priest Amandus	49	H. of M. L. Fronto
16	T. of Zeus Meikichios	30	H. of Ephebus	50	H. of the Gladiators
17	T. of Isis	31	H. of Felix the Fruiterer	51	H. of Orpheus
18	Casa del Citarista	32	Weavers' Workshop	52	Fullonica
19	H. of C. Pansa	33	H. of J. Polybius	53	H. of L. C. Jucundus
20	H. of E. Sabinus	34	H. of C. Trebius Valens	54	Casa degli Amorini Dorata
21	H. of P. Montanus	35	Schola Armaturarum	55	H. of the Vettii
22	Verecundus	36	H. of P. Cerialis	56	H. of the Labyrinth
23	Fullonica Stephani	37	H. of the Moralist	57	H. of the Faun
24	H. of Cryptoporticus	38	H. of Loreius Tiburtinus	58	T. of Fortune
25	H. of the Menander	39	H. of Marine Venus	59	Thermae of the Forum
26	H. of Lovers	40	Villa Julia Felix	60	H. of the Tragic Poet
		41	H. of C. Rufus	61	H. of Sallust
		42	H. of Siricus	62	H. of the Surgeon
		43	Lupanar Africani et Victoris	63	H. of Apollo
		44	Inn of Sittius	64	H. of Meleagro
		45	H. of the Bear	65	H. of Centaur
		46	H. of Marcus Lucretius	66	H. of Adonis
				67	H. of Castor & Pollux
				68	H. of the Little Fountain
				69	H. of the Large Fountain
				70	H. of the Anchor

shaded areas closed to public

the volcano's destructive path. The casts were made in the 1800s by injecting plaster into the hollows left by the decayed corpses, though epoxy resin is now used. The bodies are a moving if macabre sight. Other outstanding pieces in the museum are the lifesize statue of Livia taken from the Villa dei Misteri and the simple household objects such as tools and terracotta vessels.

The **Basilica**, Pompeii's largest building at 67m long and 25m wide is just down the Via Marina. Probably built in 200BC, it had nothing to do with religion, but was where judicial affairs were conducted. The large central courtyard is divided by two long rows of 28 Ionic columns, and the Law Courts were in the raised portion at the back. Much of the Basilica was badly damaged in the serious earthquake 16 years earlier, and Pompeiians had not restored it. Its main entrance to the northeast opened on to the Forum.

The **Forum** (Foro), perfectly planned and positioned, lies in what was once the centre of town. This was a large and active meeting place, lined with emperors' statues up on pedestals and paved with marble flagstones. Pompeiians would come here to vote, to have documents notarised, to buy goods at market stalls or at auction. Undoubtedly one would bump into a neighbour or a friend – this was the best place in Pompeii to catch up on local gossip and government scandal. The Forum was almost completely enclosed by the provisions market (Macellum), the voting hall, Chief Magistrate's office, temples, a cereal market and a fuller's hall for woollen-cloth merchants who sold their goods to foreign buyers.

The **Temple of Apollo** (Tempio di Apollo) runs along the western side of the Forum. This revered god was honoured with official cult status, and his temple was one of the first buildings restored after the earlier earthquake. The rectangular area is surrounded by 48 columns; copies of the statues of Apollo and Diana are in the southern corners (the originals are now in the museum in Naples). A travertine altar, where offerings were presented, sits in front of wide steps. These lead up to the sacred shrine (cella), bounded by six frontal columns, where a statue of Apollo was once placed.

The **Temple of Jupiter** (Tempio di Giove) is at the Forum's northern end, at the top of a wide set of 15 steps, once flanked by two equestrian statues. The temple was constructed in the second century BC, covered by a high roof and enclosed by tall white Corinthian columns. The cult that worshipped here venerated three divinities called the Capitoline Triad: Jupiter, Juno and Minerva. The huge marble head of Jupiter now in the Naples Museum was found upon the shrine here.

Walking north from the Forum up the Via di Mercurio, you'll be leaving civic and religious Pompeii and entering one of the town's residential districts. Turn right on Via della Fortuna and stop at nos 2–5, one of Pompeii's most interesting houses.

The **House of the Faun** (Casa del Fauno) was a luxurious dwelling, named for the little bronze statue found there. The original of this and other treasures from the House of the Faun are among the best pieces in the Naples museum. This includes stunning mosaics: the Battle of Alexander, the Nile Scene, and

The Temple of Apollo with its travertine altar, at Pompeii

that of doves pulling a pearl necklace out of a vessel. To think that Pompeiians trod on these works of art!

Before entering the house, look down at the word *HAVE* inscribed in the pavement, a Latin salutation meaning 'Welcome' (*salve* in Italian). The house is large, covering a whole block, but most of the rooms within are small and intimate. Bedrooms surround the first open courtyard and in the middle of its far end is the tablinum, a room where the nobleman Signor Cassia conducted his business affairs. The first peristyle, or columned courtyard, behind this section of rooms was decorated with a fine pavement and surrounded by 28 stucco covered columns. The largest peristyle is behind, surrounded by Doric columns to include the garden area.

The **House of the Vettii** at No.1 Vicolo dei Vettii is probably Pompeii's most famous, rich in decoration of the Fourth Style. From the House of the Faun, go north and take your first right on Vicolo ai Mercurio, and then left on Vicolo dei Vettii. This grand house belonged to the Vettii brothers, Restitutus and Conviva. They were rich merchants who owned a large estate, selling wine and other agricultural products. The wall decoration here is superb, and when you see these paintings you'll probably recognise them immediately. The house is notorious for its pornographic wall paintings, especially that of a man weighing his huge appendage on a pair of scales. Guides love to attract men to this sight for a few hundred lire extra, while with dark looks and hand signals they try to deter women from coming along for the private view.

The first room you enter is the atrium, with its delightful set of Cupids painted along a black band on the wall; I especially like the one of Cupid riding a fat crab. This room opens onto a beautiful rectangular garden (peristyle) with basins, statues and classical flowers that probably grew there. Public spaces in Pompeii were not full of greenery, and the House of the Vettii is one of the best surviving examples of how gardens came to dominate homes' interiors.

Facing the atrium, take a look at the rooms which exhibit better than any other in Pompeii the role that classical mythology had in art of the period. Off to your right is the Pentheus Room, a dining room named for the god who is being torn limb from limb by maenads, frenzied females who were followers of Bacchus. Also here is a painting of the baby Hercules strangling two snakes, the first of 12 tasks he had to perform. Off to your left in the other corner of the peristyle is another small dining room; the fresco is of Daedalus presenting a lifesize wooden cow to Pasiphae, wife of King Minos of Crete. (Poseidon has made her fall in love with a bull, and a trap door in the wooden cow's hollow back allowed her to mate with it.) The Queen looks slightly sceptical as the cow is wheeled up to her, but she must have managed somehow, as she later gives birth to the Minotaur, a monster with the head of a bull and the body of a man who is eventually killed by Theseus.

You should see one other dining room off the peristyle, the Sala Dipinta in the middle of the northern wall with rooms along its length. It was probably used for special occasions, and little Cupids are up to all sorts of tricks on a black band running around the room. They gather flowers, distil perfume, race chariots, make bread, harvest grapes and sell wine. The rooms beyond are servants' quarters and the kitchen, where bronze pots are still waiting to come to a boil on the hearth.

Walking south on Via del Vesuvio, which then becomes Via Stabiana, turn right on Via dell 'Abbondanza to enter the **Stabian Baths**. Four public bath houses were built in Pompeii, and these are the best preserved, divided like most into separate sections for men and women. People gossiped, had a swim, ordered a drink or snack at the bar, relaxed with friends, and perhaps did a little politicking between a massage and a cold plunge.

After entering the baths, you immediately come upon a large gymnasium surrounded by columns; dressing rooms and a swimming pool are on the left. The stucco reliefs and paintings here show Daedalus fixing the wax wings on his son Icarus; Hercules and a Satyr; and Jupiter with his eagle. In the lower right-hand corner are the men's baths, with pretty pale blue-and-cream coloured stucco decoration on the ceiling in the vestibule. The women's baths, in the upper right-hand corner, are not as big or well-decorated as the men's, but the mosaic floor of the triton with sea creatures in the changing room (apodytarium) is wonderfully intact.

Heading down the Via dei Teatri, turn left on the Via del Tempio d'Iside.

The **Temple of Isis** is farther down this street on your right, dedicated to the Egyptian goddess who was the wife of Osiris. She was the patron goddess of navigation. In one ceremony, called the Adoration of the Sacred Water, the high priest blessed water from the Nile which was thought to have miraculous healing powers. Egyptian forms abound in the temple – even the candelabra were lotus-shaped.

The inscription along the entrance door's architrave announces that a man named Ampliatus paid for the complete rebuilding of the temple after the earthquake in 63. To the left of the entrance are the rooms where the priest lived. Inside, steps lead up to the temple, with broken columns lining the front and niches on the sides which once held statues. The main altar was at the bottom of the steps. Behind the raised temple were a meeting hall and a chamber for initiates into the most popular of foreign cults at Pompeii.

The small theatre, or Odeon, is reached by following the Via del Tempio d'Iside and turning right on the Via Stabiana. It is adjacent to the Great or Large Theatre, which was an open-air complex accommodating 5000 spectators. The smaller Odeon, built about 80BC, held only about 800 people and originally had a wooden roof. Pompeiians attended more intimate musical performances here, along with very popular poetry readings.

From the small theatre head back up the Via Stabiana and turn right on the Via dell'Anfiteatro, which becomes the Vicolo Meridionale.

Here on the right you will find the entrance to the **House of Menander** (Casa del Menandro), a large patrician villa that had servants' quarters and its own private baths. The name of the house comes from a wall painting of the seated Greek poet. The atrium is beautifully decorated in the Fourth Style, and in a room to the left are three paintings of Trojan scenes. Off the peristyle is a green reception room with a Nile scene mosaic, and the house's best mosaic is in the caladarium of the bath area: swimmers are surrounded by eels, crabs and other fish on a black-and-white floor. In 1930, a rich cache of silver kitchen and tableware was found in the cellar here; most of these pieces — more than 100 of them — are now in the Naples museum.

The last stop within the confines of the town is the Amphitheatre (Anfiteatro), reached by walking all the way down the Via dell'Abbondanza and turning right. The large grounds of the palestra are nearby, where gladiators and athletes trained. This Roman amphitheatre, built in 80BC, is the oldest ever uncovered but it doesn't appear to have had underground chambers. It held at least 12,000 spectators; people would often come from the neighbouring towns of Stabia, Nola and Naples for wrestling matches and other spectacles. The lower walls of the arena were decorated with animal and combat scenes. Men sat closer to the action while the upper galleries were reserved for women and children.

In 59AD, a bloody scene ensued in the stands. It began with name-calling and stone-throwing between the citizens of Nuceria and Pompeii, but escalated into a full-scale riot. Many people were killed in the fighting. The Roman Senate was so outraged that they ordered the amphitheatre to be closed for ten years, and all the chief magistrates were removed from office. But Nero became emperor during this ten-year period and it is thought that he lifted the ban, which seems highly likely considering his bloodthirsty love of combat.

To the north west lies the **Villa of the Mysteries**, one of the highlights of a visit to Pompeii, beyond the excavated area of the main town. The most interesting way to reach the villa is via the Porto Ercolano Gate in the north west corner.

Floor mosaics in the House of Menander, Pompeii

You will be on the Via delle Tombe, a suburban byway once flanked by shops, villas and family tombs. Pass both the Villa of Diomedes and that of Cicero. The Villa of Mysteries is about 200m beyond.

The villa was built during the third century BC and belonged to various patrician families. Its position was carefully planned, surrounded by terraced grape vines with views to Vesuvius and out to Capri. But the building was not uncovered until 1909, and it was the remarkable discovery of a complete cycle of frescoes in 1930 which gave the villa its name.

Just inside the entrance to your right is the Sala del Grande Dipinto where the frescoes were found. These lifesize figures confounded art historians for years, though most experts now agree that the panels represent initiation rites into the cult of Dionysus. Legend has it that this cult spread quickly in Greece, especially among women. The devoted, called Maenads or Bacchae, left their homes to roam through the countryside, whirling in dance and cavorting with woodland spirits. At the height of ecstasy and with superhuman strength, they seized an animal and tore it to pieces, devouring it in a sacrificial meal to Dionysus.

An inscription found at Cumae, dating back to the fifth century BC, orders those who are not members of the cult to be buried in a separate place. Later, in 186 BC, the Roman Senate suppressed their frenzied *Bacchanalia*, which were reported to accompany a crime wave in the city! The Senate blamed citizens of Campania for 'bringing much disorder under the cover of religion'. We can't know how spirited or disruptive the Pompeiian cult might have been, but the owner of the Villa of the Mysteries was certainly a member of the cult, and perhaps one of its ministers. These ceremonial scenes, painted on a background in the Second Style, fill the whole room. The famous colour of 'Pompeiian red' features heavily in this panoramic frieze.

On the north wall, an initiate or bride walks toward a young boy who is reading the rites from a sacred text; in the second scene a seated priestess takes cloth from a basket while a female attendant pours water over her right hand, thought to be a sacrificial ceremony. An old Silenus strums his lyre, looking toward the next scene.

On the east wall a cloaked woman seems to be warding off evil. Some interpret this as a fleeing, frightened initiate who looks toward the woodland spirits of satyrs and Silenus, as well as Dionysus who lies sprawled on the lap of a woman who many think must be his wife, Ariadne. The next scene is somewhat unclear: a kneeling woman, the initiate, reaches to unveil (or protect?) a purple object – probably the sacred phallus which represents the god's fertility – in the ceremony's climax. An angel (or demon with wings?) stands ready to chastise her with a whip.

In the first scene on the south wall, the initiate is being flogged as she lies in the lap of her companion. No pleasure without pain, these scenes seem to say. But the initiation ceremony is finished, and a naked woman clashes her cymbals as if to announce 'Let the dance begin'. The cult's newest member can now perform the ritual dance of joy. The frescoed scenes end on a peaceful note, perhaps signifying purification and total acceptance.

The panoramic frieze in the Villa of Mysteries, Pompeii

Practical Information

How to get there

By car, take the A3 autostrada from Naples to Salerno. The exit for both Vesuvius and Herculaneum is the Ercolano exit (13km from Naples); for Pompeii the exit is marked Pompeii Scavi (25km from Naples). The Circumvesuviana Railway runs from Naples' main station at Piazza Garibaldi to both Ercolano and Pompeii at regular intervals. To reach Vesuvius, get off at the Ercolano station, where a bus (summer months only) or taxi (best shared) will make the 15-minute drive to the parking lot below the final walking path to the summit. At the same station, a ten-minute walk south down the main road leads to the entrance gates of the excavations. (Beware: pickpockets have a reputation for stalking this stretch.)

To reach Pompeii by railway, depart at the Villa dei Misteri station on the west side (the Pompeii Scavi station is on the east side).

Tourist Information Offices

POMPEII 1 Via Sacra (tel. 081 8631040) and at the excavations at Piazza Esedra (tel. 081 8610913).

Hotels and restaurants

Unless it's absolutely necessary, I don't recommend spending a night in the vicinity of either Herculaneum or Pompeii. It's better to head farther south along the Amalfi coast (see information section in Chapter 9).

HERCULANEUM No hotels to recommend, but quite a few good, inexpensive trattorie like **Corso IV Novembre** on its bottom half closest to the entrance of the excavations.

POMPEII The **Villa Laura**, 13 Via della Salla (tel. 081 8631024), is a pleasant enough hotel with just twenty rooms and free parking. Moderate prices. Across from the railway station in modern Pompeii is **Hotel Bristol** (Tel. 081 8631625) – somewhat noisy, but very clean and serving meals; moderately priced.

The American fast-food restaurant **MacDonald's** is open, after much controversy, on Via Roma near the Duomo in Pompeii.

Price Ranges

Hotel (double room)	Restaurant (per head)
Inexpensive: under 60–000	under 25,000
Moderate: 60–120,000	25–50,000
Expensive: 120–200,000	50–90,000
Very expensive: 200,000+	90,000+

Museums and other public sites

HERCULANEUM Excavations (tel. 081 7390963) open 09.00–15.00 except Mon and hols; until 18.00 during summer months. Vesuvian Villas such as Campolieto open 09.00–14.00 daily unless a conference or other function is in session.

POMPEII Excavations (tel. 081 8621181) open 09.00–15.00 except Mon and hols; until 18.00 at height of summer.

VESUVIUS Best climbed in the morning, catching an early train from Naples' main train station (Piazza Garibaldi) to Ercolano, then by bus or taxi from there; the road to the top of Vesuvius is often blocked after 14.00.

8. CAMPANIA'S ISLANDS: Procida, Ischia and Capri

Islands, simply by virtue of being surrounded by water, have always exerted a soothing influence on the traveller. Campania's islands remain among the most beautiful in the Mediterranean, though they haven't remained untouched. Inevitably, some will reminisce about past unspoilt charm and bemoan the age of mass tourism, but to my mind the sheer numbers of people who have already discovered the islands of Ischia and Capri (while Procida awaits them) do little to diminish their beauty. You just have to know when to go — if you like tourists and café society then travel during the summer months when the sun is strongest; if you prefer your sites less peopled, then the months of April, May, September and October are ideal.

Ischia, Campania's largest island, is in many ways just as dramatically beautiful as Capri, and has had a large number of summer residents for decades. Many Germans own homes here, and even more come as tourists. In fact on Ischia you'll find that most of its citizens have acquired a basic knowledge of German to oil the wheels of tourism, whereas Capri has traditionally been the province of the English. In recent years Americans have chosen Capri as a holiday haven too, and this island has the most 'international' character of the three. Small Procida, however, is still very much a fisherman's island, unchanged and proudly planning to remain so. They don't court tourists here — in summer months you'll find mainland Italians mixing with the locals along with day-trippers from Ischia and Capri.

Procida and Ischia share the same geological history: volcanic islands that were once connected, and broke away from the mainland near the Phlegrean Fields thousands of years ago. No volcanic activity has been recorded on either island for centuries, though Ischia is famous for its hot springs and thermal baths. Their beach sands are dark, whereas Capri shines brightly on sheer cliffs of dark creamy limestone, having the same geological makeup as the Sorrentine peninsula and Amalfi coast.

It's easy to reach all three islands, either from Naples, Pozzuoli, Sorrento or Positano. Cars with Campania license plates aren't allowed on the ferries during summer months, but rental cars, or those with foreign plates and from other Italian regions, can book passage at any time. However, you cannot take a car on to Capri unless you are a resident (it would be more of a hindrance than a help anyway) and though Ischia is larger, the bus service around that island is extremely good and will probably meet your needs unless you've rented a villa off the beaten track. Procida has a less efficient bus service which will probably prove frustrating if you aren't staying in one of the main towns. Micro-taxis at the port will take you to the few hotels on the island, but some streets are so narrow that you risk scraping side walls if driving anything wider than a small Fiat. Either take a small car to Procida or, if relying on taxis and your own two feet, stay at the port or the areas of Chaia or Chiaiolella.

Procida

The approach to Procida is a lovely sight. The Bay of Naples and Cape Misenum recede into the background, and a charming streetscape of yellow, white and pink houses stretches along the island's seafront. The port area is divided into two short sides, Marina Grande and Marina di San Cattolico (or Sancio'), where all ferries arrive and depart. The tourist office, bars, and three or four good restaurants are all along the port area's main street here.

The island is made up of four low, partially eroded craters. It's less than 4km long, and about 2km broad at its widest point on the northern side. But Procida is packed with people – more than 10,000 inhabitants – which makes it one of the most densely populated places on earth. The statistic makes it surprising that life here is not more chaotic. Fishing is still one of the island's main sources of income; almost one-fifth of the islanders employ themselves this way, with a centuries-old reputation in Europe's ports for being among the best sailors and fishermen. Procida is also known for its tangy, fragrant lemons, so don't leave the island without trying a fresh iced *granita di limone*.

One other point about these islanders: they are steadfast in their wish to keep Procida as it is, with no desire to compete with Ischia or Capri for tourists' dollars, pounds and deutschmarks. Their respect for the island's beauty borders on passion, and if you can't understand that then don't come to Procida. The beautiful islet of Vivara (attached by a walking bridge to the mainland) is a case in point. A well-known vacation club company tried to buy this island some years ago, and islanders answered, 'You want to buy our *isoletto*? Have you taken a good look at it? Please, open your eyes: wild olives, capers, berries . . . do you realize that the only foreigner permitted there was Ferdinand IV, King of the Two Sicilies? It was his hunting ground, but after others hunted there we are left without falcons, and now you want to take away the olives, the capers. Please, go back to your own country.'

The ancient history of Procida, once called Prochyta, is similar to Ischia's. It is thought that Greeks settled here too. The Romans were the first to use the island as a hunting ground, making day trips from Baia and Naples. An abbey was built by Benedictine monks in the 11th century, and the small number of inhabitants supported themselves by cultivating vines, olives and lemons. In the 13th century, the island was the property of Giovanni di Procida, a Ghibelline nobleman born in Salerno who liked his domain so much that he named himself after it. But the island was confiscated by Charles I of Anjou after he entered Naples with the victorious Guelphs. (John of Procida then took revenge in helping to instigate the Sicilian Vespers in Palermo, the revolt which killed close to 8000 Frenchmen.)

By 1340, two shipyards were constructing vessels in the port area and the population continued to grow. But the island wasn't without enemies, and during the 16th century marauding pirates such as Barbarossa, Dragut and Bolla all stormed the island. It was also occupied by the English in 1799 when Napolean proclaimed the region a republic, from 1806–9 against Napolean and Murat, and then again in 1813 for a brief period. It was during this time of French influence and upheaval that the poet Alphonse de Lamartine came to Procida and fell in love with a girl named Graziella. She renounced her island fiancé for him, but Lamartine went back to Paris never to return. Graziella didn't survive such treatment; she died two months later. Yet her name, and her island, became known throughout Europe after the success of Lamartine's novella entitled *Graziella*.

The island's three main centres are the port area, Corricella on the northwest coast, and Marina di Chiaiolella on the island's southern end near the islet of Vivara. There are a number of dark sandy beaches, but none are very long due to the nature of this rugged and sometimes high coastline. It juts in and out for 14km around the island, but that also means that you're apt to find a secluded though somewhat rocky spot for sunning. Procida's main beaches are Ciraccio, Ciraciello and the Lido on the southeastern side, and Chiaia near Corricella to the northwest.

The island's prettiest area to walk through is *Corricella*, with its fishing boats moored in the harbour beneath the abbey walls. This is Procida's oldest village. If you walk up the Via Madonna delle Grazie to the island's highest point of Terra Murata, you get a wonderful view back down to the beach with old houses rising above it. Faded pastel facades in pink, yellow and blue, arched entryways and outer stairwells are all reminiscent of Greek island architecture. Men on the beach sort their catch, fix nets or scrape the bottoms of wooden boats while women chat from balcony to balcony and children tumble in the sand. Down to the left are the abandoned ruins of a church built in 1586 called Santa Margherita Nuova. A long bay sweeps in a gorgeous band south here, from the Punta dei Monaci to the Punta di Pizzaco.

The Via Madonna delle Grazie leads up further through an archway called the Porta Mezz'Olmo, where you pass what was once a castle and is now an abandoned prison. (The whispered rumour is that Gianni Agnelli of Fiat fame is trying to buy the complex from the state in the hope of turning it into a big hotel, much to islanders' chagrin.) Turning right up a steep and narrow street leading to a small enclave of houses, you'll come to the island's most interesting church, **San Michele Arcangelo**. The richness of its marbled altars, tall candelabra and indented coffered ceiling of gold leaf is matched in literary terms by the number of expressive notes left in strategic places by the priest for his congregation. By the pews: 'Kids! Keep Quiet!' On the side wall: 'Please! The church . . . is not a museum. Do not offend the faith of God and your brothers.'

But, God forgive me, it is hard not to see the church as a museum; the objects on view here seem part of an eccentric curator's collection. The small church is stuffed with old statues, dark religious paintings badly in need of restoration, and glass cases filled with votive offerings made from scrap metal. Two important paintings are housed in the church: on the main ceiling is Luca Giordano's *The Glory of San Michele*, painted in 1699, where the Archangel is battling with Lucifer. Even more interesting is Nicola Rosso's painting in the apse: *San Michele Defending the Island*. The monumental figure with fiery sword and shield is surrounded by helpful putti, while the perfect toytown of Procida below is surrounded by ominous shiploads of Turks.

Chiaolella is the small fishing port on the island's southern end, where buses end their routes and modest restaurants line the beach. From here you can head south west for two beautiful walks. The first is to the promontory of Santa Maria Vecchia, where you'll find the ruins of a church with its Benedictine convent that was abandoned in 1586. The view back to Procida is superb.

The other walk takes you over the little bridge that leads to crescent-shaped **Vivara**, now a nature preserve protected by the state. No one lives there, but rabbit hunting is still allowed so it is open to the public. (If the chain appears to be wrapped around the gate, give it a yank because it probably isn't pad-locked.) One path leads up the hill to a number of walking trails that twist around the summit, one of which leads to the arched ruins of what was probably a hunting lodge. Other routes stop at the edge of high cliffs affording wonderful views. To the south east is the mountainous island of Ischia, and to the east is Procida's southernmost tip of Punta Solchiaro, so-named because the island receives its first rays of the day's sun here (another good place for walking).

Heading through the island's centre from Chiaolella in the direction of the northern port area (a distance of about 4km), you wind through narrow streets flanked by the stuccoed walls of small houses. Fields behind are full of olive and lemon trees, as well as grape vines. You'll come to a small quarter known as Olmo, with a square by the same name. Near here is the 17th-century church of St Anthony of Padua, with its pretty cupola. Head off to the left while going north, and you'll end up at Punta Serra, with the little beach of Pozzo Vecchio beyond. Going inland again leads to the Annunziata quarter, named after the church overflowing with votive offerings to its miraculous Madonna. From here, follow the Via del Faro north to Punta Pioppeto, with its lighthouse and a good view up to Cape Misenum. To the north east, sunlit ferries and hydrofoils carry islanders and visitors in and out of the marina, back to the mainland or off to the shores of Procida's neighbour.

Ischia

Green and mountainous Ischia easily holds its own when compared with the natural beauties of Procida and Capri. Pine and olive groves seem to cover what isn't home or street, while pink and purple bougainvillea curls and hangs from every post and gate. An extinct volcano rises high in the middle of the island, and villagers close to the summit cultivate the grapes that have given the island its famous white wine, named after Monte Epomeo. The coastline rises and falls with each bay and creek, especially dramatic on Ischia's southern edges. Much as on Capri, what you can be sure of is that each fantastic view will be surpassed by another as you make your way around the island.

Was the first Italian Magna Graecia colony here on Ischia? The prevailing theory is that Pithecusa, as it was called, was a settlement as far back as the 9th century BC but that volcanic eruptions sent the Greeks, originally from the island of Euboea, fleeing to Cumae on the mainland. According to legend, the giant Typhoeus fought Jupiter's thunderbolts with flowing lava and quaking earth from his seat on Monte Epomeo. Eruptions were recorded as early as 500BC, but not since 1301 has there been any cause for alarm.

Ischia was the province of Hieron of Syracuse, then of the Neapolitans, and by 326 belonged to the Romans. The emperor Augustus had owned the island, but exchanged it for Capri in 6AD. It was sacked by Saracens in the 9th century, and then by Pisans on their way to Amalfi. It's as if these sailing invaders sighted land and decided to give their troops drill practice before the main event elsewhere.

In the late 13th century the islanders, with Sicilian help, opposed Charles I. But Charles II recovered the island in 1299 and punished the citizens of Ischia by sending soldiers in to cut down their trees and vineyards. In another tragic episode, Barbarossa landed with his pirates in 1541 and is said to have taken away 4000 prisoners. Kings, queens and consorts came and went, whose fortunes are connected to the Aragon Castle. Ischia, like Procida, played a part in the Napoleonic Wars by serving as Nelson's base, and in 1815 was a refuge for Murat on his way out of Naples when the shortlived Parthenopean Republic was overthrown.

Ischia is now an island with a population of about 45,000. The island is 9km from east to west and six from north to south. Inland it's high and hilly, but there are quite a few good stretches of dark sandy beach. Many of the islanders work in the tourist trade – in hotels, restaurants, thermal baths and boutiques. The season runs well beyond the summer months because of the many Scandinavians, as well as Germans, who come for thermal treatment from April to October. But some of Ischia's citizens still make a living through growing grapes, olives and fruit; fishing is a viable occupation for very few.

Visitors arrive by boat at **Ischia Porto**, a perfect ring of a harbour that's packed with all the amenities a tourist might need: information office, bus terminus, restaurants, pharmacy, T-shirt shops, and ice-cream vendors. Small boats line

The island of Ischia

the shore; there's always a ferry or hydrofoil disgorging passengers. The main shopping street in Ischia Porto is Via Roma, heading south, and this is the place for people watching during the evening *passeggiata*. The square where almost all the island's buses begin and end their routes is just up the street from the harbour, and a cable-car to take you to the extinct crater of Montagnone – a short trip affording fantastic views – is a five-minute walk from there.

A far more interesting little town on the island is **Ischia Ponte**, a ten-minute bus ride south of Ischia Porto. Once a fishing village, this quarter is dominated by the **castle** on its rocky hilltop, connected to the mainland by a causeway built in 1438.

One of my favourite hotels in Campania is within this castle complex. It is called Il Monastero, after the monastery it once was, and some of the best sunset views in Campania can be enjoyed from its terrace. It is a simple place (accommodation is in small bedrooms that were once monks' cells) and the spartan setting leaves one feeling tranquil, serenely able to relish the island's history and landscape.

The castle is surrounded by thick stone walls, and tall arched passages lead to structures in various states of ruin. Ferdinand II retired here in 1495 after abandoning Naples to Charles VIII, but he almost didn't get on to the island. When he sailed up to the castle with 14 galleys, the Catalonian castellan refused him entry. At last he acquiesced – the king and queen could enter, but Ferdinand would have to send his retinue back to Naples. When the king entered the castle, he drew his sword and killed this huffy castellan, whereupon the whole crew came ashore. Six years later Ferdinand's uncle and successor also retired to Ischia, where he stayed until he travelled to France to surrender to King Louis. So ended the Aragon dynasty.

But the castle's most celebrated inhabitant was the 16th-century poetess Vittoria Colonna. She was from a famous Roman family whose ancestors included cardinals, generals and Pope Martin V. Betrothed at the age of four, she married the Marquis Pescara Ferrante D'Avalos in the castle's church in 1509 when she was 17. Widowed at the age of 33, she turned to poetry and her *Rime spirituali* were widely praised, especially by the poet Ludovico Ariosto. But she was probably best known for her warm friendship with Michelangelo, who composed sonnets to her.

The church, dedicated to the Assunta, where Vittoria Colonna was married lies in the heart of the complex, built in 1301. This romantic expanse is nothing but arched ruins now, with a Gothic substructure and remnants of Baroque renovation in the 1700s. The church was completely destroyed in 1809 by the English fleet when they were chasing the French.

Farther along the wide stepped passages is the Gothic arched entrance to the Abbey of Basiliani di Grecia, also ruined. At the castle's high southern edge is the small hexagonal church of San Pietro a Pantaniello, built in the 16th century. This out-of-the-way sanctuary has a wonderful view. The abandoned prison above held prisoners such as Carlo Poerio, Nicola Nisco, il Settembrini and other patriots from 1851 to 1860. Continue up the cobbled pathway to a secluded, terraced café, a fantastic place to contemplate the lives of those who were walled within.

Once you've descended and crossed the castle's bridge, you will be on the Via Mazzella in Ischia Ponte. On the side closest to the sea is the island's **cathedral**, also called the Assunta, first built in 1300 and renovated in the Baroque style. Within are lavish marble *intaglio* altars. The Church of Santo Spirito, almost opposite, is more interesting however. Its cupola of green-and-yellow tiles is much like those on the Amalfi coast, built with the money of sailors who were keen to inject an Eastern influence into their architecture. The sacristy in this church is charming: the ceiling is a beautiful faded fresco in shades of olive green; on the wall is another fresco of a tall ship in the port by the still recognisable causeway, probably done in the early 16th century.

If you continue to walk north on Via Mazzella, and then turn right on Via Pontano, you'll come to a good beach called the **Spiaggia dei Pescatori**. The **Lido**, on the same stretch of coast but farther north, is one of Ischia's nicest beaches. It is best reached by one of the side streets leading from the main avenue of Corso Vittoria Colonna.

Heading down toward the southern edge of the island, follow road No.270 through mountain villages, many of which are untouched by the tourists crowded into the seaside towns. You'll pass through Fontana (not to be confused with Serrara Fontana), the highest town on Ischia. This is the best place to start the ascent of **Monte Epomeo** (788m), either by a challenging one-hour walk or by hiring mules well used to making the trip. On a clear day, and for those with very good eyesight, the view extends to 100km from the top. (The iron

Punto Sant' Angelo, Ischia

crucifix towering above was erected in memory of 44 people killed in an air crash.) Far to the north are Lazio's Pontine Islands; closer to Ischia are the Gulf of Gaeta, the Phlegrean Fields, Vesuvius and the Sorrentine Peninsula. The whole island is spread below, ringed by water of cobalt blue. You don't have to return by way of Fontana – a two-hour descent down the other side leads to either Forio or Casamicciola.

After stunning mountain-top views the next best are witnessed while following road No.270 south to **Punto Sant' Angelo**, a teardrop of land descending into the Tirrhenian Sea. Buses and cars stop at the top of a hill where a wide paved path then leads to the village. This fishing port, though very crowded in summer, is a great place to hire boats for a tour around the island, or for a drop-off at either Maronti Beach or Ischia's oldest hot springs of **Cavascura**. A series of baths cut into the hillside is said to have been used by the Romans, and I'm not sure hygiene standards have improved much since then. I'd choose one of the island's newer establishments on the hill above the town, such as the kitsch **Thermal Gardens Tropical** which sports lots of healthy vegetation and masses of monstrous white statuary.

Back on route 270, heading northwest now, you'll come to another pretty village called **Forio**. Here too are boutiques and restaurants, but one gets the feeling that these villagers have better things to do than simply cater to passing tourists. Kids run off to school, while adults head to the vineyards, for this is the island's most important wine-producing centre.

This area of the coast was plagued by marauders more than any other, and

Model ships rest on columns in San Soccorso, Ischia

12 towers were constructed along the shore to guard the sea and relay messages. The largest, and one of the few still standing, is the **Torrione** near the Piazza Matteotti. It was reconstructed in 1480 and now serves as a gallery to exhibit the work of many artists who work here in Forio. The Baroque church of Santa Maria di Loreto is nearby, erected in the 14th century with two tiled bell-towers.

Even more picturesque is the small, white sanctuary of **San Soccorso** down by the water. This church is unusual for its harmonious blend of architectural elements: a Gothic bell-tower, Renaissance portal, a Baroque pedestal for the cross. The outer stairway is decorated with majolica tiles. This is where fishermen and their families have been praying for centuries. Beautifully carved model ships rest atop columns; above the side chapel are 15 highly-varnished *putti* carrying crosses, chains, arrows, and crown of thorns – all symbols of the Passion and Crucifixion.

Just below San Soccorso, on its southern side, is the Pensione Umberto a Mare. This is a clean and quiet place to stay, also serving lunch and dinner to travellers on its enclosed terrace overhanging the sea. One of the finest gardens in the region (open to the public) is just north, toward Punta di Caruso on Via Francesco Calisa. Called **La Mortella**, the late Sir William Walton and his wife Susanna began building their home and garden in 1956. The extensive plantings cover a fertile valley, filled with palm, magnolia and tulip trees, along with water lilies and lotus, tree fern and camellia. Along with overseeing the garden, Lady Walton runs a foundation for promising young musicians who come here to study.

On Ischia's northern side are the towns of **Lacco Ameno** and **Casamicciola Terme**. Lacco Ameno still retains a personality strongly linked to its past, while Casamicciola is best left to the patrons of hotels and hot springs.

In Lacco Ameno, the pink-stuccoed church of **Santa Restituta** and its underground museum are worth a detour. Santa Restituta is the island's patron saint, a North African Christian whose body was found on the nearby shore of San Montano in 304. She'd apparently survived many forms of torture in Carthage before being forced out to sea, but while her captors tried to set fire to the boat they were engulfed in flames instead. She died at sea but when her boat landed here, lilies sprang up on the beach, and the saint's remains were buried in the house of a woman who claimed to have dreamed of Restituta's arrival. Villagers still celebrate the coming of the saint each year on May 17th. The church is filled with the white lilies that bear her name; fireworks and symbolic bonfires are part of the festivities.

The sanctuary of Santa Restituta is really two churches: the more modern one was reconstructed in 1800 with a façade that dates to 1910. Within this church are ten paintings telling the story of the life of the saint. The smaller church dates from 1036, built on the remains of a Paleo-Christian basilica. Behind the altar here is a statue of Santa Restituta, dating from the early 16th century. Below is the excavated crypt, only discovered in 1951. These ruins, with tombs and old sections of pavements, form part of the underground museum. Glass cases displaying ceramic fragments and iron tools attest to Greek colonisation, along with Egyptian and Syrian objects that must have been traded when Ischia's port was included in the sailors' route from the eastern Mediterranean.

The pretty inlet beach of **San Montano** (no lilies growing here now) is just west of Lacco Ameno. Seven kilometres east along the northern shore is the town of Casamicciola Terme. Greek colonists probably settled here first, and legend has it that the Sibyl of Cumae prophesied the coming of Christ while in Casamicciola. (Does this mean that she practised here, and left for Cumae on the mainland with the other settlers?) Henrik Ibsen began *Peer Gynt* here in 1867, but this area was devastated by an earthquake in 1883 and was completely rebuilt at the turn of the century.

As in Lacco Ameno, many hot springs bubble forth in Casamicciola, accounting for the large number of hotels. These waters, high in carbonate and muriate of soda, are said to relieve symptoms of rheumatism, arthritis and sciatica, while Lacco Ameno's waters are purported to be the most radioactive on the island. *Murray's Handbook* of 1855 recommended these waters for 'scrofulous swellings' and 'gunshot wounds'. If you're sensitive to smells, these springs just might do your system more harm than good; near the famous Gurgitello spring in Casamicciola is another called *Agua di Cappone* because it's supposed to smell like chicken broth.

The next town along the coast is lively Ischia Porto again – the completion of a clockwise tour around the island.

Capri

Whenever I go to Capri I find myself thinking that surely this time it won't be the same. I'll find more crowds than before, or yet another useless boutique, and will vow never to return. But the island remains alluring. The Blue Grotto has lost none of its ultramarine glow; the Faraglioni stand as solid and serene as ever; the whitewashed homes of the islanders have been coated anew, their gardens overflowing with flowers.

However, thousands of other travellers are attracted to Capri for all the same reasons. Be warned: it becomes very crowded during the summer months. As inaccessible as its tall cliffs seem, thousands of tourists scramble on and off the island each day in the months of July and August. If you are able to travel during low season (there is consistent sun as early as April and as late as October), you'll find a seat on Piazza Umberto, and will be able to take splendid walks without others bumping into you from behind. Let me add one other word of warning, depending on your state of health: you'll do a lot of walking on this island, especially from the main town of Capri itself. Make sure to check just how far your hotel is from the main square, because some are quite a steep hike from the centre.

The island seems bigger than its ten square kilometres suggest, due to an undulating landscape upon sheer limestone cliffs. Ferries and hydrofoils dock at the **Marina Grande** on Capri's northern side; fishermen and those in smaller private boats sometimes dock at the **Marina Piccola** on the southern coast. Above the Marina Grande is Capri's main town, also called Capri, arrived at from the port by taking the quick funicular railway, or by taxi up a steep winding road. The island's only other main town is Anacapri, connected to Capri by a high corniche road that affords beautiful views down to the sea. Anacapri sits on a flat plateau, and is therefore less strenuous on the legs and lungs.

Capri and Anacapri have traditionally been involved in a tug-of-war for power and prestige, and have evolved distinct personalities. Capri is more pretentions, seemingly more elegant with the Quisisana Hotel, designer boutiques and the much photographed main square with its tall clock-tower. Anacapri is best known for quieter pleasures such as Axel Munthe's Villa San Michele, the small enchanting church of San Michele and Monte Solaro. The connection between the two towns can be made by riding in some of the best taxicabs I've ever seen – gleaming bulbous convertibles, circa 1950, proudly maintained by their owners.

Tourists are constantly transported back and forth between Capri and Anacapri, a hard job for the small local buses in high season. The thousands of day trippers I mentioned are mainly from Naples, along with tourists from coastal resorts such as Sorrento and Positano. Islanders would like to put a stop to this heavy influx of tourists, and the police force has started to levy fines on those who wear too little clothing, carry noisy radios or are judged to be making a general nuisance of themselves. I doubt this method will deter many day-trippers, but the suggested addition of much higher boat fees, and restricted ferry schedules, probably would. That tactic might not seem fair to mainland Italians, but locals are finding it harder and harder to cope with so many people on such a small island.

This love for Capri is nothing new. First came the Greeks, then Emperor Augustus built villas and baths as a retreat from a stressful life in Rome. He was followed by Tiberius in 26AD, who ruled Rome from Capri for the last 11 years of his life. He gave Capri its racy reputation, highly exaggerated to entice the tourists. It's said that he constructed 12 villas on Capri, one for each deity (or one for each mistress depending on who's doing the telling). Some historians would have us believe that Tiberius spent his days in orgiastic pleasure, contrasted with the pain of tortured prisoners who were then thrown over the cliffs at his hilltop palace of Villa Jovis.

But about Tiberius I side with Norman Douglas, the English writer who immortalised his adopted home of Capri and other parts of southern Italy in *Siren Land* and *South Wind*. He came to the emperor's defence in *Siren Land*, writing in one passage that:

> Tiberius at Capri is supposed to have suffered from the mania of persecution, ending in senile dementia. In proof of his madness is adduced the fact that he complained of the debauched habits of his (adopted) grandson Nero. As if Tiberius had not been making complaints of this kind, and with perfect justice, all his life!

When the Roman Empire fell, Capri belonged to Naples, and then to powerful Amalfi during the ninth century. The Saracens terrorised these islanders too, until the Normans came to power in the 11th century. The island's fate shadowed that of Naples for many centuries – changing hands from Anjou to Aragon – and during the Napoleonic War was occupied by both the British and the French. In 1813, Capri was back in the hands of the Italians under Ferdinand I of the Two Sicilies.

The island's history as tourist attraction blossomed with the so-called discovery of the Blue Grotto in 1826 by a German poet called August Kopisch. But islanders certainly knew that it existed; it was marked on a 1696 map with the name of Grotta Gradola and the district above is still sometimes referred to by the same name. As Norman Douglas points out in *Siren Land*, 'Beezlebub himself could never keep a Capri fisherman out of a sea cave if there were half a franc's worth of crabs inside it.' And as for the romantic names of so many caves cut into Capri's coastline, Douglas wrote:

> The foreigners liked colour in caves. The foreigners brought money. Colour in caves is cheap. Let them have it! Therefore, in a twinkling, the two-mouthed Grotta del Turco became the green grotto; the venerable Grotto Ruofolo put on a roseate hue sufficient to justify the poetic title of Red Grotto . . .

And no harm's been done. The island's caves are definitely worth viewing, whatever they may be called and, if you've got the time and money, hire a boat with knowledgeable guide for a trip along these 17km of coastline. The lovely island landscape, at sea level and above, is home to more than 800 species of plant life. It's not at all surprising that Capri has been found agreeable by every sort of traveller – from politicians and philosophers such as Lenin, Rilke and Nietzsche, to writers such as Turgenev, Conrad and G. B. Shaw. The Swedish doctor Axel Munthe added to the island's fame with his *Story of San Michele*, and more recently the music-hall legend Gracie Fields made her second home here.

Some of these famous characters are buried in the foreign cemetery, a short walk from Capri's Piazza Umberto Primo down the Via Marina Grande. Norman Douglas was buried here in 1952. The consolatory inscription on his tombstone, a quotation from Horace, reads *Omnes Fodem Cogimur* (We are all in the end driven to the same place). This small, scruffy cemetery begs so many questions: what were they like, the foreigners who chose to live here? How in the world did Dr Ludwig Schroeter, a physician born in Poland who practiced in Buffalo, New York, end up here in 1912? One couple from Pontiac, Illinois, engraved on their joint monument: 'Within this bit of foreign earth there lies the dust of two who loved this Italy.' The best inscription of all belongs to both Salvatore Vuotto and his wife Irma Schwarze: 'Citizen of the world and free thinker'. The island's Catholic cemetery is stepped above; graves are carefully tended by island relatives who are near enough to pull the weeds and repot the flowers.

Walking up the Via Marina Grande to the enclosed **main square** brings you back to the center of life on Capri. The cafés here are see-and-be-seen venues, and you pay highly for the privilege. Narrow walking streets radiate off the square, leading to shops, hotels and restaurants. Right on the piazza is the 17th-century Baroque church of **San Stefano**, interesting for its mosiac floor at the foot of the high altar. The inlaid marble pavement was taken from the Villa Jovis, Tiberius' most elaborate dwelling. In the chapel to the right are the tombs of Vincenzo and Giacomo Arcucci, both sculpted by Naccherino. Count Giacamo is the one holding the little church, for he founded the island's monastery.

Near the church is the **Palazzo Cerio**, named for the physician and amateur archeologist who dedicated so much of his time to studying the island's history. This small museum was originally a 14th-century castle, now housing various artefacts and fossils. Even Augustus, according to the historian Suetonius, found 'tremendous limbs of huge monsters and wild animals', attesting to the accepted view that Capri was once part of the mainland near Sorrento. When the Hotel Quisisana was enlarged in the early 1900s, Cerio was there to help label the skeletal remains of an elephant, hippopotamus and a rhinoceros from the quaternary era.

Not far from the main square is the Carthusian monastery, the **Certosa of San Giacomo**. Follow the Via Vittorio Emanuele down to the Hotel Quisisana, and then go right on Via Federico Serena to Via Certosa. The monastery, at the end of this street, was founded in 1371. Though it was destroyed by Torgud in 1553, monks restored it soon after. As a religious retreat it was supressed in

1807, then used as a prison and a hospice throughout the 1800s. Today the convent buildings are occupied by a secondary school as well as a library.

The cloisters and the dark Gothic church are open to the public. The church's most interesting feature is the 14th-century fresco above the outer doorway, called *Madonna and Child Enthroned Between Sts Bruno and Giacomo*. To the right of this central panel is the fresco *Founder with Two Sons*; to the left of the central panel is *Three Praying Women*, the first of whom is Angevin Queen Joan I, who died here on the island.

The Great Cloister here does not impress me. This is a bleak open space carpeted with cement, such a contrast to the abundance of flowers hidden in the back garden just over the walls. The Small Cloister nearby is much prettier, with 18 columns and a well at its centre. There's also a permanent art gallery attached to the monastery, called the **Museo Diefenbach**. This space exhibits about thirty dark and crusty oils painted by the German artist Diefenbach who died on Capri in 1913. I found nothing inspiring in these large works, but the first room on the left after entering the gallery is worth a look. It holds a painting by American genre scene painter C. Caryl Coleman called *Sorrow*, very much influenced by the Pre-Raphaelites. (Coleman is another lover of Capri buried in the foreign cemetery, having died in his Villa Narcissus in 1928.) Here also are pitted sculptures dredged up from 20m below the surface of the Blue Grotto, which help to support the hypothesis that this cave was used to worship nymphic divinities in Roman times.

From the monastery, walk back up the Via Certosa, turning left on Via Matteotti. On your right is one of Capri's two perfumeries – a pretty little shop for truly Caprese gifts, such as one of their small jars of cream, wrapped with exquisite care. The Monastery of San Giacomo began producing perfume on the island in 1380. This industry flourished for a few centuries, but died out as the monastery lost its prestige in the late 18th and 19th centuries. In 1948, inspired islanders began to produce these old formulas once again.

Past the perfumery are the **Gardens of Augustus**. More gorgeous views await you from the terrace here, this time down to Marina Piccola and the Faraglioni rock formations. The winding path below is Via Krupp (also called Augusto), excavated from the rock by German arms manufacturer Friedrich Krupp. The easy walk down, of about one-half hour and highly recommended, leads to the Marina Piccola, a much prettier port area than Marina Grande. Small beaches along the shore are connected to restaurants, called *stabilmenti* because you pay a small fee for beach chairs, mattresses and shower. A bus or taxi is available for the trip back to Piazza Umberto Primo.

One of the island's most spectacular walks is from Capri's main square to the **Faraglioni** and the **Arco Naturale**. Steps and steep pathways are positioned high above the southeastern coast, and the walk takes about an hour. From Via Vittorio Emmanuele, turn left on Via Camarelle past the Hotel Quisisana. After shops and a scruffy sort of animal farm over the wall on your right, you'll be passing private villas on Via Tragara, along with another luxury hotel called La Scalinatella. Rounding a bend, you'll see a sign pointing down to the Faraglioni, the three tall rock sentinels beyond the Punta di Tragara. One of the three is said to harbour a species of blue lizard – the *Lacerta caerulea Faraglionensis* – found nowhere else in the world. It would be hard to check the accuracy of this statement, as it is thought that the lizard may now be extinct.

You can cut this walk short by spending a day at the beach, climbing down the steps here (a long way down and no other way up), but fisherman from the Marina Piccola will also take passengers by boat. This is a popular spot for sunbathing, so if you want to assure yourself a prime position, head down early. Rocky sections have been connected by flat cement areas; you can rent chairs or foam mats, and dive into clear deep pools. Two restaurants with terraces make it very easy to spend a day lazing around.

Back at the top of the stairs, continue along the well-tended pathway past private homes in enviable positions. The flora bordering the walkway is astonishing for its variety – rosemary, heather, juniper and myrtle – one or another plant is fragrant and flowering. You will see a long, rectangular red house on a rocky plateau below, but without any way of reaching it. This was the home of Italian writer Curzio Malaparte, author of *The Skin* and other books about Neapolitan life. Designed in 1940 by Adalberto Libera, the building is a strong simple shape, and its position is astonishing – if not stupefying.

The path now climbs up and down constantly, sometimes through dense pine woods, and then suddenly open to sun and sea again. You'll pass the **Grotta di Matromania**, a damp cave with a semicircular apse. This is believed to have been a Roman sanctuary for those dedicated to the cult of the Cybele, a fertility goddess also known as the Mater Magna. From here it's a 15-minute climb to the Arco Naturale, a tall arch which has eroded its way through craggy golden limestone. In the distance are Punta Campanella and the Sorrentine Peninsula on the mainland, 6km away. Just beyond this beautiful spot is a small terraced bar, very welcome after a long climb. Soon the path evens out and, flanked by islanders' homes with their welcoming ceramic plaques, you'll be descending to the main square.

From the town of Capri, there is one other site to see before heading to Anacapri. This is the **Villa Jovis**, the biggest and best-preserved Imperial villa on the island. It's high on a hill, at the end of one of the walking streets passed on the way back from the Arco Naturale. (If you're refreshed enough after a rest at the bar mentioned above you could head up to the villa before returning to the main square.) From Piazza Umberto Primo, however, the Via Delle Botteghe climbs to become Via Fuolovado and then Via Croce, which takes you left to the Via Tiberio (ceramic signs will also help point the way). Just before reaching the villa's entrance the street becomes Viale Amedeo Mauri. I suspect this stretch has been named as an avenue not for its size but for the great amount of respect Italians have for this famous archaeologist. He supervised the villa's excavation from 1932–35.

You won't find elaborate mosaic floors or statues in place here, and at first glance the site might seem disappointing. Many of the villa's treasures were plundered in previous centuries, but the sheer extent of the ruins in such a superb setting makes them worth a visit. Built in the first century, Villa Jovis was apparently 12 storeys high but only partial remnants of three remain. A

The towering rock sentinels of Faraglioni, Capri

warren of passages leading to many small rooms makes it clear that this villa functioned almost as a mini city, with baths, stores and servants' quarters. The remains of a tower, called il Faro, are near the entrance gate. It's thought that Tiberius sent signals (smoke by day, fire by night) from here to the mainland when urgent answers were needed on political matters in Rome. Nearby is il Salto, or the Leap, where the emperor may have tossed his enemies to their death.

The walls and pavement of the villa are interesting for their methods of construction, now stripped bare of stucco and marble facings. In the middle of the villa was a huge cistern, mainly to supply the extensive baths in the front section. On the upper terrace stands a small ugly chapel called Santa Maria del Soccorso, along with a bronze statue of the Madonna flown in by US Navy helicopter in 1901. But these odd elements are easily ignored when you consider the incredible panoramic view from this terrace. At the villa's northern edge is the **Imperial Loggia**, reached by a path covered with some of the only original mosaic pavement remaining at the site. The loggia is almost 100m long, enough uninterrupted space for Tiberius to stroll along while pondering problems of state.

Anacapri

The town of Capri is on the slope of the island's east mountain; Anacapri lies west at the foot of Monte Solaro. Until the 1870s, the only way to reach Anacapri was by way of 881 steps cut into the rock, called the Scala Fenicia; donkeys scrambled up and down them more quickly than people did. The steps were probably first formed by the Greeks to connect the marina to this town, then reconstructed by the Romans. But now the Scala Fenicia is impassable, and the corniche road connects Capri to Anacapri. A bus or taxi will drop you at Anacapri's main square, Piazza Vittoria. From here small streets fan out leading to the Villa San Michele and the church of San Michele. Just above the piazza is a chairlift to the top of Monte Solaro. Once away from the main square, you'll find that Anacapri is a quieter town than Capri, especially if you wander through the maze-like back streets past whitewashed homes cascading with bougainvillea.

The **Villa San Michele**, the famous home of Swedish doctor and psychiatrist Axel Munthe, is what draws most tourists to Anacapri. His charming *Story of San Michele* was published in 1929. A profitable practice in Rome allowed Munthe to buy land here in the 1890s, though throughout his life he devoted time to the poor. His reputation for generosity was sealed after his work in Naples during the cholera epidemic there in 1884, and he was also a volunteer doctor with the British Red Cross during World War I.

The villa is reached by Via San Michele, a flat path about 1km long, from steps at the top of the main square. You might wonder, as you pass shops filled with straw donkeys, mohair jumpers and stuffed blue bears, what all this has to do with Axel Munthe, but it seems quite acceptable to the islanders who manage to sell so many silly trinkets. Don't despair, you are well rewarded

The Villa San Michele, former home of Swedish doctor Axel Munthe, Capri

at the end of the trail when you enter the beautiful whitewashed villa on a promontory.

When Munthe was building his dream house the ruins of a much older villa were discovered. It's possible that this was the site for one of the 12 villas of Tiberius, though there's no substantial proof. The elegant interior, cool and dark, is filled with small swirling columns, arched windows, Latin inscriptions and other spoils inserted into the walls. One piece of sculpture to look for is the Roman original of Medusa, along with another thought to be Tiberius or his nephew Germanicus. In the outer courtyard is a beautiful table of exquisite inlaid marble in the Cosmati tradition. Everywhere is green, surrounded by cypress, pine and palm.

I couldn't help envying Axel Munthe his discovery of so many island 'treasures'. Though he bought numerous antiques in Rome and Naples, some of the precious objects here were found on Capri at a time when one didn't have to turn every shard and fragment over to the state department of archeology.

The gardens here are gorgeous, and so are the views. Walk through the sculpture garden to the pergola by the granite sphinx (another little 'find' from a villa on the Calabrian coast). Looking below you'll see a section of the Scala Fenicia, now boarded up. Just above is a small chapel, with the Roman figures of mother and child beside the door. On the hillside above is the Barbarossa Castle, raided by the pirate Red Beard (Kheir-ed-Din) in 1535. However, unless you're keen to view the surroundings from a bit higher up, it's not worth trekking to these ruins.

Once back in the main square, head for the island's most interesting church, **San Michele**. It's reached by taking Via Orlandi and then turning right on Via San Nicola. This street leads to a small enclosed square; the octagonal church with its beautiful tiled floor is on the left side.

San Michele was built in 1719 to a sober Baroque design by Domenico Antonio Vaccaro. The high altar (not so sober Baroque!) and those in the side chapels are worth viewing for their soft colours, but it is the floor that overwhelms. Walking around its edges on wooden planking, you can see the story of Adam and Eve unfold in colourful detail. The sinister snake has wrapped itself around the central tree; monkeys, unicorns, camels and dozens of other creatures fill the scene. Climb the spiral staircase up to the choirloft (with its pretty wooden-cased organ) from where the floor can be fully appreciated. The majolica tiles were made in 1761 by Leonardo Chiaiese, and shipped to Capri from Naples. Chiaiese was also responsible for the beautiful tiled cloisters in the Neapolitan church of Santa Chiara, worked from a design created by Francesco Solimena.

By returning to the Via Orlandi and turning right, you come to the **Piazza Diaz** and the Baroque church of **Santa Sofia**. It has three assymetrical cupolas and a surprisingly soothing interior in the softest of yellows. The piazza is surrounded by majolica-tiled benches, a good place to rest and read though it lacks shade. Little streets from here lead to Anacapri's most typical neighbourhoods.

One of the island's highlights awaits if you take the chairlift to the top of **Monte Solaro** from Piazza Vittoria. This is easily equal to a trip into the Blue Grotto below, because sitting atop this summit plants you in one of the world's prime picnic spots. (Buy sandwiches from the Salumeria on Via Orlandi near the corner of Via San Nicola.) Gazing down on the Faraglioni while munching on a mozzarella and prosciutto *panino* is an unforgettable experience. The chairlift is a one-seater; feet dangle above grape vines, tomato plants, ferns and chestnut trees on the 12-minute ride to the top. Bring a windbreaker or a jumper even if it's a sunny day, because even though there are many spots to choose from for your picnic, it's scrubby ground without many trees for protection from sun and wind.

Last but not least, drop to sea level to row inside the **Blue Grotto** on the northwestern coast. It's close to Anacapri, by bus or a walk down the Strada della Grotta Azzura. From the bottom you can hire a small boat with sailor to take you into the grotto. Or, from the Marina Grande, motor boats carrying from four to twenty people ply from the harbour to the cave. Most guidebooks suggest reaching the grotto between 11.00 and 13.00, but Norman Douglas (who certainly visited more than once) insisted that the afternoon hours are really when the light within is best. I wonder whether the morning rule recommendation has anything to do with the Italian rite of a large lunch and an undisturbed siesta . . .

If you're in a boat with lots of people, you'll be transferred to a smaller rowboat outside the mouth of the cave. The entrance through a rocky arch is very low, so you must sit on the bottom while the boatman (on his back now) leads the boat in by pulling hand over hand on a length of fixed chain above. The blue light inside is close to indescribable – the sun's rays enter beneath the water and anything in it shimmers with this light when submerged. Don't foolishly deny yourself the joy of this excursion for fear of being labelled a 'typical tourist'. It's a wonderful treat on an island that has more than its fair share of them.

Practical Information

My preference is to see the islands during the months of May or September. These are both reliably sunny months, and even mid-October can be warm enough to spend a few hours of the day on the beach. From October to March, some hotels and restaurants will be closed, but all three islands have much to offer to fewer tourists during the quiet months.

Getting there

You won't be sorry if you bring a small car to Procida, and it's also easy to manoeuvre with one on Ischia (though not at all necessary). On Capri, however, visitors' cars are not allowed. A reliable and frequent ferry and hydrofoil service is available from Naples at both Mergellina and the Beverello port areas; less extensive service during high season is maintained from Pozzuoli, Sorrento and Positano. There is also a twice-daily hydrofoil service from Rome's Fiumicino airport to Capri from 15 June until 30 September, calling at Ponza, Ventotene and Sorrento en route. The trip takes 4½ hours and costs about £35. Tickets are purchased in Rome from Med Mar, Piazza Barberini (tel. 081 4828579). The dock near Fiumicino is on Viale Traiano (tel. 081 6521577).

If you're island hopping, the only connections you can't make are between Procida and Capri, and between Ischia and Capri from late September to May. Take a ferry to Ischia from Procida and connect to Capri during summer months, or travel via Naples from Procida and Ischia to Capri. The trip from Naples to Capri, the island farthest from Naples, takes about forty minutes by hydrofoil and 1½ hours by ferry. The cost of transporting a car by ferry, one-way, varies from about £10 to £30 depending on size.
The main boat companies are:
ALILAURO Via Caracciolo 13, Naples (tel. 081 682017).
CAREMAR Molo Beverello, Naples (tel. 081 5515384).
SNAV Via Caracciolo 10, Naples (tel. 081 7612348).

A helicopter service is available from Naples's Capodichino Airport to Ischia and Capri during the summer months, an expensive 15-minute trip. Contact Società Eliambassador, Naples (tel. 081 8370644).

Tourist Information Offices

CAPRI   AAST offices at Marina Grande where ferries dock (tel. 081 8370634), in Piazza Umberto I under the clock (tel. 081 8370686) and in Anacapri at 19A Via G. Orlandi (tel. 081 8371524). Close to the town of Capri's main square are agencies that will book island tours and excursions for you.

ISCHIA   AAST, Via Iasolino (tel. 081 991146); bordering the port area near ferry line ticket offices.

PROCIDA   138 Via Roma (tel. 081 8969594 or 8969624).

Hotels and Restaurants

CAPRI   Many hotels and pensione are scattered down side streets off Capri's main square of Piazza Umberto Primo. The doyen of high-class hotels here is the very expensive **Quisisana**, 2 Via Camarelle (tel. 081 8370788). If you don't stay here, splash out by ordering drinks on the raised terrace. Much smaller but almost as expensive is **La Scalinatella**, 8–10 Via Tragara (tel. 081 8370633), and nearby is the expensive **Hotel Punta Tragara**, 57 Via Tragara (tel. 081 8370844), built as a private villa by Le Corbusier in the 1920s. On a more moderate scale and up the street from the Quisisana is the **Gatto Bianco**, 32 Via Vittorio Emmanuele (tel. 081 8370203), with its vine-covered terrace and décor that harks back to the 1960s. The very pretty and peaceful **Villa Sarah**, 3a Via Tiberio (tel. 081 8377817), is a whitewashed home with a newly added wing of comfortable rooms, situated a steep ten-minute ascent from the main square, also moderately priced.

ANACAPRI,   the **San Michele**, Via G. Orlandi 1/3 (tel. 081 8371427), is in a villa just off the main square; moderate.

The island had one restaurant accorded a Michelin star, but it has recently been demoted to 'two fork' status – **La Capannina**, 14 Via delle Botteghe (tel. 081 8370732), near Piazza Umberto Primo in Capri town; Its *ravioli alla caprese* and *linguine* with fish sauce are very good, and now they are working harder than ever to rejoin the upper ranks; expensive. Just up the street is the **Aurora Grill**, 46 Via Botteghe (tel. 081 8377642), good for pizza and grilled meats and fish; moderate.

One of Capri's most elegant eateries is probably **Ai Faraglioni**, 75 Via Camarelle (tel. 081 8370320), with a dining room overlooking the Faraglioni; very expensive. Have a swim, and take in lunch, at the delicious but pricey **Canzone del Mare** (tel. 081 8370104) down at Marina Piccola. Back near the main square **Da Gemma** is a sound choice, with its mouthwatering display of *antipasti* in the room's centre; 6 Via Madre Serafina (tel. 081 8370461); moderate.

In ANACAPRI, try two inexpensive places: **La Rondinella**, 295 Via Orlandi (tel 081 8371223), on a continuation of the street after it forks to left. A more unusual restaurant is **Da Gelsomina**, 6 Via Migliera (tel. 081 8371499). It is found near the Belvedere di Migliara, a thirty-minute walk south of Anacapri, where the family offers home-made wines, sausage and tasty mushrooms from the slopes of Monte Solaro.

ISCHIA   This island has more than 200 hotels, so you won't be left out in the cold, whatever the season. My favourite place is **Il Monastero**, 3 Castello Aragonese, Ischia Ponte (tel. 081 992435). Accommodation is simple but comfortable, and the view is fantastic. There is a lift for which you'll get a pass, though there's still some climbing to do before reaching the hotel entrance. The price includes breakfast and dinner (which is nothing special) but the room rate is low enough to warrant skipping the evening meal here to dine elsewhere; closed mid-Oct to mid-March. Inexpensive.

A small moderately priced place I recommend is **Pensione Umberto a Mare** in **Forio** on the island's western side, 2 Via Soccorso (tel. 081 997171). All 14 rooms have lovely views, as the hotel practically hangs over the sea. Prices are for full board (slight reduction for half), but food is good, and the terraced restaurant is pretty; closed Nov–March. On to more superior places: in Lacco Ameno, the **Regina Isabella e Royal Sporting**, Piazza S. Restituta (tel. 081 994322), closed mid-Oct to mid-Apr, and the **San Montano**, Via Monte Vico (tel. 081 994033), closed mid-Oct to late March. Both have tennis courts, a pool, pretty gardens, hot springs and spa, and both are very expensive.

In PORTO D'ISCHIA, the **Excelsior Belvedere**, 19 Via Gianturco (991522), is the plushest, out on a spit protruding from the ringed harbour, surrounded by pines and pretty gardens, along with a heated pool; closed mid-Oct to mid-April. Very expensive. Not far from this hotel is a less expensive alternative hidden in lush gardens with a small pool, **La Villarosa**, 5 Via Giacinto Gigante (tel. 081 991316); closed Nov-late March; Moderate.

Better known for hot springs than haute cuisine, Ischia doesn't have any outstanding restaurants. But like Procida, fresh seafood is plentiful and pasta never disappoints.

In the port area, **Gennaro**, 66 Via Porto (tel. 081 992917), is good, and close to where boats come in and out of the harbour; closed Nov to mid-Mar. Moderate.

Near the castle at Ischia Ponte is **Di Massa**, 35 Via Seminario (tel. 081 991402), for typical southern Italian dishes; closed mid-Nov to mid-Feb. Inexpensive.

Another inexpensive restaurant good for seafood is **Dal Pescatore** in tiny Sant'Angelo (tel. 081 999206); closed Dec–Mar.

In **Forio**, **Lacco Ameno**, **Casamicciola** and **Ischia Porto**, you'll find many pizzerias and trattorias offering modestly priced meals.

PROCIDA   The island has three fairly basic, clean hotels. **The Riviera**, 36 Via G. Da Procida (tel. 081 8967197), is south near the eastern beach of Ciraciello, and less than 1km from the small bay of Chiaolella. Nice views from some of the rooms here; closed Nov–Mar; moderate.

The **Savoia**, 32 Via Lavadera (tel. 081 8967616), is near Chaiolella and has six bedrooms, none with bath. The small, family-run pensione was one of the first to open on Procida many years ago. They are open year round and offer full board during the summer months. Inexpensive.

The **L'Oasi**, 16 Via Elleri (8967499), is northwest, down a very narrow street and somewhat cut off from island life, open year-round; moderate.

You'll find small restaurants and trattoria throughout the island, though mainly at the port area, Corricella and Chiaolella. You'll get a good meal if you opt for island specialities of seafood or rabbit. Along the Via Roma in the port area are five or six places – try **La Medusa** (Inexpensive). In Chiaolella, try **Da Crescenzo** (they've also got a few bedrooms), 33 Marina di Chiaolella (tel. 081 8967255); inexpensive.

Price Ranges

Hotel (double room)	*Restaurant (per head)*
Inexpensive: under 60,000	under 25,000
Moderate: 60–120,000	25–50,000
Expensive: 120–200,000	50–90,000
Very expensive: 200,000+	90,000+

Museums and other Public Sites

CAPRI   Carthusian Monastery of San Giacomo: Open 09.00–14.00 except Mon and hols.
Church of San Michele: 10.00–18.00 Mon–Sat, 10.00–14.00 Sun April–Oct.
Foreign Cemetery: 07.00–17.00 daily except Thurs 07.00–13.00, and hols 08.00–12.00.
Monte Solaro Chairlift: 09.30–sunset daily.
Villa San Michele: 10.00–sunset daily.
Villa Tiberio (Jovis): 09.00–one hour before sunset daily except mon and hols.

ISCHIA   Aragon Castle, Ischia Ponte: open 09.00–18.00 daily except during months of Jan, Feb and Mar.
La Mortella Gardens, Via Francesco Calisa, Punta Caruso: open 09.00–19.00 Tues, Thurs and Sat from Easter until end Oct. Entrance fee of about £4.
Santa Restituta Museum, Lacco Ameno: 09.00–12.00, 15.00–18.00 except Sun, March–Oct.

9. THE AMALFI COAST: From Sorrento to Salerno

The Amalfi coast road is the best known drive in Italy, a geographical wonder separating the Bay of Naples from the Bay of Salerno. The road winds, climbs and swoops relentlessly from Sorrento to Salerno, flanked by tenacious groves of lemons, oranges and olives. From the top of limestone cliffs which edge the Lattari Mountains, you catch glimpses of fishing villages beside the sea, and pass through towns crammed precariously onto the high ridges. Some, like Positano, have terraced themselves into a set of solid white steps down to the water's edge, whereas Amalfi is serenely situated on a gentle slope. Ravello, one of the prettiest towns I've ever seen, sits back in proud isolation high above sea level.

The ride along the coast can be hair-raising, but I offer the following advice for safe passage: allow yourself to be overtaken, sound your horn around corners, and prepare to reverse when an oncoming coach needs room to manoeuvre. Don't try making the trip from Sorrento to Salerno in one day – there are enough bends on the Amalfi Drive to send you round one. It's a distance of about 80km, closer to 100 if you include the northern section from Castellammare to Sorrento. With so many picturesque towns to stay in, and hotels of a high standard, plan to spend at least three or four days exploring the Amalfi coast. In high season you must book well ahead and be prepared for crowded resorts; spring and autumn are a more pleasant alternative, as the weather can still be glorious, though a number of hotels will be closed.

Like Naples and Capri, towns along the Amalfi coast – especially Sorrento – have a well-established tradition of attracting travellers. Initially, this popularity was partly because of the bad press Naples received from guidebook writers during the 1800s, but it developed quickly due to Sorrento's superb position above the Gulf, within easy reach of Naples, Pompeii, the islands and Paestum. Charles Dickens came here in the 1840s, Tolstoy and Longfellow too, while Henrik Ibsen worked on *Peer Gynt* here in 1867.

English writer Norman Douglas evoked the Sorrentine peninsula's past in *Siren Land*, published in 1911. His tales of the elusive sirens and their rocky

The Amalfi coastline is one of the most famous in the world

homes on the outlying islets of li Galli conjure up images of helpless sailors struggling back to Amalfi's safe harbour. And indeed, when one explores the coast by boat, a host of pirates and sea-monsters seem to beckon from the hills and hidden sea caves. Regional myths abound – from capricious gnomes called *monicelli* to golden lambs and chickens buried in the hills near Punta Campanella.

Sorrento

Sitting 50m above the sea, Sorrento is one of the most popular towns on the Amalfi Coast. In an enviable geographic position, it possesses superb views, with the Sorrentine Gulf below and the islands out to sea. Hotels perch on the edge of the cliff, and a sliver of beach rims the bay far below. Small streets wind through the town's historic centre, easily explored in a day. Though Sorrento has become increasingly devoted to tourism and its more tawdry trinkets, local craftsmen still create beautiful objects of inlaid wood (their method is called *tarsia*), leather, and jewellery of coral and cameo in side-street workshops.

Many travellers base themselves here when touring the area, as it has scheduled ferry and hydrofoil services to Naples and the islands. Sorrento has lost some of its character simply because there are too many hotels, and too many foreigners staying in them. But it is a very pretty town, and the hotels above the marina have unbeatable views from windows and balconies. Most offer lift service to the north-facing beach below, which consists mainly of deck chairs and mattresses lined up along cement piers. Sorrento also has a good choice of restaurants, despite a proliferation of English 'pubs' (or poob as the Italians call them).

Sorrento was known as Syrentum to the Greeks, cementing its connection to the place where Odysseus resisted the call of the Sirens by tying himself to his ship's mast. Then, for the Romans, Surrentum was a pleasant escape, a colony during the reign of Augustus. From 830 to 1109 the town was an independent republic. Its citizens repelled a series of Saracen raids, and battled against Amalfi seafarers for the right to remain independent in 892. Conquered by Normans in 1133, Pisans helped them rebel four years later. But in the 16th century, Sorrentines could not hold back the bloodthirsty Turks, who carried off 2000 citizens; only 120 ever returned. The population constantly allied itself with groups trying to overthrow the monarchy, but eventually came under the power of the dukes and kings of Naples.

Sorrento's main square is **Piazza Tasso**, named after its most famous son, the poet Torquato Tasso (1544–95) whose best known work is the epic poem *Jerusalem Freed*. Two years before his death he composed *Jerusalem Conquered*, about the First Crusade. If he had stayed in Sorrento he might have led a happier life; for seven years he was confined in the northern city of Ferrara, declared insane. In later years, after much restless wandering, he was summoned to Rome by Pope Clement VIII to be crowned Poet Laureate, but he died in the capital before receiving the honour. His home is now part of Hotel Sirenuse along the town's eastern edge.

Sorrento's main street, Corso Italia, runs north and mainly south from the Piazza Tasso. The town's prettiest tourist attraction is the 14th-century **Cloister of St Francis**, south of the square near the corner of Via Vittorio Veneto. Attached to the Baroque church with its big bell-tower, the arched cloister is filled with palms and tumbling purple bougainvillea. The surrounding walls are often used for local art exhibits, as the convent is now an art school.

On nearby **Piazza Antonino** is the church of the same name, dedicated to the city's patron saint. Traces of the original 11th-century basilica have been uncovered, but the present features are mainly Baroque. The church's three most interesting elements have little to do with the grander aspects of ecclesiastical architecture: a beautiful pulpit crafted in the Sorrento style of inlaid *tarsia* by the Fiorentini Brothers in 1938; the animated *presepio* created in the 1700s by the Neapolitan school of Solimena in a room to the left of the high altar; and, in a chamber beneath the high altar, an amazing collection of ex-voto offerings from sailors to the saint buried here. These paintings and metal decorations read like a logbook of divine intervention.

Sorrento's **Cathedral**, located on the southern half of the Corso Italia, is not much to look at. Its pale, plain façade was unfortunately rebuilt in the early 1900s, but at least the bell-tower on the left, unattached to the Duomo, retains its graceful Romanesque arch. More Sorrentine *tarsia* work is displayed in the choir stalls inside. Behind the Duomo are the remains of a Roman arch, at the end of the Via Sersale off Corso Italia. Also near the Duomo, heading south

The cloisters of St Francis, Sorrento

this time off the Corso down Via Tasso, is a strange corner building called the **Sedile Dominova**. Recognisable by its bright green-and-yellow tiled dome, this was the seat of the Sorrentine nobles in the 15th and 16th centuries; their coats of arms are displayed within. The dark forecourt is now the *Società Operaia*, a men's social club where a lot of serious card-playing takes place beneath the faded frescoed ceiling. The Via San Cesareo runs to one side of the building, filled with fruit and vegetable stalls on most mornings.

Sorrento's only museum is in the 18th-century **Palazzo Correale**, recently reopened after extensive earthquake damage forced curators to close it in 1985. It is reached by walking north on Via Correale off the Piazza Tasso. The works within were donated to the town by Alfredo Correale, Count of Terranova, and his brother Pompeo. The museum houses an impressive collection of furniture and Neapolitan paintings, as well as other Campanian works of art – porcelain, majolica tiles, more Sorrentine *tarsia* work – from the 15th to 18th centuries. Some of Tasso's manuscripts are kept in the library here, guarded by his death mask poised on a corner pedestal.

Excursions from Sorrento

Sorrento is ringed by many small hill towns worth exploring, such as Sant'Agata, Vico Equense and Massa Lubrense. The area is especially good for long walks with spectacular views to coves and coastline far below, such as the highly recommended trek to the abbey of Il Deserto south of Sorrento. If you haven't climbed Vesuvius, or been to the summit in either Ischia or Capri, spend half a day on top of Monte Faito north of Sorrento. Or take to the open sea – hire a boat in Sorrento and visit the hidden fishing village of Marina di Puolo just south.

Sant'Agata sui Due Golfi and Il Deserto

The old monastery of Il Deserto, with its many terraces and spectacular views, is best reached by first driving to **Sant'Agata sui Due Golfi** south of Sorrento. This small town, inland off state road No.145, sits high between the Gulf of Naples and the Gulf of Salerno. Park near the church of Santa Maria delle Grazie, built in 1622, and peek inside if you're lucky enough to find the doors open. The high altar here is a magnificent example of Florentine inlaid marble work. Mother-of-pearl, malachite and lapis lazuli are swirled in intricate patterns on all four sides. The altar was made in the 1500s, and moved here from a church in Naples in 1845.

A road climbs north from the left side of the church, a walk of less than 2km up to the abandoned site of **Il Deserto**. (This is a good place for a picnic, almost sure to be free of other travellers.) Suppressed by the French, the Franciscan monastery's red buildings are crumbling now. But their fading beauty only helps to enhance the impact of the view – especially to the north, as the convent was built on the Sorrentine side of the ridge.

Marina di Puolo and Massa Lubrense

The small fishing village of **Marina di Puolo** is just around the Punta del Capo, also south of Sorrento. In a protected cove, it is one of the Amalfi coast's unspoilt havens where life simply carries on regardless of tourists. If you take a boat from the Marina Grande in Sorrento, you'll pass the ruins of the Roman villa of Pollio Felix on the way around the point. Nearby is the **Bagno della Regina Giovanna**; light enters the sea pool through a cleft in the rock, causing the water to be tinted with hues of blue, green and violet.

Marina di Puolo is enclosed in a gorge between Punta del Capo and Capo di Massa. The faded red, white and pink façades of fishermens' homes are squeezed together along the shore. It's a good place to come for lunch if you're skirting the coastline by boat (though the village can also be reached by parking above and walking down). There's a small beach for sunbathing, and a few modest restaurants serving fish guaranteed to be fresh.

The town of **Massa Lubrense** is about 5km south, and if driving from Sorrento you'll have many open views of the sea. The town is situated on a cliff, with homes stepped gently down to the small harbour which is still an active fishing port. Massa is of Lombard origin, recorded in the first half of the 10th century as Massa Publica; the name Lubrense then came from the church of Santa Maria della Lobra. This church was probably built upon the remains of a Roman temple, though no one knows for sure who the temple was dedicated to – perhaps Minerva or Jupiter.

The town's history is similar to Sorrento's, but when Massa was incorporated under the domain of that bigger town in the 1300s, its townspeople successfully rebelled and regained their independence. The Turks ravaged this town in 1558 too, capturing many prisoners. Murat watched his French troops take Capri from here in 1808.

Massa Lubrense's two churches both have pretty majolica-tiled floors. Santa Maria delle Grazie, built in 1512 but reconstructed in 1760, has 18th-century paving in the transept and in the presbytery. Santa Maria della Lobra, dated 1512, is the second built on this site. Its tiled floor is also from the 18th century, and the organ here is unusual: supported by two antique columns that were possibly salvaged from the original temple. A peaceful cloister lies beside the church, part of the small Franciscan convent built here in the 17th century.

From Castellammare di Stabia to Vico Equense

Castellammare lies over the ancient ruins of **Stabia**, about 12km north of Sorrento. Stabia was also engulfed by the eruption of Vesuvius in 79, and on the shore here is where Pliny the Elder met his death. Stabia's uncovered sites have been overshadowed by the excavations at Pompeii and Herculaneum, and though the town does offer ruins dating from the period they are more spread out and many of them are best left to keen lovers of archaeology. Vico Equense and its little port of Marina di Equa are about halfway between Sorrento and Castellammare di Stabia.

In Stabia, visit the Antiquarium. It is within walking distance of the train station in Castellammare, near the corner of Via Denza on Via Mario Marconi. Eleven rooms are filled with artefacts found in the excavated baths, villas and burial ground – frescoes, pavement fragments, terracotta busts, bas relief sculptures and sarcophagi.

Between Castellammare di Stabia and Vico Equense is **Monte Faito**, worth the climb if you haven't had your fill of the view from other points. For a trip to the summit (1131m), return to Castellammare di Stabia. A small railway (open April–Oct) runs to the top, taking eight minutes from the Stazione Circumvesuviana. A more challenging route by car starts from the old Hotel Quisisana, reached from state road No.145 at Castellammare. If coming from Sorrento, pass the towered Angevin castle on the left and bear right on the Via Quisisana about 1km farther on. A sharp right again will start your serpentine climb of 15km up the mountainside. The surroundings of tall oak, cedar and chestnut trees mean that the view will not open out fully until you reach the top, but it's an absolutely magnificent one when you do. From the Belvedere of Monte Faito, the Gulf of Naples is spread below, with Vesuvius just north and Punta Campanella and Capri stretched south. The word Faito stems from the Italian *faggeti* for beech trees, and there are soothing walks beneath them which circle the summit.

Heading back down the coast again, southwards out of Castellammare di Stabia on state road No.145, **Vico Equense** makes a pleasant place to stop. At its centre is Piazza Umberto I, and on the nearby Via Corso is a small museum called the Antiquarium. It has a few interesting pieces, particularly from a necropolis found in the area which dates to the 7th century BC. At the end of Via Corso is the church of Sts Ciro and Giovanni, topped by a colourfully tiled cupola, one of the Amalfi coast's trademarks. Another pretty church is that of the Annunziata, poised above the sea at the very end of Via Vescovado. Its square bell-tower rises in three sections over an arch. Within the church is the tomb of Gaetano Filangieri, a Neapolitan economist and jurist who died in the Angevin castle here in 1788. Below is the small cove of Marina di Equa, a popular spot for swimming and relaxing. From Vico, a turning on Route No.269 inland provides a shorter alternate route to Positano. You'll pass through the town of **Moiano**, well-known for its creamy **fior di latte** cheese, the cow's milk version of buffalo mozzarella.

Positano and li Galli

The journey to Positano is almost as enjoyable as reaching your destination. From Sorrento through Sant' Agata the 'Strada del Nastro Azzurro', or Blue Ribbon Road, takes you over hills clothed with olive and orange trees. All the while the road remains true to its name: a wide band of blue never disappears as you drive south toward Positano. But the town itself plays a game of hide-and-seek while you wind along State Road No.163. Moorish-style houses glint like uneven stacks of white cubes in the distance, but suddenly you've rounded yet another bend and the vision is temporarily out of sight.

Positano

Positano has remained unchanged for centuries, and retains a unique atmosphere because of its Moorish architecture and terracing. What land was available has already been built upon, and there doesn't appear to be a single hectare left to develop. The town has far more steps than streets, so check how high above sea level your hotel is if you're concerned about too much climbing. (The less expensive pensioni tend to be higher up.) Apart from the small church of Santa Maria Assunta, there isn't another site to see in Positano, but this may come as a relief, and the town makes a good base from which to view other towns and ruins. (You just have to be prepared for the coast drive back and forth.)

Positano is first and foremost a great place to relax: marvel over its position, read on your hotel's terrace, drink *cappuccini*, or just soak up the sun while deciding where to eat the next meal. Of course, no one will deny that Positano has been 'discovered'. So fashionable are the boutiques that even the clothes-conscious Romans come here in May to buy their summer wardrobes. But

Moorish terracing characterises the town of Positano

Positano attracts all sorts of people. I have one friend (so oblivious to fashion that he can't match his socks) who is in love with this town, happy as a drunken sailor to read his book in a beachside bar all day, the quintessential Englishman Abroad.

Positano doesn't really have a town 'centre'. The town's only main street of Via Pasitea is one-way, but even so it is tight enough when buzzing motorinos and pedestrians crowd the pavement. This system does mean that if you need to come through town again you've got to go all the way down, around and out before re-entering. If you're driving and don't have a place to stay, or haven't yet located it, leave the car at the bottom of Via Pasitea in one of the car parks there. People congregate at the lower end of Via Pasitea where buses stop, but one of the few open areas immune to traffic (reached on foot only) is the Marina Grande. The other is Fornillo beach, reached by a cliffside walkway from Marina Grande or from steps higher up Via Pasitea. Both beaches are extremely crowded in summer, but it's the Marina Grande that hums from morning to midnight, lined with bars and restaurants.

Just above the Marina Grande is the church of **Santa Maria Assunta** with its brightly tiled cupola. The dark Madonna and Child over the high altar is a 13th-century Byzantine work. The local legend of this Madonna is illustrated in the painting to the right of the altar. Hostile Turkish sailors were ready to attack, whereupon the Madonna spoke to them, repeating the soothing word *'posa'*, meaning rest or lay down. This miracle of speech apparently converted them: they came peacefully to shore and christened their town Positano. A more widely accepted theory has it that citizens of Paestum founded Positano after fleeing from the Saracens, and that the town's name is also a corruption of the Greek Poseidon.

Li Galli

From Positano you can rent a boat to explore the coastal caves and the rocky islets of **li Galli** about 6km west. By tradition, these three outcroppings are the home of the Sirens, made so famous by Homer in the trials of Odysseus. The largest one was the summer residence of Rudolf Nureyev. He carried on a tradition of Russian ownership, after Diaghilev at the turn of the century. The other two, with barely a flat surface upon them, are uninhabited except for scrub pines and seagulls.

Li Galli, or the Roosters, hardly seem attractive enough to lure lovesick fishermen. What then did the Sirens make of their homes? Perhaps they only frolicked around and beneath them in large hidden caves, which my boatman told me do exist if you're willing to hold your breath and dive deep enough. And who were these so-called Sirens? I refer to Norman Douglas in *Siren Land*, who knows how to keep a reader within the realm of myth:

> The Sirens, says one, are the charms of the Gulf of Naples. No, says another; they were chaste priestesses. They were neither chaste nor priestesses, but exactly the reverse. They were sunbeams. They were perilous

cliffs. They were a race of peaceful shepherds. They were symbols of persuasion. They were cannibals.

Whatever the mysterious Sirens were made of, it's obvious that their islands are chunks of Appenine limestone. They must have broken from the mainland thousands of years ago, but still seem to be sliding down into the sea with their long laminated sections of rock poised at such high angles. The first one viewed from Positano, il Gallo Lungo, is the largest. Close by is the smallest one named la Castelluccia for the remains of a tower on its edge. Locals prefer to call this island il Brigante, saying that brigands used this spot for hiding themselves and their stolen treasure. The third islet, la Rotonda, is . . . well, just a little bit rounder than the other two.

Point your boat in the direction of Nerano, about 4km farther west. You'll pass two more outcroppings on the way – the rock called Scoglia Vetara and another closer to shore called Scoglia dell'Isca, which was the summer home of Neapolitan actor Eduardo di Fillipo and is now owned by his son. The protected cove of Nerano, a quiet fishing village, has a couple of good restaurants on stilts by the water's edge. (Anchor off-shore by either one and the restaurant owners' sons will pick you up in a rowing boat.) Feast on fresh fish and the day's pasta, helped along by a local white wine.

Heading back toward Positano you'll pass secluded coves ideal for swimming, along with small grottoes emitting loud groans when the waves pound up against them. The limestone cliffs rise like an immense sea wall to restrain the land above, and the remains of towers – said to have signalled from one to the next all the way to Sicily in case of Saracen raids – are scattered on the grassy hills. One of the best things about this boat trip is being able to return to Positano and admire it from the sea, especially as the sun is setting. Tiny golden lights glimmer from houses that now look like so many tiers of theatre boxes, and soon you're back on the stage of Marina Grande.

South of Positano

The Amalfi drive continues its snakelike path south of Positano, full of hairpin turns and deep ravines. The **Punta San Pietro**, with its small church, is your first reference point out of town. The San Pietro, a luxurious cliffside hotel, is built below the upper terrace; hidden from view are sumptuous bedrooms with views back to Positano. From here, state road No.163 becomes a series of sharp curves intersected by small deep valleys; the view out to sea includes Capri and its Faraglioni rock formations. Three kilometres from Punta San Pietro is the small town of **Vettica Maggiore**, followed by **Praiano**. As the local saying goes, 'Whoever wants to live a healthy life spends the morning in Vettica and the evening in Praiano.' These are both simple villages, their homes scattered on the slopes down to the coast. They aren't as overrun with tourists as Positano and Sorrento, but the beach areas are small (though it's a nice sandy one at Marina di Praia) with a limited amount to do in each place.

You'll be driving through tunnels here, as the rock face juts out and falls in a sheer drop to the sea. Just past Praiano is a huge fissure in the limestone cliffs, a deep valley called the **Vallone di Furore**. The sea laps its way to a pebbly beach under the viaduct, a pleasant place to swim if you can find a safe place to park the car above. Steps beside the viaduct lead down to the beach, while a much longer set leads up to the windswept outposts of Sant' Elia and Furore. The valley and the village probably owe their name to the furious noise created when stormy weather sends the wind and water rushing into this deep gorge.

The **Emerald Grotto** is not far from the Furore Valley, and it's worth taking the lift or steps down to this huge cave (then entered by boat) if you won't have a chance to see Capri's Grotta Azzurra. The Emerald Grotto was discovered in 1932, and the eerie green light in the cave enters just as it does in Capri – filtered through indirectly and beneath the surface of the water. The emerald light also plays on the mineral formations in the cave – stalactites have dripped down to join stalagmites in columns that reach a height of 10m.

The coast road then swings past the small fishing villages of Conca dei Marini (once the most active sea-trading town on the coast) and Vettica Minore before introducing you to the whitewashed shapes of Amalfi, a total distance of about 6km from the Emerald Grotto.

Amalfi

This famous town's importance as a maritime power faded centuries ago, but sea trade has been effectively replaced by the tourist trade. Instead of the tall-masted sailing ships that once anchored in the small bay, double-decker coaches sit in the seafront parking lot. If you're driving the car must be left here, unless you're staying at one of the beautifully situated converted monasteries up on either edge of Amalfi, the Cappuccini Convento or the Luna. The town itself, with its impressive mass of a cathedral squeezed onto one side of the inner main square, climbs up the steep curved slope behind the bay. As in Positano, most streets are narrow lanes of stairs winding from house to house.

Despite constant sea-front traffic and the great number of tourists paying homage to the town that gave the coast drive its name, Amalfi is still one of the most picturesque spots on the Tirrhenian Sea. The Corso Roma above the beach area is the scene of the *passeggiata*, the evening stroll down the avenue performed in every town in Italy. You can continue up the Via Amendola near the remains of the Torre di Amalfi; the view back to town is the only one needed to prove why so many people visit Amalfi. Narrow streets off the Piazza Duomo, full of little restaurants, are reminiscent of a medieval town. Covered passageways lead to staircases which then open onto small squares as you climb higher into the town's residential quarters.

Amalfi was populated as early as the fourth century, possibly by shipwrecked Romans who had been trying to make their way to Constantinople but instead stopped at Palinuro to the south, then inland near Eboli and finally settled here.

Another version of the town's founding tells of a settlement in 320 headed by an official in Emperor Constantine's army called Amalfo. But Amalfi was a Byzantine dominion in the sixth century; then slowly, due to the distance and weakening state of Constantinople's governing power, it began to enjoy semi-independence. In 812, it was able to fend off Saracen invaders, and smaller towns along the coast depended on it for protection.

Amalfi became a republic in about 850, and until the 11th century rivalled the ports of Venice and Genoa in its ability to attract wealth and power through sea trade. Its population today is about 7000; but 1000 years ago it totalled 60,000 and was governed by enlightened doges. Amalfi owned warehouses and banks in Byzantine and Islamic ports; Amalfi sailors and merchants set up shop in such places as Cyprus, Jerusalem, Beirut and Alexandria. Its influence in Italy extended from Naples and Benevento down to Syracuse in Sicily. Amalfi became famous for devising the *Tavole Amalfitane*, said to be the world's oldest maritime code, a set of regulations for shipowners, merchants and seamen which was in use until the 1500s. But Amalfi was annexed to the Kingdom of Sicily under Roger II in 1131, then plundered twice by the Pisans. Until 1582, it was under the dominion of the Colonna, Orsini and then the Piccolimini families, and was never again able to regain its former power and prestige.

Little remains in Amalfi of its illustrious past – most historians will tell you it lies buried beneath the sea. Powerful storms in 1013 and 1343 destroyed most buildings along the seafront. The ruins of the **Arsenal**, two halls with Gothic arches, can still be seen on Via Camera near the bayside Piazza Flavio Gioia (named for the presumed inventor of the compass in the 11th century). The arsenal is where ships were constructed, some with as many as 116 oars. Amalfi's maritime laws are preserved in the Municipio near the Piazza Duomo.

The town's great architectural treasure, the **Cathedral of St Andrew**, overwhelms the central square. Its best features are the façade, the attached Cloisters of Paradise and the top level of the bell-tower. The cathedral is faced in striking bands of black and white, with small intertwined arches and alternating squares patterned with stars, crosses and animals. At the top is a bright gold-and-blue mosaic, *Christ Enthroned by Symbols of the Evangelists and Earthly Powers*, designed by Neapolitan artist Domenico Morelli. From the piazza, 56 wide steps lead to the cathedral's arched porch.

The Duomo was first built in the ninth century, reconstructed in 1203, and then again in 1701 in keeping with its earlier Lombard-Norman style. It partially collapsed in 1861, and was then heavily restored from 1875–94. Among its most impressive monuments are the carved bronze doors, inlaid with silver and made in Constantinople before 1066 by Simeon of Syria. Unfortunately, the designs have worn and are difficult to decipher.

The cathedral's interior is Baroque, divided into three naves on the plan of the Latin cross. The marble pulpit and the tall Easter Candelabra are interesting for their intricate Cosmati mosaic style; the only other objects within that I found worthy of inspection were the relics of St Andrew, which were brought from Constantinople in 1208 and are buried beneath the high altar. (He is missing one important body part though, since his head has been in the Vatican since 1462.) A sort of oily liquid is said to have oozed from his body in the 14th century, called the 'manna' of St Andrew. Amalfi's cathedral was a place of pilgrimage for such luminaries as St Francis of Assisi and Pope Urban IV in the 13th century, but when word spread about the 'manna' many more Christians came to pay their respects. Up until the 1500s, miracle health cures were attributed to the manna of St Andrew.

The **Cloisters of Paradise** are reached through a door from the left-hand side of the porch. They form an intimate courtyard, graced with slender double columns which are surmounted by tight pointed arches. Frescoes, sarcophagi and coats of arms along each aisle make it feel like an open-air museum; the Cosmati mosaic work embedded in the walls is the best I've seen, and the only opportunity I know of to see these fine geometric patterns displayed in daylight.

The Campanile, to the front of the church and on the same side as the cloisters, was completed in 1276 and is the only remaining portion of the earliest building work. Its central tower at the top, with four corner turrets, is criss-crossed with playful arches in tiles of yellow and green. I love everything about it but the bells. Perhaps being a manual bell ringer is not a very prestigious job, but was it really necessary to install an electrical system that allows these bells to ring every quarter hour?

Amalfi's quietest locale is up beyond the highest residential quarter, in the **Valle dei Mulini** or Valley of the Mills. About 150 years ago there were 16 paper mills (among the oldest in Europe) and 15 macaroni factories operating in Amalfi; many were based in this part of town. In fact, the only papermaker left, by the name of Cartiera F. Amatruda, still operates in a 14th-century mill near here. They produce beautiful stationery which you can purchase at the mill, a five-minute walk north of Largo Marini on Via delle Cartiere.

From Piazza Duomo, follow Via Genoa up to Via Capuano which leads you into the valley. The rushing stream is below, the way lined with gardens and citrus groves. In about an hour's time you reach the walk's prettiest point at the ruined mill, or *mulino rovinato*. The head of the valley is reached after another 45-minute walk, but most people make the ruined mill their stopping point.

Amalfi's other treasured and peaceful spot is on its western hillside: the Cappuccini Convento Hotel. Even if you're not staying at this 12th-century former monastery, it's worth the trek up a long flight of steps (or by lift) on the Via Camera. The view is superb; the restored cloisters and flower-covered loggia are soothing spots. On the other side of town is another hotel with a gorgeous 13th-century cloister called the Luna Convento. Part of the whitewashed hotel is in the Saracen Tower by the sea, Amalfi's last landmark on the eastern edge of town before the road rejoins the coast drive south to **Atrani**. This small town, so close to Amalfi that it seems like a beachside extension, is well known for its production of colourful ceramics. The bronze doors on the church of San Salvatore de' Bireto here (just off Piazza Umberto I) are as well-wrought as Amalfi's, and were made in Constantinople at about the same time.

Ravello

The steep turning left uphill to Ravello is just past the town of Atrani. This picturesque road off the Amalfi Drive ascends for about 7km, through the vineyard-laden Valley of the Dragon. The small villages of Pontone, Minuto and Scala (this last worth a detour for its views) can be seen in the distance on flat patches among the hills.

When you reach **Ravello** much of its beauty will be hidden from view until you leave the car and stroll up the narrow streets around Piazza Vescovado. One of the town's central avenues is simply a path of wide stone steps beside the Duomo which leads to the top of the hill. You're apt to pass schoolchildren whom the local priest is admonishing to slow down, and always a handful of other travellers who have discovered that this is a worthy place of pilgrimage. Ravello has some excellent hotels, amongst them my own favourite: the friendly, old fashioned Caruso Belvedere. A more formal (and more expensive) alternative is the Hotel Palumbo. The town's two most elaborate villas, the Rufolo and the Cimbrone, are set among gorgeous gardens and open to the public.

Ravello was probably established by the Romans in the sixth century, but the first accurate records point to settlement in the ninth century when this area of the coast was under Amalfi's rule. It became an independent episcopal seat in 1086, and by then had 13 churches and 4 monasteries. The ruins of these are hard to find, and many of Ravello's houses have been built upon them. Despite the town's isolated position, it came under very heavy attack by Pisans in 1135. Roger the Norman came to the citizens' aid, but Pisa retaliated two years later when the town was decisively destroyed by the northern invaders. Ravello recovered, however, and its period of greatest wealth was during the 13th century when rich merchant trading familes had ties with Sicily and the Orient. The town retained its independence until the early 1800s, when it then became part of the diocese of Amalfi.

In 1086, Ravello's first bishop, Orso Papirio, founded the **Cathedral of San Pantaleone** that dwarfs the town's only piazza. The church was rebuilt in the 12th century, probably around the time when the justly famous bronze doors were brought here from the Apulian city of Trani in 1179. They were made by Barisano da Trani, divided into 54 panels depicting the lives of the saints and Christ's Passion. (Since they are protected by wooden doors inside and out, appeal to the Sacristan within the church to open them for you.)

Inside the cathedral (well restored in the 1970s when the 18th-century Baroque additions were dismantled), the floor slopes slightly upward. When I asked the Sacristan whether I was imagining this, he solemnly said, 'No, it slowly makes its way to God's altar.' (A less pious explanation is that it makes it easy for the water to run out when the floor is being washed.) Along the walls of the right nave are traces of ancient frescoes and two Roman sarcophagi. The raised pulpit in the central nave is a real beauty, created by Niccolo di Bartolomeo da Foggia in 1272. It is supported by six twisted columns encrusted with bands of mosaic resting on the backs of lions.

The mosaic pulpit in the cathedral of San Pantaleone, Ravello

Pantaleone is the town's patron saint, a doctor who was the favourite physician of Emperor Maximian. The saint was beheaded in the year 206, on 27 July, and Ravello claims for him an annual miracle on a footing with San Gennaro in Naples. An ampoule of San Pantaleone's blood is stored in the chapel to the left of the high altar; it's said that every year on 27 July it also becomes liquid. (According to H. V. Morton, the marble floor of this chapel was paid for by an Englishman named Captain John Grant, because he was so impressed by the ceremony in 1925.)

To the right of the church off the piazza is the **Palazzo Rufolo**. The rich Rufolo family elaborated on its earlier construction in the second half of the 13th century. Did Boccaccio's Landolfo Rufolo, hero of one of his stories in the *Decameron*, live here? As the story goes 'this Rufolo was a very rich man indeed. But being dissatisfied with his fortune, he sought to double it, and as a result he nearly lost every penny he possessed, and his life too.' By the story's end, after selling his cargo at bargain prices in Cyprus, turning to piracy and then being shipwrecked, Boccaccio has our hero 'secure at last in Ravello . . . no longer interested in commerce . . . living in splendour for the rest of his days.'

Once inside the walls of the Villa Rufolo, it is obvious to see how easy that would be. Wagner found inspiration for his *Parsifal* in the tropical gardens here (in summer still the scene of wonderful concerts); the villa was occupied centuries earlier by Pope Adrian IV, Charles of Anjou and Robert the Wise. In the late 1800s it was owned by Scotsman Francis Neville Reid, but is now the property of the Italian State. One of the two remaining towers can still be climbed, and the small enclosed Moorish cloister nearby is dark and quiet. Paths lined with palms and cypress trees lead to a wide terrace with a wonderful view along the coast.

The garden of **Villa Cimbrone** is slightly wilder and even more stunning, reached by Via San Francesco from the same side of Piazza Vescovado. The palazzo was built in the late 1800s by Lord Grimthorpe, a wealthy English lawyer and an authority on architecture and horology, who designed Big Ben. He had his ashes buried here beneath the Temple of Bacchus near the cliffside Belvedere. Villa Cimbrone is now owned by the Swiss Vuilleumier family, hoteliers who have run the Hotel Palumbo since 1875. They claim that not even a generous offer from Fiat magnate Gianni Agnelli has enticed them to sell the villa. One can't blame them: this has to be one of the most spectacular properties in southern Europe. (The American author Gore Vidal has managed to purchase one cliffside patch; inevitably though, animosity has developed over foot-path rights.)

Acres of lush garden are unevenly and sporadically pruned, which only adds to their charm. This is a place for lingering along paths lined by roses, camellias, begonias and hydrangea – and those are just the most easily identifiable plants in this flowering paradise. To the north, the ground slopes down to a wooded area covered with pine and chestnut trees, where the Temple of Bacchus is hidden. Within is the seductive bronze statue of the god, rubbed to a high sheen by appreciative hands. Just beyond is one of the highlights of the Amalfi Coast – an astounding view from the Belvedere, a clifftop balcony 350m above the sea. The railing at the outer edge is interspersed with busts of emperors, set bravely on pedestals; stone benches line the inner boundary. The panorama beyond is breathtaking – this is another perfect place for slicing the cheese and sausage, and uncorking the wine of Ravello . . .

Towards Salerno

The coast road continues to convolute, winding past the two seaside resorts of Minori and Maiori. The ruins of a **Roman villa** were uncovered in Minori during the fifties, found on the Strada S. Lucia before heading down into the main part of town. Built in the 1st century, only the villa's ground floor remains though some of the rooms are very well preserved. The villa was constructed around a central courtyard which once had a swimming pool. In the barrel-vaulted hall are faded frescoes and stucco decoration. In the course of excavation here, two other villas were uncovered. They are not open to the public but their existence points to the fact that Minori has been a holiday resort for almost 2000 years.

Minori is – as the name implies – smaller than Maiori, and so is its beach. **Maiori** draws more crowds in summer, and hotels line its long, grey, sandy beach. The church of Santa Maria a Mare is a pretty one, its golden-tiled cupola dominating the low skyscape and reached by climbing 108 steps from Corso Reginna Maior (the town's original name). Originally built in the 12th century, it was modified for the second time in 1836 and has a small, idiosyncratic museum in the sacristy. A beautiful ebony and ivory casket, used to store relics, dates from the 16th century. There are silver crosses, collection plates from the 1400s, even 15th-century English art in the form of an alabaster altar-frontal with Gothic bas reliefs of Gospel scenes. The little balcony with its view out to sea is unusual in a church. If you are down by the shore here, take a quick boat trip to the Pandona Grotto – much bigger than Capri's Blue Grotto but with similar light effects.

From Maiori, you'll round the **Capo d'Orso**, the last point along the drive to really get a good, long view back along the coast. This chunky spur of oddly shaped rock separates the valleys of Tramonti and Cava de'Tirreni. Driving out toward the lighthouse, the view will include Punta Campanella and Capri. Rounding this point, the view east now takes in the wide Gulf of Salerno. Below is one of the Amalfi Coast's best beaches at the **Marina di Erchie**, guarded by the square Saracen tower at its far end. Farther on is **Cetara**, a small fishing village which hasn't embraced tourism in a big way. I'm not sure why – all the requisite elements are there to exploit. Maybe it hasn't quite shaken off the reputation acquired in the late 1700s of being a 'nest of pirates'.

Vietri sul Mare is the next town along the coast, and marks the end of the Amalfi Drive. It's a popular holiday resort, but without the charm of a place like Positano. It's well known for ceramics that are produced in many factories among the inland hills, and buying in bulk means you'll easily slash chainstore prices in half. Another beautifully tiled dome is part of the landscape here, attached to the hilltop church of San Giovanni Battista built in 1732.

Up in the hills behind Vietri is a strange and interesting monastery, the **Abbazia dell Trinità**. It nestles in a deep, green valley, and the strong harsh lines of the buildings here don't seem in keeping with the soft surroundings, which only serves to emphasise the power and prestige this monastery once had. From the coast road in Vietri, a sharp left turn takes you on to a wide road which climbs for about 8km. Follow signs for Corpo di Cava, and also yellow signs for the 'Badia'. Once in Cava, you'll pass a small monument to Pope Urbano II who consecrated the abbey in 1092; the road from here (a distance of 3.8km) will lead down to the piazza by the monastery's church.

The powerful Benedictine abbey was founded in 1011 by Sant'Alferio Pappacarbone, a nobleman from Salerno who was the monastery's first abbot, and who apparently died here in 1050 at the age of 120. It is also the resting place for King Roger of Sicily's second wife Sibylla who died in Salerno, and the antipope Theodoric who died here in 1102 living as simple monk. The monastery was most powerful under its third abbot, Alferio's nephew San Pietro, with jurisdiction over about 500 abbeys, priories and churches from Rome to Salerno. It even maintained a fleet for commercial trading in the Orient, and along with artistic treasures the monks amassed an impressive and important collection of documents. Many are still preserved in the archives and library, including a Bible in Visigothic script and the *Codex Legum Longobardorum* (a complete survey of Lombard laws, dated 1004).

The abbey's church was first constructed toward the end of the 9th century, enlarged in the 11th, and then renovated in a Baroque style in the late 1700s. The façade is a restrained version of the style, but the interior is too modern for my taste. Highlights here are the 13th-century ambo, or pulpit, another beautiful example of Cosmati mosaic work and the Easter candelabra with its trunk in a spiralled mosaic pattern.

Passing through a massive hall to the left of the church, doors at the end lead to the vast and varied monastery complex. (Visitors are taken through by guided tour only, in English if requested.) The small Romanesque cloisters is one of the first areas within, with delicate marble columns marking the four sides. To the left is the Gothic Sala Capitolare, paved with majolica tiles and decorated with frescoes that portray celebrated popes, monks and emperors. The Lombard cemetery, a 12th-century crypt beyond the Chapel of the Crucifix, is below ground, supported by columns that are even older. A museum is located along one side of the cloisters, with some fine pictures by Andrea da Salerno, Luca Giordano, and the school of Lorenzo Monaco.

Though thoroughly diminished in power, it appears that the monastery has enough money for extensive and careful renovation work. Glassed balconies lead to monks' quarters; floors are highly polished; restoration experts have been called in to renew frescoes. The complex of buildings seems to extend indefinitely up the valley, some low passages from one room to the next are carved right out of the rock face. Despite the vast number of rich works accessible to the public here, Trinità di Cava feels extremely remote and hauntingly still, as if it has refused to come to terms with its lowered status in the eyes of the outside world.

Salerno

This sprawling industrial city is the capital of the province also called Salerno, built in a wide arc on the hillside above the gulf. It is in a pretty position, but a population of more than 150,000 creates planning problems, and the town's medieval quarter is almost hidden within an ugly urban sprawl. Salerno was badly damaged during World War II and much was rebuilt along the waterfront during the 1950s. On 9 September, 1943, the US Army landed just south of here, and with British commandos launched their attack on mainland Europe which signalled the turning point in the war.

The city's past is illustrious: a famous School of Medicine founded in the 11th century and capital of the Kingdom of Naples under Norman ruler Robert Guiscard. But in my opinion Salerno's present state doesn't warrant a lengthy visit. I wouldn't choose this city as a base for touring the Amalfi coast or for visiting Paestum and Campania's southern coastal region.

Yet the town's small medieval quarter is wonderfully intact, and the **Cathedral** here is one of the best examples of Norman architecture in southern Italy. From the Lungomare Trieste (very pretty along its western section closest to Amalfi), the tight Via Duomo cuts up left to the old quarter and you are at the back of the big church. Dedicated to St Matthew, the Duomo was begun in 1076 under the orders of Robert Guiscard near a previous church founded in 845; it was consecrated in 1085 by Pope Gregory VII, who is buried here. It was completely remodelled in the early part of the 18th century. The recent earthquake damaged the church, but surprisingly revealed Norman columns hidden inside the Baroque piers.

The Duomo's atrium is a delight, entered through the Romanesque Porta dei Leoni up a short flight of steps. It is surrounded by columned arches on all four sides and has a small fountain in its centre. The 28 marble columns were taken from Paestum long before one needed permission for such plundering, and there are some very well-preserved sarcophagi in the side galleries. The 12th-century bell-tower rises on the right, its decorative upper storey similar to Amalfi's.

It is thought that part of the medical school existed here, in what are now side rooms off the atrium. Its origins are obscure, first mentioned in documents dating from the early 9th century. Benedictine monks had a directing hand in the school's growth from the 10th century; but it reached its zenith in the 12th and 13th centuries. Students came from all parts of Europe (their teachers from as far afield as Africa), and no one could practise medicine in southern Italy without the school's certificate: seven years of study with public exams, and a year practising under a qualified physician. La Scuola Medica Salernitana also gave students a firm grounding in theology, and the philosophy and laws of medicine. Its Code of Health was a standard reference guide throughout the Middle Ages.

The cathedral is entered from the atrium through a tall bronze door of 54 panels, another import from Constantinople in 1099 and once also inset with silver. The decorated pulpits within are superb works, especially the bigger one on the right side of the middle aisle. It rests on 12 granite columns with exquisitely carved capitals. The Easter candlestick nearby was also made in the early 13th century; at more than 5m it's the tallest I've ever seen.

Though the Duomo is loaded with Roman sarcophagi and other monuments to the dead, the most splendid tomb was carved for Margherita di Durazzo. She died in 1412, the mother of Angevin King Ladislau and wife of Charles III of Durazzo. Supported by four symbolic figures of Prudence, Regality, Faith and Fortitude, the tomb is in the last chapel in the left aisle, just before the steps which lead to the high altar area. It was completed in 1435 by Alessio di Vico and Antonio Baboccio da Piperno (who also worked on Milan's Duomo).

The **Museo del Duomo** is nearby at No.2 Via Monterisi, and houses an interesting collection of art commissioned in Salerno through the centuries. Its best works are a large set of ivory relief tablets showing scenes from the Old and New Testaments. Four of the 54 panels are missing, one exhibited at the Louvre, another in Berlin, a third in Budapest and the fourth at the Museum of Metropolitan Art in New York. They were carved by various artists in the 12th century, probably made as the large frontispiece of an altar. A painting by Ribera, *St Peter and St Jerome*, is worth viewing in Room II; the museum's first room displays diplomas from the School of Medicine.

Via Mercanti, south of the Duomo, is the best street for absorbing the atmosphere of the medieval quarter. On the Piazza Matteotti at the street's eastern end is the **Church of the Crucifix**, first constructed in the 10th century. A

14th-century fresco under the altar in the right apse is a real oddity, *The Martyred Saints Clemente, Paolina and Cassiano.* The remains of each saint are said to be contained in the gold urns beneath the figures. At the other end of Via Mercanti is the Arco di Arechi, all that remains of a palazzo built in the 8th century by Lombard Prince Arechi.

The **Castello di Arechi**, stronghold of the same family, was constructed by the Byzantines, enlarged by the Lombards, and then reinforced by the Normans and Aragons. It sits on the hill above Salerno, and the view from here takes in the city and the gulf beyond, with the Cilento mountains to the south. The city plans to turn this site into a museum, but restoration of the castle ruins continues slowly.

Practical Information

Getting there

The Amalfi coast road, about 70km from Sorrento to Salerno, is reached by car from Naples on the A3 Autostrada. The motorway stops at Castellammare di Stabia, and parts of the coast road (No.145) from there to Sorrento can be just as breathtaking and time-consuming as the drive past Sorrento. An alternative route is to drive directly to Salerno on the A3, and make your way back up the coast in the opposite direction. Trains from Naples's central station leave often for Sorrento (the Circumvesuviana line), and blue Sita buses along the coast will connect one town to the next.

Tourist Information Offices

AMALFI   Azienda Autonoma di Soggiorno e Turismo: Corso Roma 19 (tel. 089 871107).

CASTELLAMMARE DI STABIA   Piazza Matteotti 34 (tel. 081 8711334).

POSITANO   Via del Saracino 2 (tel. 089 875067).

RAVELLO   Piazza Vescovado 10 (tel. 089 857096).

SALERNO   Piazza Amendola 8 (tel. 089 224744) or Piazza Vittorio Veneto at the train station (tel. 089 231432).

SORRENTO   Via Luigi De Maio 35 (tel. 081 8782229).

VICO EQUENSE   Corso Umberto I (tel. 081 8798343).

Hotels and restaurants

AMALFI Cappuccini Convento Hotel, Via Annunziatella 46, 84011 (tel. 089 871877), has a wonderful situation above town in a 12th century monastery (lift from Via M. Camera, or with car follow signs up hill on town's western side); cloisters and columned dining room; private car park below at road level; expensive.
Luna Convento Hotel, Via P Comite 19, 84011 (tel. 089 871002). This old hotel has been in the same family for five generations, with claims that St Francis of Assisi stayed here in the 13th century. Beautiful Byzantine cloisters and nice swimming pool, private garage; expensive.
Hotel Fontana, Piazza Duomo 7 (tel. 089 871530), right across from the cathedral, clean and friendly, but you'll have to put up with the constant clang of church bells. Inexpensive.
Hotel Lidomare, 5 Largo Piccolomini (tel. 089 871332), a small hotel with friendly owners, right by the sea; clean, simple décor and inexpensive.
La Caravella Restaurant, Via Nazionale (871029), near the tunnel by the beach, very popular and known for tangy seafood sauces over generous helpings of pasta; closed Tues and Nov. Moderate.
Da Barracca, Piazza dei Dogi (871285) is on a side street west of the Duomo, with a pleasant outdoor terrace. Inexpensive.

CONCA DEI MARINI Hotel Belvedere (tel. 089 831282) just beyond Amalfi on the way to Positano. Terraced rooms lead down to the water, tucked under the coast road with calming sea views; great swimming pool and private parking; moderate.

MASSA LUBRENSE Antico Francischiello-da Peppino Restaurant, Via Villazzano 27 (tel. 081 8771171), on the coast road connecting Sorrento to Massa. (A number of clean and simple bedrooms available, private beach, moderate prices.) The restaurant's antipasto offerings are outstanding, cannelloni superb, good house wines. Expensive.

POSITANO Casa Maresca, Viale Pasitea, 84017 (tel. 089 875140), simple, whitewashed hotel not far from the water. Run by an Englishwoman and her Italian husband, it's inexpensive, with good food to boot.
Conca D'Oro, (tel. 089 875111), 16 Via Boscariello, off upper end of Via Pasitea above Fornillo district. Rooms here have balconies with views over town, and the covered terrace is a crazy-quilt pattern of coloured tile chips. A long walk down many steps to beaches and town, but comfortable and inexpensive.
Palazzo Murat, 23 Via dei Mulini (tel. 089 875177), just behind the Duomo in a fantastic Baroque palazzo with profusely flowering plants; a new addition has rooms with bigger balconies. The architecture and atmosphere are worth the price. Expensive.
San Pietro Hotel, Via Laurito 2 (tel. 089 875455) just beyond Positano on a spur off the coast road. This is one of southern Italy's most luxurious hotels, its

suite-like rooms cut into the cliff with views across the bay to Positano. The formal dining room with very good food is for guests only; a lift serves the hotel's private beach and tennis court. Very elegant and understated; extremely expensive.

Buca di Bacco Restaurant, 8 Via Rampa Teglia (tel. 089 875699), right on the beach and also with rooms available from April to mid Oct. All sorts of tempting specialities are displayed in the dining room; the pasta is made fresh daily, for seafood try the *zuppa di cozze*. Moderate.

La Cambusa (875432), again on the beach, but up steps and set in a small square. I liked the *risotto pescatore* here, and pasta with zucchini which is a popular offering on this coast. Moderate.

RAVELLO Hotel Bonadies, 5 Piazza Fontana Moresca, 84010 (tel. 089 857918). A pleasant, family-run hotel with 33 rooms; its restaurant has stunning views to the south. A minibus runs guests to the seaside. Moderate prices.

Hotel Caruso Belvedere, Via San Giovanni del Toro 52, 84010 (tel. 089 857111). Opened in 1903 by the Caruso family, this is a relaxed old-fashioned place with loads of atmosphere. Comfortable rooms come in all shapes and sizes, some with arched windows and small balconies. A terraced garden affords marvelous views; Caruso family wines and delicious local specialties are offered at dinner. Expensive.

Hotel Palumbo, Via San Giovanni del Toro 28 (tel. 089 857244), closed Feb. This hilltop hotel has been host to such luminaries as Humphrey Bogart and D. H. Lawrence; it's more pretentious and more elegant by modern standards than the Caruso down the street. Most bedrooms have their own terrace; the Moorish-style courtyard is cool and quiet. Very good food, and Episcopio wine produced since 1860. Very expensive.

Hotel Toro, Viale Wagner 3 (tel. 089 857211), is near the piazza, entered through a pretty garden. The converted villa is small, and bedrooms are unexceptional, but food here is good, fresh fare (open to non-residents for dinner); moderate.

Villa Cimbrone (tel. 089 857459) is a moderately expensive but special place to stay, with only ten rooms – splash out if you can. Half the rooms have spectacular sea views, and breakfast is served on the lovely terrace; closed Nov to April.

Compa 'Cosimo Restaurant (tel. 089 857156), closed Mondays from November to March; also a pizzeria in the summer months and always a friendly relaxed atmosphere. The Bottone sisters make their own pasta, as well as ice cream.

Garden Restaurant (tel. 089 857226), also has ten bedrooms, each with terrace. Wonderful place to eat in warm weather, on shaded terrace with fine views. Moderate prices.

SALERNO Unfortunately, nothing to be recommended in the medieval quarter, but the **Jolly Hotel**, Lungomare Trieste 1 (tel: 089 225222) is a known quantity as it's part of a chain – high in services and low on character – in a very good location. Expensive.

Antica Pizzeria del Vicolo della Neve in the old quarter (at No.24, tel: 089

225705) serves excellent pizza evenings only. Closed Wed; inexpensive.
La Brace, Lungomare Trieste 11 (tel. 089 225159), closed Sun and two weeks late December, is near the Jolly Hotel. Good local dishes, moderate prices.

SORRENTO Bellevue Syrene Hotel, 5 Piazza della Vittoria, (tel. 081 8781024), positioned on the cliff edge, originally a private villa built in the 18th century, garden terrace and lift down to beach, along with over-the-top décor of the attached Villa Pompeiana (great for drinks on its far terrace), expensive prices.

Grand Hotel Excelsior Vittoria, Piazza Tasso 34 (tel. 081 8071044), is also on the edge of the cliff, its large, comfortable rooms in four grand villas. Beautifully frescoed breakfast room, a long terrace with sweeping views, pool behind and private beach below reached by lift, very expensive.

La Tonnarella, Via del Capo 31 (tel. 081 8781153), heading out of town toward Massa Lubrense but with good views of the sea. Also a popular restaurant, and gardens filled with lemon and eucalyptus trees. Lift to the beach, but only 16 double rooms; inexpensive.

Bar Santa Anna at the Marina Grande is a very simple trattoria by the sea. But you've got to go down and place your order in advance so there's enough time for them to fish it out of the sea. The nearby **Taverna Azzurra** operates under similar conditions. Both inexpensive.

Davide Ice-Cream Parlour, Via P. R. Giuliani 39 (tel. 081 8781337) is justly famous, to the extent that they even print their own brochure offering 'the largest range of sweetness in Italy'. You'll bump into lots of foreigners here, but what's the difference − it's fantastic stuff.

La Favorita-o'Parrucchiano, Corso Italia 71 tel. 081 8781321), closed Tuesdays November to May, is one of Sorrento's best restaurants. Try the amazing mozzarella rolled in lemon leaves, the *panzarotti* (little pies stuffed with mozzarella, tomato and basil), and the house speciality of *gnocchi alla sorrentina*. Moderate prices, but it could get expensive if you go all out on every course.

La Pentolaccia, Via Fuori Mura 10, (heading north off Piazza Tasso) prepares excellent regional dishes in unpretentious surroundings; a local favourite with moderate prices.

Price Ranges

Hotel (double room)	*Restaurant (per head)*
Inexpensive: under 60,000	under 25,000
Moderate: 60–120,000	25–50,000
Expensive 120–200,000	50–90,000
Very expensive: 200,000+	90,000+

Museums and other public sites

AMALFI Arsenal: corner of Via M. Camera. 10.00–13.00, 16.00–20.00
Municipio: entrance on the square behind the Municipio, off Corso Roma. 09.00–14.00, closed Sun.

CASTELLAMMARE DI STABIA Antiche Terme Stabiane: Via Sorrentina, by Piazza Amendola at port. 09.00–sunset.
Antiquarium: Via Marco Mario 2. 09.00–15.00, (09.00–13.00 Sun), closed Tues.

CAVA DE' TIRRENI Abbazia della Trinità di Cava, in the hamlet of Corpo di Cava. Guided tours and museum 09.00–12.30 weekdays, 09.00–11.00 Sun and hols.

MONTE FAITO By cable car from Piazza Circumvesuviana in Stabia from 1 April to 31 October; 8-minute ride timed to leave after arrival of trains en route from Naple to Sorrento.

RAVELLO Villa Cimbrone: fee; 09.00–sunset.
Villa Rufolo: fee; 09.30–13.30, 15.00–sunset.

SALERNO Museo del Duomo; Via Monterisi. 09.30–12.30, 16.00–20.00, closed Sun and hols.

SORRENTO Museo Correale di Terranova: Via Correale. 09.30–12.30, 16.00–19.00 Apr-Sept; 09.30–12.30, 15.00–17.00 Oct-Mar; 09.30–12.30 Sun, closed Tues.

10. PAESTUM AND THE CILENTO PENINSULA

The Cilento is Campania's least appreciated area, steeped in contrasts between its rocky coastline and mountainous inland areas. It is criss-crossed by rivers and wide valleys – its fertile plain a patchwork of greens, the mountains terraced with hundreds of olives trees. The name Cilento stems from the name Alento, one of the territory's central rivers.

It's hard to compare this part of Campania with any other. Remote hill-towns here have more in common with Basilicata to the east than agricultural areas closer to Naples and Caserta. Coastal resorts like Palinuro resemble those of nearby Calabria more than those on the Amalfi coast. What the Cilento does share with the rest of Campania is its western boundary on the Tirrhenian, and a host of mythical associations.

Then there are the wondrous temples at Paestum, the best examples of classical Greek architecture outside modern-day Greece. Two of the three massive temples are older than the Parthenon, all standing within the ruins of a city founded nearly 2500 years ago. It would be a great mistake to miss them, just 40k south of Salerno. Between Paestum and Palinuro are the rarely visited ruins of Velia, famed in antiquity for its school of philosophy. And about 60km inland, near the Basilicata border is the architecturally stunning monastery at Padula called the Certosa of San Lorenzo. North of here are the strange caves of Pertosa, more than 2km long and full of stalactites and stalagmites.

The town of Eboli, which just touches the northern tip of the Cilento, southeast of Salerno, was made famous by the title of Carlo Levi's book, *Christ Stopped at Eboli*. But it is the people from hill-towns south of Potenza, in the region of Basilicata who are the subject of Levi's book, which is well worth reading. When travelling through the Cilento though, one realises that Levi could just as easily have been describing the rural Italians here in southern Campania. Mountain trails traversed on the back of a mule are still favoured over paved versions, and small villages offer only the community comforts of a church and local coffee bar.

Travelling through the Cilento is easily worth three or more days of your time, perhaps based in Palinuro where hotels are of an acceptable standard. The A3 autostrada from Salerno zips down the eastern side of the Cilento, and the fairly good state road No.18 passes Paestum and then cuts inland (in part tortuously sinuous) toward the Gulf of Policastro. In the high season, you're less likely to run up against the large number of visitors to be found on the islands or Amalfi Coast, and more of them will be Italian than British, German or American.

Paestum

The temples at Paestum are overwhelming in their sheer size and beautiful simplicity. When staring up at them I feel an even stronger sense of the awe felt when visiting the city of Cumae near Naples. They are part of the same mysterious pattern etched on this landscape by Greek settlers. After their centuries of slumber, we now gaze at these monuments like children introduced to a new sibling. How in the world did they get there, and what secret knowledge is stored within their massive ancient columns?

It is not true to say that these Doric temples were 'rediscovered' in the 18th century. Italians in the hilltop town of Capaccio always knew they were there, though the ruins were partially covered in riotous vegetation. Small columns were carted away to Salerno in the 11th century; the troops of Ferdinand I fought Neapolitan barons on the Sele river banks nearby during the 15th. What guidebook writers condescendingly mean is that foreign travellers were not apprised of the temples' existence by their Italian contemporaries. What they were told was that this area was a nasty malarial swamp and a route for bandits, all true enough. Paestum was still slightly infested in 1944, when travel writer Norman Lewis (then a soldier) was admitted to hospital here.

The Latin poets Virgil, Ovid and Ausonius make no mention of malaria in their verses dedicated to Paestum, and we have no records to show that Greeks in the 6th century BC had to contend with the disease in their city. It was then called Poseidonia, City of Neptune, founded by the citizens of a settlement farther south called Sybaris (who were supposedly so decadent and unenterprising that they begat the term 'sybaritic'). Two hundred years later, the town's name was changed to Paestum when ruled by a local tribe called the Lucanians. It was then taken by the Romans in 273 BC, remaining loyal to the Empire when Hannibal charged through in the 3rd century. But malaria did finally cause the town to collapse, after a savage attack by the Saracens in 877. Paestum's dwindling population headed for the hills, where they founded the village of Capaccio in fresher air.

Along with the temples, the outlines of the old city of Paestum can be covered in a few hours, and the small museum across the street can be seen in the space of an hour or so. The site is about 1km long, and half that from the main street back to the farthest edges of excavated buildings. Old Paestum is surrounded by thick walls of travertine and is a fairly open site, though shade is supplied by the temples' huge round columns and the square blocks of stone

The Doric temples at Paestum

connecting them. The highest buildings are the temples of yellow limestone; most of the walls of other city dwellings, behind and between the temples, are less than waist high. It is a pleasure to wander in this open landscape: lizards bask on crumbling stone foundations and snails cling to the stems of flowering rosemary bushes. In the distance, people become Lilliputian as they make their way around the temples.

After walking through the entrance gates, the **Temple of Neptune** dominates the scene before you – the largest and best preserved, built about 450BC. Its 36 fluted columns are 9m high, those in the corners slightly more elliptical to counterbalance the thinning effect of light hitting them from more than one angle. The Basilica to the left was built 100 years earlier, with a single row of columns down its central space. Both temples were probably dedicated to the goddess Hera, Queen of Heaven and venerated symbol of fertility.

About 200m to the right of the Temple of Neptune is the wide open space of the **Forum**. It was once surrounded by a variety of Roman buildings; on the southern edge are ruins of baths and the Senate's Curia, to the north are the Roman Temple of Peace, a Greek theatre and an amphitheatre which, sadly, the modern main road has ploughed through. Also on this side of the Forum is a round area called the Bouleterion, thought to be where the city Senate (or Boule) met.

Farther north and to the right of the Forum is the **Temple of Ceres**, built about 500BC. It was in fact not dedicated to this goddess of tillage and corn (known to the Greeks as Demeter) but to Athena – or Minerva as the Romans called her – the goddess of wisdom. It is surrounded by 34 fluted columns, its interior more open than the other two large temples. In the Middle Ages it was turned into a Christian church: three tombs have been found near the south wall.

161

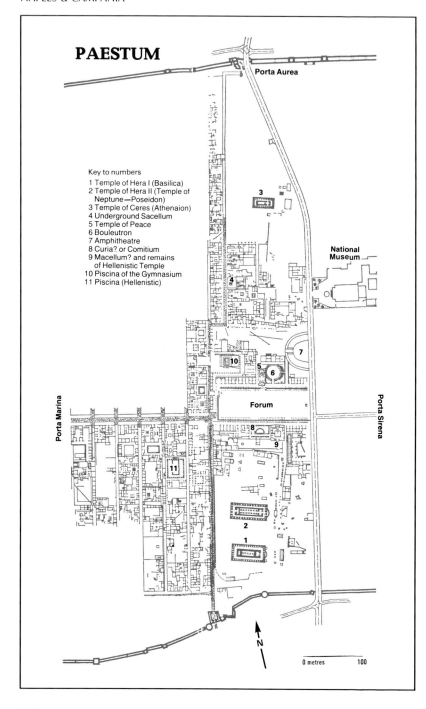

PAESTUM

Porta Aurea

Key to numbers
1 Temple of Hera I (Basilica)
2 Temple of Hera II (Temple of
  Neptune—Poseidon)
3 Temple of Ceres (Athenaion)
4 Underground Sacellum
5 Temple of Peace
6 Bouleutron
7 Amphitheatre
8 Curia? or Comitium
9 Macellum? and remains
  of Hellenistic Temple
10 Piscina of the Gymnasium
11 Piscina (Hellenistic)

National
Museum

Porta Marina

Porta Sirena

Forum

N

0 metres   100

The Tomb of the Diver, Paestum

Across the street near the Temple of Ceres is the **museum**, containing objects found in and around Paestum, including a series of metopes uncovered in a sanctuary devoted to Hera outside the city walls. (Metopes are the bas relief depictions found on a frieze between the triglyphs, which are the stone blocks decorated with three vertical bands so evident on the Temple of Neptune.) These richly carved scenes date from between 800 and 480BC, the pre-Classical Archaic age in Greece. The metopes are in the first three rooms, presented as if still intact on a frieze, and are delightful episodes from Greek mythology and illustrations from poems by Stesichorus.

But the museum's highlight is in Room VIII at the back: the **Tomb of the Diver**. It was discovered in 1968, and is thought to be one of the few existing examples of Greek mural painting ever found. This amazingly serene cycle of internal tomb paintings was done in the 5th century BC, and most art from this period is intact only on vases and is rarely seen in a larger format like this. The diver appears to plunge untroubled into the pool beneath him; other sides of the tomb are banquet scenes which add to the sense of carefree transfer from one world to another.

On the same side of the street is the Ristorante Museo, a shaded terrace and inner dining room well placed for a snack or lunch. The modern town of Paestum is little more than a cluster of hotels and campsites, and the railway station is about half a kilometre from the entrance to the ruins, just outside the Sirena Gate which formed part of the city's eastern boundary.

From Paestum to Velia

Two routes lead 50km south to the Roman ruins of Velia. Inland is by way of state road No.18, a more rewarding alternative if you've spent a lot of time driving along the coast already. This road climbs east and then south through hilly country to the small towns of Ogliastro and Rutino, which were even smaller when mule tracks were the only routes of transportation here. Beside old stone homes are newer buildings in various states of completion, and more and more roofs are now topped with TV antennae. But the landscape hasn't changed that much. Hills are covered with olive groves, nets cast below each tangled tree to prevent the oily green fruit from rolling away.

From on high, an occasional glimpse of the sea near Agropoli is a perfect foil to the scrubby green hills surrounding you. West of Rutino are ruins of the castle at Rocca Cilento. The state road finally flattens out on the Salento Plain after passing through Omignano Scalo, and before joining the coast road you must turn right at the T junction. Velia will then be viewed up on the left, most notably the tower on the hill. A left turn on the main road leads to the ruins.

An alternative route is by coast road No.267, passing through Agropoli, Santa Maria di Castellabate and Acciaroli. The fishing villages strung along the coast here have been taking in summer visitors for some years now, mainly in July and August. Many Italians come to camp in this area, spending most of their time on the beach and exploring the coastline by boat.

The coastal resort closest to Paestum is **Agropoli**. It was probably founded in the 5th century by the Byzantines, and its oldest quarter is one of the more interesting and best preserved of any to be found along the coast. This area on the top of town is dominated by a castle, constructed by the Byzantines but enlarged by the Aragon dynasty. If you're looking for a place to eat lunch or dinner, good pizzerie and trattorie are to be found on the narrow streets here, but it's difficult to take a car all the way up. The rest of Agropoli is a modern sprawl of nondescript buildings, though bayside hotels near the port are clean and reasonably priced.

Farther along the coast is smaller **Santa Maria di Castellabate**, with a fine sandy beach on its northern side. The small marina of San Marco a little to the south also has a good beach and a short side trip of about 4km off the main road from San Marco takes you to **Punta Licosa**, one of the best places on the coast for a view out to sea. The name stems from Leucosia, one of the sirens whose legend says that she threw herself into the sea here after her failed attempts to lure Ulysses. The tiny island of Licosa, with its lighthouse and ruins of ancient walls, is just beyond the point. It's a beautiful walk up to the headland by mule track, but a paved road also leads there by way of Hotel Castelsandra – one of the nicest hotels the Cilento has to offer, though its position is the main draw.

About 15km south is the seaside town of **Acciaroli**, where Ernest Hemingway is reputed to have stayed. If so, he picked one of the prettiest resorts on the coast. The small harbour is packed with colourful fishing boats, dominated by a thick square Angevin tower. Acciaroli makes very few concessions to tourists, though they come just the same. There's not much to do here once you've walked its streets and studied the 12th-century Church of the Annunziata (much remodelled) at the marina. But it's a fairly quiet and unpretentious spot; the Hotel Scogliera with its view of the port serves a good meal in its terraced restaurant even if you aren't spending the night.

Pioppi is the only other place of interest passed on route No.267 south to Velia. Positioned on a small inlet protected by the surrounding hills, it retains a Saracen tower and a 17th-century castle. The Church of Santa Maria dei Pioppi was first built in 994, though you wouldn't know that from the unfortunately modern façade. There's a great view from here down to Cape Palinuro as the road climbs and continues on to Velia, flanked by fig and olive trees.

Velia

The sprawling hillside ruins of **Velia**, or Elea to the Greeks, are all that remain of what was once a thriving community 2000 years ago. They were discovered in the 1880s, and various archeological projects undertaken in fits and starts since then (notably by Amedeo Maiuri in the 1920s) have uncovered more areas of the city. But by scanning the hillside and walking its borders today, one realises that there is much more excavation to be done at Velia. This is a little visited site well worth exploring; very few of its walls and foundations are off limits, and you'll find yourself playing amateur archaeologist by sweeping sand away from a mosaic floor to find out whether there's anything worth seeing beneath. Though enough areas have been uncovered to give one a sense of Velia's overall plan, it's what is still buried that stimulates the imagination here.

Velia was founded in the 6th century BC by immigrants from Phocaea in Asia Minor who, first fleeing from Persian invaders by landing on Corsica, were then driven south by the Etruscans and Carthaginians. The town had strong trading ties with Marseilles, which was also settled by Phocaeans. Within 100 years, Velia was highly regarded for its Eleatic school, founded by Xenophanes who emigrated from Colophon. The school was then headed by one of his followers, the philosopher Parmenides. He stated that nothing changes, that one can logically only affirm existence and say 'it is'. Aristotle described him as the founder of 'the science of truth'.

The school continued to flourish under Zeno, one of Parmenides's favourite pupils. His four arguments against motion, 'Achilles and the Tortoise' (portrayed in one of the metope fragments in the museum at Paestum), 'The Flying Arrow', 'The Stadium' and 'The Row of Solids', are his best known contributions to philosophy, hotly contested by Aristotle.

By the 3rd century BC, Velia was a *municipium* under Roman rule. Villas sprang up as wealthy Romans discovered its beautiful setting by the sea – the orator and statesman Cicero and the poet Horace both came to stay, though no villas have yet been uncovered. The two harbours slowly silted over, reducing the town's importance, and it was probably completely destroyed by the Saracens during the 8th or 9th century. A village called Castellamare della Bruca sprang up along the ridge in the early 12th century, but was abandoned some time in the 1600s.

The extensive ruins first seen on the right after entering from the car park were part of the lower city at the south marina, once on the shore but now half a kilometre away. The waist-high walls of homes and shops fill this area; to the south is a necropolis where the Romans buried their dead. A wide road of paving stones leads up the hill, past baths on the left. Constructed in the first half of the 2nd century, the floor of the frigidarium retains its mosaic design. On the right side of the road is a vast cistern.

At the crossroads beyond, the simple and stunning Porta Rosa finally comes into view, having been hidden by a high side wall until now. A left turn leads to the Acropolis. As you walk up toward the castle tower, down to the left are ruins of houses built in the 6th century BC. Farther on is a semicircular theatre from the Hellenistic period. On the summit near the castle are the remains of an Ionic temple. The castle dates from Norman times, though some of its foundations are the city's earliest; the circular tower was built during the Angevin period. This is where, according to H. V. Morton, the Scottish writer Ramage was so beseiged by fleas in 1828 that he ran to the sea, tore off all his clothes, and dived in. After reading that story, I was convinced I saw a fair number still jumping around.

Walking back through the Porta Rosa and along this path for about 300m, you turn left to the north marina with a good view down to the theatre and acropolis. If you head straight on instead, the path is flanked by tower ruins which once stood above the city walls. On your right are the excavated remains of a sacred area with its terrace and long altar; a few hundred metres beyond is the city's north-eastern boundary at the Castelluccio tower.

Palinuro

State road No.447 continues south from Velia along the sea, and views from this portion of coast road are among the best in the Cilento. The pretty town of **Pisciotta**, with its large church of Saints Peter and Paul, dominates one prominent hilltop. Winding down to the marina from the eastern edge of town, you pass grove after grove of olive trees, for Pisciotta produces more olives per square acre than almost any other town in the region. The small port area has a fine stretch of beach to one side, a popular place for summer boaters and campers.

Twenty kilometres south is **Palinuro**, named for the pilot of Aeneas in Virgil's *Aeneid* who legend says was buried here. The ruins of what is called his tomb are at the entrance of the harbour by the beach. Palinurus died while at the helm, and Book V closes with the ship drifting along Italy's coast:

The fleet ran its course none the less
Safely and without fear, for Father Neptune's
Promises held. Borne onwards, it drew near
The Sirens' rocks, so dangerous in old time
And white with the bones of many men.
(Meanwhile the rocks moaned hoarsely as the salt
Constantly flooded round them.) But Aeneas
Sensed that the pilot was gone and his ship was drifting.
And himself steered her through the waves of night,
Sighing and numbed at what had befallen his friend:
'Trusting too much to clear skies and calm seas,
The end is, Palinurus, you will lie
Naked upon an unfamiliar shore.'

Palinuro is famed for its position on a small bay, and though the modern town has grown for the sake of tourists with nothing to recommend it to those interested in history and architecture, the coast has remained rugged and wild. The town has two main streets: the Via Pisacane runs along the hillside; the Via Indipendenza runs parallel, closer to the sea. Both are lined with small hotels and restaurants, crowded in summer. But the grottoes and sandy inlets just north and south of Palinuro are this area's best features, and most can only be reached by boat (always for hire at the small port). Scuba divers come here by the dozens, attracted by the clean clear water and the abundance of marine life.

'From here the storms are born,' say fishermen in these parts. Winter winds whip fiercely around Cape Palinuro, and their erosive powers have created ragged natural arches and tall pointed cave openings. Heading down the coast near the cape is the **Grotta Azzurra**, not quite as splendid as Capri's but with big stalactites and still a beautiful shimmering blue. The **Cala del Ribatto** is farther on, a cove that opens on to four grottoes. There are yet more grottoes to explore in the **Cala del Salvatore**, **Cala della Lanterna** and **Cala Fetente** (dubbed the 'stinking' cove for its spring of sulfurous water). Just east is the natural arch called the Archetiello; farther south is the **Cala del Buon Dormire** (Cove of Good Sleep), so-called after a group of foreigners who once spent the night here for some odd reason. Out to sea is a rocky outcropping called **Il Coniglio**, though its shape hardly resembles the rabbit it's named after.

The vast cave beyond, **Grotta delle Ossa**, is interesting for the bone particles encrusted in stalactites and stalagmites and even in the cave walls. For a long time it was thought that these were the bones of shipwrecked victims of both the Second Punic War's Roman fleet and of seafarers during the reign of first Roman Emperor Augustus. But more recent studies conclude that these are the Neolithic remains of bears and horses – either trapped here or eaten by prehistoric man.

On the hillside above are the remnants of a town once called Molpa, thought to be an outpost of Velia. The river Lambo meets the sea here, once known as the Melpio. The city was sacked by Goths and then Saracens, and completely destroyed by Barbarossa. Built on what was once an acropolis are the ruins of a castle, and the view from this deserted spot is wonderful if you walk the half hour needed to get there. (From state road No.447, head toward Centola until it crosses the river, then turn right on No.562 for a short stretch, turning right again toward the sea and the ruins.)

The Gulf of Policastro and north to Padula

Once out of Palinuro, state road No.447 becomes No.562 along the coast. Around the headland of Cape Palinuro lies a gorgeous stretch of sandy beach, belonging to the town of Marina di Camerota just south. The Touring Club Italiano has a holiday village here, along with six campsites and a host of hotels and bungalows. The old town of **Camerota** rises on a hill 300m from the marina, known since the 11th century for producing ceramics, especially the long terra-cotta amphorae used to store wines and other liquids. Oddly enough, the town also produced vast amounts of fishing line. It must have been a profitable venture considering the number of Cilento fishermen who still make their living from the sea.

But Camerota is not a charming place, nor are the towns of Policastro, Villamare and Sapri surrounding the beautiful blue Gulf of Policastro. They look as if they sprang up when the tourists came to town, lacking character and saved only by the scenery. Just before reaching them, state road No.562 heads inland, climbing through green hills that make one forget that the sea is sometimes less than a kilometre away. The road snakes on, reaching degrees of intestinal intensity matched only by sections of the Amalfi Coast drive. Then at Scario you are suddenly on the wide Gulf of Policastro, its colour an intense blue even on a grey day.

Padula

The Carthusian monastery of San Lorenzo in Padula is the Cilento's architectural wonder, about 35km north-east of Sapri. The drive from the Gulf of Policastro through the inland hills is beautiful, cutting through the heart of rural Cilento. Farmers tend olives and grapes, slow carts are piled high with produce. Mule tracks trace their way up and over the hills, while cows and goats always take precedence over cars as they cross the main roads.

Vibonati

From the coast road between Villamare and Sapri, turn left on the secondary road that climbs toward **Vibonati**. Within a few kilometres you'll see this charming hill-town, its stone homes clustered around the church and bell-tower. Stop here for a walk around, for this is one of the province's most evocative small

The charming hill-town of Vibonati

towns. Hundreds of years ago Vibonati provided shelter away from the coast for those escaping Saracen incursions. Streets are narrow and steps lead from one terraced home to the next. Some of their portals retain elaborately carved stone surrounds dating from the 16th and 17th centuries. The church of **St Anthony Abbot**, with three asymetrical naves, was built upon the ruins of the Carafa castle built in the 15th century.

Leaving Vibonati, and after successive bends and dips for about 12km, the road near Caselle in Pittari joins state road No.517. From here, the climb is slow to Sanza; the road then forks right toward Buonabitacolo. Within 15km after this town, the A3 autostrada and state road No.19 running north to south are reached (the exit off the A3 is Padula/Buonabitacolo). You are now in the lush Valley of Diano, but it won't really appear as such until viewed on high from such hill-towns as Teggiano farther north. To reach the monastery at Padula, yellow signs off cluttered state road No.19 will point the way east.

Certosa di San Lorenzo

Today the recently restored Certosa di San Lorenzo in Padula appears totally out of context in its 20th-century setting. When it was founded in 1306 by the feudal lord Tommaso da Sanseverino, the valley was a rich source of agricultural income in a strategic position between Naples and Reggio di Calabria. Surrounded now by modern homes not far from the highway, the monastery sits like some majestic remainder on a deserted film set whose size overwhelmed

The Certosa di San Lorenzo in Padula, one of the most elaborate and extensive monasteries in Italy

the carpenters sent to dismantle it. One finds it hard to imagine the monastery as a concentration camp, which it was during both world wars.

Tommaso set out to construct the most elaborate and powerful monastery in southern Italy, and he certainly succeeded. With a total area of 52,000 square metres, the Certosa's architectural statistics are staggering: 600 rooms, 13 cloisters, 41 fountains, 51 internal staircases, and lavish quarters for the monks. This is one of the biggest monastic complexes in the world, and flourished as the Order of San Bruno until it was supressed by the French in 1866.

The monastery was continually embellished until the end of the 18th century; the Baroque interiors are outstanding examples of the period. This was always an obligatory stop for the aristocracy and in 1535 Charles V just happened to drop by with his army, for which an omelette of 1000 eggs was said to have been made. (The size of the kitchen attests to the probability.) Painters, sculptors and architects from Naples and other parts of the south were commissioned to decorate altars, ceilings, cloisters and pavements.

The gridiron pattern appears everywhere, most obviously in the overall plan (which mirrors Spain's Escorial). The gridiron is a symbol of St Lawrence, who was burned to death while chained to the frame of iron bars. The symbol appears over the entrance, on the majolica tiles, and is always in the saint's hand or by his side in a number of sculptures and paintings.

The most noteworthy interiors are close to the monastery's entrance. The **small cloister** dating from 1561, paved in a delicate herringbone pattern with

The Fathers' Choir and high altar in the church at San Lorenzo in Padula

a central fountain, is to the right after entering the complex. The **church** is off to the right side; its Gothic doorway with bas relief scenes from the life of San Lorenzo is one of the only remaining elements from that period. The choir stalls within are remarkable. The section of the Lay Brothers has a grey-and-white geometric floor; wooden inlay scenes on the stalls are the early 16th-century work of Giovanni Gallo. The more elaborate Fathers' Choir with the faded majolica-tiled floor has 36 scenes from the New Testament on the seat backs. The high altar is a florid testimony to the Baroque, encrusted with mother-of-pearl, lapis lazuli and coloured marbles.

Farther along the main corridor is the kitchen, as big as a church hall and housing a hefty stove with a chimney that must be nearly 3m wide. The walls are skirted in scallop-shaped tiles of brilliant green and yellow, and on the far wall a fresco of the Deposition of Christ was uncovered during the course of restoration. When I visited recently, a group of old-age pensioners from Salerno was being taken through by a tour guide. They were most animated in the kitchen, excited by the length of the worktables and musing over the famous omelette they'd mistakenly increased to 10,000 eggs!

The monastery's most beautiful room is the **library**, reached by a spiral staircase near the edge of the Great Cloister. The floor is a pattern of soft blue-and-cream majolica tiles, and the curved ceiling painted in the 18th century by Giovanni Olivieri has recently been restored. When the monks were not praying or sleeping, many were to be found here. The Carthusian order (founded in Grenoble in 1084) was among the most cultivated and literate in Europe. The monks collected and studied classical Greek and Latin works, transcribed laws and manuscripts, as well as studying medicine and natural science.

Just beyond the library is the monastery's most outstanding attraction – the

Great Cloister, finished in 1690. The rectangular quadrangle is surrounded by 84 pilasters supporting arches which are topped by a covered walkway. The monks' cells are off the courtyard, six on each side, de luxe suites by an ascetic's standards. Each cell consisted of a small sitting room, bedroom, study and a covered walkway leading to a back garden. The monks' cemetery is just outside their doors, its low walls carved with skulls. At the opposite end to the cemetery is an elegant elliptical staircase designed in 1761–63 by Vanvitelli's pupil Gaetano Barba. This takes you to the upper walkway around the Great Cloister, built so that the steps would lead somewhere.

Teggiano

The 15km drive from Padula to Teggiano along state road No.19, following the course of the Tenagro river, is nothing but a line of shops, petrol stations and badly built modern houses. But once off the main road (follow signs left to Teggiano) you will find the Cilento's agricultural riches all around you. Fields stretch out along the long valley, filled with fruit trees, tobacco plants and vegetables. It's about 12km to the pretty town of Teggiano, seen on high before the climb round the hill's rim.

This is one of the region's best preserved towns, called Tegia when it was a municipality under Roman rule. After the 4th century it was known as Diano, taking the name of the valley it towers above. In 410 the town was destroyed by the Visigothic King Alaric I, who wrought havoc from Rome to Sicily. There is little left to discern the town's role during the Dark Ages, but in subsequent centuries it came under the jurisdiction of the monastery at Padula, and then shared the territory's fortune under Aragon and Angevin rule.

By the 15th century, a baronial family had planted itself here. Baron Antonello Sanseverino, Prince of Salerno, refused to be removed by Frederick of Aragon after the Rebel Barons conspiracy of 1485. His family had built the 13th-century **castle** which still dominates the town (now privately owned). With its arched and crenellated details, the stone castle is a rather heavy-handed reminder of feudal times.

Teggiano's **Cathedral of Santa Maria Maggiore** on Via Roma is a testament to the town's rich history. Its carved portal by Melchiorre di Montalbano dates from 1279, though the church was basically rebuilt after an earthquake in 1857. Within are an elaborate Pascal candlestick springing from a lion at its base, and a marble pulpit with symbols of the Evangelists carved in 1721. The other noteworthy work is the sculpted tomb of Enrico Sanseverino (on the wall of the internal façade up to the right), done in 1336 by followers of Tino di Camaino.

The Angevin church of **Sant' Andrea** is farther along the Via Roma, constructed on the remains of an ancient temple dedicated to Juno, wife of Jupiter. It's interesting for the two 14th-century triptychs done by disciples of Andrea da Salerno. The nearby church of San Pietro was also built on the remains of a temple, probably dedicated to Aesculapius, god of healing. The church is now a civic museum, exhibiting fragments of Roman capitals, coats of arms and tombs from medieval and Renaissance times. San Pietro has a very pretty bell-tower, and the nearby church of **Sant' Agostino** boasts a 16th-century cloister. The Gothic **Church of the Pietà's** small cloister was built in the 1400s.

Teggiano packs a lot of churches into a town of 8000 people. Its narrow streets are flanked by ancient homes that have been squeezed side by side for centuries; the winding alleyways make for a wonderful walking tour, past stairwells terraced with flower pots and lengths of red peppers hanging to dry from stone balconies. The one annoying thing about Teggiano is that though there's a bar or two on Via Roma, there isn't a single trattoria or pizzeria in town. But one hotel, the Eldorado, is situated above the castle. It's run by a very friendly family who make their own wine and sausages, and typically keep the TV on in the dining room during lunch and dinner. Most rooms have a view of either the castle or the valley below. The one view that can't be ignored before leaving Teggiano is from the Belvedere at the end of Via Roma to one side of the castle. Six hundred metres below is the Valley of Diano – immense rectangles of green and brown punctuated by the ochre-coloured dots of old farmhouses.

Pertosa

These long caves are extraordinary for the number of stalactites and stalagmites hidden within. You begin by boat, and continue on foot; the interior caverns are illuminated by artificial light. Round and twisted shapes distend from the ceiling and sprout from the floor, conjuring up the oddest images – one can become immersed in creating a fantasy world peopled by these formations.

From Teggiano, state road No.19 continues north (as well as the A3 autostrada) past towns such as Sala Consilina, Atena Lucana and Polla. These are among the Cilento's oldest towns, dating back as far as the 4th century BC. But though they harbour churches and ruins of some interest, they have lost their charm due to modern development. Driving through them from Teggiano to the caves of Pertosa is not a very uplifting experience, and I don't recommend taking the time to search out the one or two hard-to-find sites they offer to travellers.

However, **Pertosa** is such a strange and magical place that it's worth the trip if you're heading back north. (The A3 then shoots up to Salerno, about 80km to the northwest.) The Grotte di Pertosa are about 3km off state road No.19; signs will send you down the valley past a handful of houses to the car park. From here you walk up past a small hotel and bar to the cavernous entrance. Once inside you step into the boat that travels slowly through a man-made canal. The underground caves are almost 3km long.

It is thought that these grottoes were inhabited during the Bronze and Early Iron Ages, but most recently only bats have found refuge here. Our guide revelled in disclosing the amount of excavation work carried out in the 1930s: thirty tons of bat faeces removed, he claimed. He also prided himself on knowing their nocturnal schedule: out at 9pm and back at 4am. Whatever the creatures' habits, the caves seemed very clean and relatively bat free during the daytime.

The only other living things within are the stalagtites and stalagmites, some joined over centuries of steady dripping to create damp white columns up to 4m long. The process starts with soluble bicarbonate of calcium within the rock. When it reaches the surface, higher temperature and lower water pressure combine to change the bicarbonate into a hard material which adheres to the rock face. Over the centuries, strange forms have taken shape and the guides have identified a fantastic array of characters for their visitors – from the Sphinx to the Madonna of Lourdes and a garden of smurfs. You pass through the Throne Room, the Tabernacle, the Sponge Room and on to the Castle and the Waterfall. This is certainly fertile ground for the imagination, provided you have no fear of sleeping bats and dark spaces!

Practical Information

Getting there

Trains run from Naples and Salerno into the Cilento, stopping at Paestum and Palinuro on a fairly frequent basis. However, without a car you are confined to the coast and a limited number of towns, so it's best to drive through this area. Rent a car from either Naples, Sorrento or Salerno. The A3 autostrada, from Naples or Salerno, runs down the eastern border of the region. Choosing that route, you would then turn inland down state road No.517 to the Gulf of Policastro before heading north along the coast. Alternatively, follow the coast road from Salerno south, or state road No.18 which takes you inland before reaching Agropoli.

Tourist Information Office

PAESTUM   Via Magna Grecia 151/156 near the Archeological Zone (tel. 0828 811016).

Hotels and restaurants

ACCIAROLI   La Scogliera Hotel and Restaurant, port area, (tel. 0974 904 014). Clean and pleasant hotel; 14 rooms with good views of port and sea; nice terrace restaurant. Closed 15 Dec–15 Jan. Moderate.

AGROPOLI   Carola Hotel and Restaurant, near port at 1 Via Carlo Pisacane (tel. 0974 826422). Closer to the old town than the stretch of dull modern establishments on Agropoli's northern beach edge. Most rooms have small balconies, though some without views. Closed Nov through March. Moderate.

CASTELLABATE Castelsandra Hotel at San Marco, Via Piano Melaino (tel. 0974 966021), 5km south overlooking the bay. Bigger rooms here are best; all have terraces. The hotel's position is wonderful, but it's a modern place and not as cosy as it could be. Closed Nov to late March. Expensive. **Palazzo Belmonte** (tel. 0974 960211) is a remarkable find in this part of Italy. Originally a 17th-century hunting lodge, the villa is on the outskirts of Castellabate, with a pool and five-acre garden bordering the sea. The Principe di Belmonte still lives in one wing; 19 self-contained apartments are on the first and second floors, along with a separate 18th-century cottage for rent called Eduardo's House. All have sitting rooms and kitchens. Highly recommended; expensive.

PADULA Certosa Hotel, 57 Viale Certosa, across from the monastery (tel. 0975 77046), is an undistinguished place but valuable if you just don't want to get back into the car. Has a tennis court and pool. Moderate.

PAESTUM   Park Hotel, in the Linora district (tel. 0828 811134). Set in a small pine grove, with tennis and beach access. Moderate prices.
Schuhmann Hotel, on the sea in the Laura district, Via Laura Mare, (tel. 0828 851151) with slightly lower prices than the Park Hotel. Closed Nov. Moderate.
Nettuno Restaurant, Via Principi di Piemonte 1 (tel. 0828 811028), has unpretentious, fresh dishes, with a good view of the temples. Closed Mon, and dinners only in July and August. Inexpensive.
Ristorante Museo, in archeological zone near the museum (tel. 0828 811135). Simple dishes, taken either inside or on shaded terrace. Inexpensive.

PALINURO   King's Residence, Via Piano Farrachio (tel. 0974 931324) is one of the town's top hotels, with a great view of the coast and a nice pool. Closed Oct–March. Expensive.
Grand Hotel San Pietro, Corso Carlo Pisacane (tel. 0974 931466) is less posh, but still with good views and all modern amenities. Closed Nov–March. Moderate.
Hotel La Torre, 5 Via Porto, Capo Palinuro (tel. 0974 931107) is a friendly unpretentious place tucked into the hillside down by the port. All rooms have their own terrace with view, and the family-run restaurant here is good. Moderate.
La Pergola Restaurant, Corso Pisacane, is one of Palinuro's best examples of a typical, family-run restaurant. Tables are set on a shaded terrace, and the friendly family cooks are known for their pastas, *fusilli* and *orecchiette* especially. Inexpensive.

TEGGIANO   The Eldorado, 14 Via Castello, (tel. 0975 79044) is the only hotel in town, situated above the castle. Nothing fancy here, but it's a very clean and friendly family-run place (their own kitchen is just off the guests' dining room). Since there are no restaurants in town except the local bar for snacks, the hotel offers full board at inexpensive prices.

Price ranges
Hotel double room
Inexpensive: under 60,000
Moderate: 60–120,000
Expensive: 120–200,000
Very expensive: 200,000+

Restaurant per head
under 25,000
25–50,000
50–90,000
90,000+

Museums and other public sites

PADULA   The Carthusian Monastery of San Lorenzo: Open daily 08.00–sunset, by guided tour only, conducted hourly.

PAESTUM   Archeological Zone: two entrances, open daily 09.00–16.00 but closed on major hols. Entrance fee. **Museum**: open 09.00–14.00 Mon–Sat; 09.00–13.00 Sun. Closed hols. Entrance fee included in ticket to archeological zone.

PERTOSA   The caves are open 09.00–17.30; in low season closed for lunch 12.30–14.00. The guided tour lasts about one hour; entrance fee.

**VELIA   Open 09.00–one hour before sunset. No entrance fee.

INDEX